The Philosophy of F. H. Bradley

THE PHILOSOPHY
OF F. H. BRADLEY

Edited by
Anthony Manser
and
Guy Stock

CLARENDON PRESS · OXFORD
1984

Oxford University Press, Walton Street, Oxford OX2 6DP

London Glasgow New York Toronto
Delhi Bombay Calcutta Madras Karachi
Kuala Lumpur Singapore Hong Kong Tokyo
Nairobi Dar es Salaam Cape Town
Melbourne Auckland
and associated companies in
Beirut Berlin Ibadan Mexico City Nicosia

Oxford is a trade mark of Oxford University Press

Published in the United States
by Oxford University Press, New York

© Oxford University Press 1984

British Library Cataloguing in Publication Data
The Philosophy of F. H. Bradley.
1. Bradley, F. H.
I. Manser, Anthony   II. Stock, Guy
192   B1618.B7
ISBN 0-19-824688-9

Library of Congress Cataloging in Publication Data
Main entry under title:
The Philosophy of F.H. Bradley.
Includes index.
1. Bradley, F. H. (Francis Herbert), 1846–1924 –
Addresses, essays, lectures.   I. Manser, Anthony
Richards.   II. Stock, Guy.
B1618.B74P47 1984   192   8323918
ISBN 0-19-824688-9

Set by Hope Services, Abingdon, Oxfordshire
Printed in Great Britain
at the University Press, Oxford

Preface

The idea of producing a volume of specially written papers on the philosophy of F. H. Bradley originated from a discussion we had at the Welsh Philosophical Society Conference at Gregynog in the spring of 1979. We felt strongly that Bradley was to be considered one of the greatest British philosophers. Yet for the last forty or so years he had become almost completely inaccessible to students of philosophy, except for some consideration of the early essays in *Ethical Studies*. One reason for this neglect was the dearth of good secondary literature. With the notable exceptions of some of the work of Brand Blanshard and Richard Wollheim's book, there was virtually nothing that could enable a student to relate Bradley's thought to the issues currently debated in the Anglo-Saxon world. We therefore decided that a collection of papers aimed at correcting this situation would mark in a fitting way the centenary of the publication in 1883 of Bradley's *Principles of Logic*. It would also prepare for the sixtieth anniversary of his death, in 1984.

The idea was taken further at the Joint Session of the Aristotelian Society and Mind Association of 1979; we received considerable encouragement from those we met there. Consequently we began to approach other potential contributors; most of those we contacted appear in the present volume. At that time we had no guarantee that the work would be published, although Oxford University Press had shown an interest in the project.

At the July 1981 Joint Session in the University of Manchester we organized an informal seminar, during which earlier versions of a number of the papers published here were read and discussed. We certainly found this a valuable opportunity to try out ideas, and we believe that the others who attended did also. At the beginning of 1982, Oxford University Press agreed to publish the volume. We would like to thank them for the assistance and encouragement that they have given us.

Those whom we would like to thank for their assistance in this enterprise, apart from the contributors themselves, are too numerous to mention individually. We trust they will accept our gratitude expressed in this general form.

However, Guy Stock would like to thank particularly the German Academic Exchange and the British Academy for enabling him to accept.for two terms the generous hospitality of Harald Delius and the Philosophy Department of the University of Mannheim. Anthony Manser would like to express his gratitude to his ex-secretary Heather King, who was of such sterling assistance in the preparation of the manuscript.

Anthony Manser

Guy Stock

Contents

List of Contributors

James Allard	Associate Professor of Philosophy, Montana State University, Bozeman, Montana.
David Bell	Senior Lecturer in Logic, University of Glasgow.
Simon Blackburn	Fellow of Pembroke College, Oxford.
Brand Blanshard	Emeritus Professor of Philosophy, Yale University.
James Bradley	St Edmund's House, University of Cambridge.
Stewart Candlish	Senior Lecturer in Philosophy, University of Western Australia.
J. N. Findlay	Bowne Professor of Philosophy, Boston University.
David Holdcroft	Professor of Philosophy, University of Leeds.
Peter Johnson	Lecturer in Philosophy, University of Southampton.
Anthony Manser	Professor of Philosophy, University of Southampton.
Peter P. Nicholson	Senior Lecturer in Politics, University of York.
T. L. S. Sprigge	Professor of Logic and Metaphysics, University of Edinburgh.
Guy Stock	Senior Lecturer in Logic, University of Aberdeen.
W. H. Walsh	Emeritus Professor of Logic and Metaphysics, University of Edinburgh, and Emeritus Fellow, Merton College, University of Oxford.
Crispin Wright	Professor of Logic and Metaphysics, University of St Andrews.

List of Abbreviations

All references in the text to the works of Bradley employ the following abbreviations.

PL   *The Principles of Logic*, Oxford, 1883; 2nd ed., 1922; corrected impression 1928.

ES   *Ethical Studies*, Oxford, 1876; 2nd ed., 1927.

AR   *Appearance and Reality*, 1893; Oxford, 1897.

ETR   *Essays on Truth and Reality*, Oxford, 1914.

CE   *Collected Essays*, Oxford, 1935.

CHAPTER 1

Introduction

Anthony Manser and Guy Stock

I

The dominant tradition in British, American, and Australasian philosophy could be said to be empiricist, analytic, and pragmatic. For reasons which are doubtfully to be located within the sphere of philosophic argument itself it seems likely that this dominance will continue. A conspicuous aspect of what may loosely be called the 'Anglo-Saxon' tradition in philosophy has been the rejection of metaphysics. One feature of this rejection, exemplified in the early work of Russell and Moore, has been its treatment of F. H. Bradley. He was taken to be the archetypical metaphysician, and *Appearance and Reality* quarried for examples of typically 'metaphysical' statements to be held up for ridicule. Ayer, for example, in *Language, Truth and Logic* uses a quotation 'taken at random' from that work to show the way in which metaphysicians are prone to make remarks which 'have no literal significance, even for themselves'.[1] Even the lectures given by G. A. Paul in the late 1940s were concerned to dissect *Appearance and Reality* as a specimen of a kind of activity which could not survive in the modern world. The underlying assumption was that the whole enterprise had been mistaken, in ways which hardly needed to be spelt out in detail, though it was interesting to see how an intelligent man could have been taken in by the notion that there could be an overall distinction between 'appearance' and 'reality'. Again, the oddity of such statements as the following was emphasized:

Reality is one. It must be single, because plurality, taken as real, contradicts itself. Plurality implies relations, and, through its relations, it unwillingly asserts always a superior unity. To suppose the universe plural is therefore to contradict oneself and, after all, to suppose that it

is one. Add one world to another, and forthwith both worlds have
become relative, each the finite appearance of a higher and single
Reality. And plurality as appearance (we have seen) must fall within,
must belong to, and must qualify the unity (*AR*, p. 460).

Passages like this, and there were many to be found in
Bradley, were taken as evidence of the way in which confusions were engendered. For the first three-quarters of this
century those who thought of themselves as the heirs of the
Anglo-Saxon tradition and as the progressive element in
philosophy regarded metaphysics as an exotic discipline and
Bradley as the last surviving specimen of the breed.

There were three reasons why it was Bradley who was
singled out for this role. First, in the opinion of the general
public he had been the greatest philosopher, being awarded
the Order of Merit for his contribution to the subject. Second,
one of his books, *Ethical Studies*, continued to be studied.
Essay I, 'The Vulgar Notion of Responsibility', fitted well
with the fashionable views, with its appeal to what the man
in the street thought and its use of this as a reason to reject
certain philosophical claims. Third, Russell, even though he
had acknowledged a debt to Bradley in 'On Denoting',
seemed to direct a barrage of criticism at him and at Hegel,
considered his master. The connection with Hegel was seen as
particularly damaging to Bradley.

Hence it might seem surprising that a number of philosophers writing in English should have been willing to contribute to a volume on Bradley, one hundred years after the
publication of the *Principles of Logic*, and nearly sixty years
after his death. Nor do the authors here represented constitute
in any sense a school. Most have turned to Bradley because
of their own philosophic interests, interests which include a
wide variety of topics, sometimes apparently remote from
what has been thought of as typically Bradleian. Nor do they
all accept Bradley's main conclusions or suggest that there
should be a 'back to Bradley' move in contemporary philosophy. It is rather that they have all found, in his writings,
arguments which can be used in their own thought and which
they see as furthering topics which are in the forefront of
philosophical advance. There is always a danger that the
reconsideration of a dead philosopher will become a mere
piece of intellectual history, an attempt to show that, in the

context, his ideas were reasonable or to be expected. Such an attitude seems to us as wrong as that which would totally reject Bradley. It is another way of burying a philosopher. To place any figure in a museum of philosophy is not to honour him. The way to show respect for a dead philosopher is to make use of him for one's own concerns, even if those concerns seem to point in a direction of which he would not have approved. For it is only in this way that the validity of his arguments can be shown, that it is possible to give reasons why it is worth while for any philosopher to read Bradley's writings.

It is not our intention to summarize here what the various contributors have said, but rather to try to give a general answer to the question asking why so many different thinkers have found something of value in his work. The justification for the publication of this volume lies in the individual contributions. Here we are concerned to show how it was possible for thinkers from a variety of backgrounds to find Bradley relevant to their interests. We do this by locating him within the history of recent philosophy. In so far as the normal image of him is of a systematic metaphysician, working within a framework imported from Germany, we wish to show how wrong this picture is and to bring out what is unique and individual about his writings.

There are reasons for thinking of him as a systematic metaphysician. He did believe that metaphysics was the proper object of philosophical thought, and that its goal was 'to produce a rational system of first principles' (*AR*, p. x). Only such a study would 'satisfy the intellect' (*AR*, p. 491). A partial study would fail:

The full and proper defence [of a general view of reality] would be a systematic account of all the regions of appearance, for it is only the completed system which in metaphysics is the genuine proof of the principle (*AR*, p. 403).

However, he himself could not give such an account. Here it is significant that all his three major books end with what can be called sceptical conclusions, which cast doubt on what has, throughout the rest of the work, been argued for with apparent confidence. In the Appendix to *Appearance and Reality*, written for the second edition of 1897, he says: 'It was not within my power to write a systematic treatise...'

(*AR*, p. 491). After answering some criticisms, he says: 'The want of system in my book is another matter, and this I admit and regret' (ibid.).

Again, the charge of being a follower of Hegel he rejected on numerous occasions:

I never could have called myself an Hegelian, partly because I can not say that I have mastered his system, and partly because I could not accept what seems his main principle, or at least part of that principle . . . As for the 'Hegelian School' which exists in our reviews, I know of no one who has met with it anywhere else (*PL*, p. x).

Referring both to the need for system and to Hegel, he says in reply to a critical notice of *Appearance and Reality*:

Now this whole doctrine may of course be mistaken in principle. I have failed, I know well, to grasp it and carry it out as it should have been carried out. Nay, if I had been able to keep closer to a great master like Hegel, I doubt if after all I might not have kept nearer to the truth (*CE*, p. 687).

To say that he was neither a systematizer nor a Hegelian is merely to suggest that the popular view is wrong; it does nothing to show that he is worth reading now. It may be important to put the historical record straight, to remedy an injustice perpetrated by a recent generation of philosophers, but to do this is not to do philosophy. To get thinkers to reread Bradley it may be an essential step, but what will maintain their attention is the discovery of his relevance to today's concerns. Such a proof, we have suggested, is given in the essays here collected. However, there are also some general considerations about his method and style which are appropriately discussed in an introduction.

It is possible to see the one 'great problem' which recurs throughout the *Principles of Logic*, *Appearance and Reality*, and the *Essays on Truth and Reality*. In Bradley's own words it is 'the great problem of the relation of Thought to Reality' (*AR*, p. 492). In the contemporary mode the problem might be expressed by asking about the relation between Language and Reality, and it is here significant that accusations of 'linguistic idealism', as well as defences against the charge, have become common. To see this fact is to realize that description of Bradley as an idealist does not mean that he is beyond consideration at present, but that what is needed is detailed examination of what he actually said. This may reveal that he is different from the image that analytic philosophers have held.

In his pioneering study of Bradley, Richard Wollheim contrasted his style with that of other 'metaphysicians':

> In contrast to so many metaphysicians who have the air of bold, perhaps reckless, travellers setting out with determination from familiar surroundings for a distant though just discernible destination lying upon the horizon of thought, Bradley is more like a man forced backward, step by step, down a strange labyrinth, in self-defence, until at last finding himself in the comparative safety of some murky cave he rests among the shadows.[2]

Wollheim is correct in the first part of his characterization; Bradley has none of the self-confidence and certainty exhibited, for example, by Kant in the preface to the *Critique of Pure Reason* or by Wittgenstein in the preface to the *Tractatus Logico-Philosophicus*. To describe this as the result of 'self-defence' and the final position as a 'murky cave' is to miss and to misunderstand the course of Bradley's arguments. He found himself unable to be systematic. He saw himself engaged, contrary to the image that later philosophers often have of him, in something like the work of a Lockean 'underlabourer':

> What we want at present is to clear the ground, so that English Philosophy, if it rises, may not be choked by prejudice. The ground can not be cleared without a critical, or, if you prefer it, a sceptical study of first principles (*PL*, p. x).

Although Bradley never occupied the position, he could be characterized as doing this in a way not too dissimilar from that of a typical Oxford tutor. The views of other philosophers are subjected to the scrutiny that is given to an undergraduate essay. Without any presuppositions it is shown that a particular view involves inconsistencies, that it is within its own terms confused, or that it fails to explain what it purports to explain. Bradley's positive view only emerges as the result of the failure of other candidates, notably the opinions of his immediate predecessors or contemporaries. This positive view, however, is advanced with a degree of diffidence which is characteristic of his style.

It is important to realize, however, that he came to his conclusions as a result of working in a manner which was more typical of the native British tradition than the result of imported doctrines. His attack on the foundations of empiricism, above all in the form presented by J. S. Mill, was not based on a doctrine accepted prior to the argument, but as the only alternative available after the destruction of other positions. And this conclusion was itself subject to revision, either as the result of outside criticism, or as a result of his own further work. At all times it is arguments that he presents to his readers, not bare conclusions. The best example of this tendency is the second edition of the *Principles of Logic*, which argues that many of the conclusions of the first edition were mistaken.

There is a further point brought out by the latter work. The aim of philosophy, or in Bradley's terms, metaphysics, is to present a complete account, one which would cover all sides of our experience. Even though what a logician had said was satisfactory from the point of view of logic, it might well turn out that it was not so from a more general view-point. The same would be true of any of the special sciences. As Bradley says, the task of metaphysics is 'to comprehend the universe, not simply piecemeal, but somehow as a whole' (*AR*, p. 1). Thus the purpose of metaphysics is characterized by contrast with the purposes, theoretical and practical, of the various special sciences. The metaphysician, unlike the logician, mathematician, natural scientist, moral philosopher, theologian, etc., cannot at any point rest content with an account the adequacy of which depends on an arbitrary delimitation of the field from which its data are drawn. And this is so for Bradley no matter how successful (evaluated either simply theoretically in its own terms or in terms of its wider practical applications to the achievement of human purposes) a particular science might become. Hence a meta-physics after the style, for example, of contemporary *scientific realism* or Quine's pragmatically based *naturalism* would be un-acceptable to Bradley. Nevertheless, for the purpose of this introduction, it is convenient to compare Bradley with Quine, because of the latter's stature as a metaphysician whom Bradley would certainly have recognized as a competitor in the field.

II

Quine sums up his naturalist metaphysics as follows:

With Dewey I hold that knowledge, mind and meaning are part of the same world that they have to do with, and that they are to be studied in the same empirical spirit that animates natural science.[3]

Bradley would have been sympathetic to Quine's impulse towards monism. The latter requires there to be one universe containing both the knower and the known, symbols and the symbolized. Everything that exists is to be construed as lying within the scope of that single system of logically interrelated sentences having logic, mathematics, and natural science at its centre, and touching 'experience' at its periphery. The whole system is construed as confronting experience in a Duhemian manner. Conflict with experience will always require a redistribution of truth-values somewhere within the system. But there will always be a choice as to precisely how the truth-values are to be redistributed. No class of sentences, neither those deeply entrenched at the centre of the system nor observation sentences at the point of contact with experience, is such that its members are beyond the possibility of revision with respect to the truth-values they are taken to have at a given time.[4] Metaphysics, concerned with the ultimate nature of what exists, must itself lie within the system, and it is clear that the activities of the metaphysician must in some way be subordinate to those of the natural scientist, mathematician, and logician. Moreover, it is clear that if knowledge, mind, and meaning are to be successfully portrayed as part of the same world they have to do with, the whole project will require some kind of reductionism — although one resting on a postulated scientific advance rather than one of the traditional phenomenalistic sort.[5] As Quine puts it:

Our three levels [of explanation] thus are levels of reduction: mind consists in dispositions to behaviour, and these are physiological states ... Until we can aspire to actual physiological explanation of linguistic activity in physiological terms, the level at which to work is the middle one; that of dispositions to overt behaviour.[6]

This provides one of the points at which Bradley would resist Quine's naturalistic monism. The intelligibility of the postulated reduction of linguistic behaviour, and dis-positions to such behaviour, to physical and physiological processes and states is crucial to Quine's naturalism, to the project of portraying knowledge, mind, and meaning as part of the same world they have to do with. On the other hand, the inability to make sense of meaning being part of the same world it has to do with can be seen as lying at the foundation of Bradley's idealism.

On Bradley's view the notion of *meaning* is fundamental in this context. Knowledge and the development of mind require an ability to make judgments (true and false), and this, Bradley insists, cannot be achieved independently of achieving mastery of the use of meaningful signs or symbols. 'Before we use symbols, we cannot judge' (*PL*, p. 2). What Quine would describe as a disposition to assent to and dissent from queried sentences would be, for Bradley, the faculty of judgment. Moreover, on Bradley's view, it is an animal's inability to master language and therefore to exhibit behaviour of the kind which requires the use of linguistic symbols, that makes it impossible to ascribe to the animal any degree of mind or soul:

The animal could never say, Yesterday I was sad but I shall be happy tomorrow ... It has, in brief, no world sundered from the world of its immediate practical interest.

And later in the same passage he continues:

I regret to be unable to explain and defend this brief statement. It may serve, perhaps, to point out the interval which in my judgment separates memory from the lower level of mind. How in detail that interval is filled up and crossed I cannot here discuss. I agree that it is the use of language for social needs which is the principal agent (*ETR*, p. 357; cf. also *PL*, pp. 307-11).

Thus there would not be much disagreement between Bradley and Quine on the superficial aspects of the matter. Bradley would agree with Quine that a child initially acquires a language through a process of 'inculcation' by others in the face of objects in their common sensible environments — and primarily in the face of objects of the child's 'immediate practical interest'. Without acquisition of language by such means a child could not come to be in a position to make that 'ideal construction', that people like ourselves do make, of our *real* world of more or less permanent physical objects etc., 'sundered' from *these* egocentrically demonstrable objects of our current perceptions and immediate practical interests. Bradley would be the first to agree with Quine that 'conceptualization on any considerable scale is inseparable from language, and our ordinary language of physical things is about as basic as language gets'.[7] Both Bradley and Quine take it to be a singular virtue in their accounts of the development of mind that they can represent a 'non-Cartesian' continuity between man and the higher animal species with respect to their mental capacities.[8] Possession of a power of symbolic thought within the human species is not a yes–no matter and the developed faculty, as we possess it, must be taken to rest on essentially cognate prelinguistic capacities which are recognizable in the behaviour of human and non-human species alike.

However, the fundamental question is: Is the nature of the faculty of symbolic thought which is inculcated through the agency of others such that its existence could be satisfactorily explained in terms of a theory falling within the compass of natural science? The project of a Quine–Dewey naturalist metaphysics requires that the answer to this question should be 'yes'. Bradley would clearly answer 'no'. Donald Davidson, it seems, would be on Bradley's side here.[9]

Bradley would admit that any truth or falsehood accessible to human beings must have been in fact symbolically articulated, perceptibly or at least in the head, and thus possess particular existence in our real world of objects and events in space and time (*PL*, p. 704 n.). However, he is equally insistent that, when faced, as the *logician* is, with giving an account of the nature of judgment (true or false) and inference, we are forced to abstract from and to ignore the particular existence, mental or physical, of symbols and to treat them simply as vehicles of *communicable* meanings. The logician must take himself to be concerned with things that are *universal*, both in the sense of being *contents* expressible on different occasions by the use of different perceptible symbols and in the sense of being things that can *hold of* (or fail to hold of) indefinitely many different objects. And if by 'exist' we mean being locatable in our real world of particulars in space and time, then the objects the logician is concerned with do not exist at all. In words like those of the later Wittgenstein, Bradley says:

It is a mistake in principle to try to defend the reality of universals by an attempt to show them as psychical events existing in one moment. For if the universal we use in logic had actual existence as a fact in my mind, at all events I could not *use* it as that fact. You must at any rate abstract from the existence and external relations . . . (*PL*, p. 7 n.).

Here lies the foundation of Bradley's anti-psychologism in logic and his attack on the doctrine of the association of ideas when it is taken to be capable of explaining the existence of discursive symbolic thought. Bradley argues that we can only make sense of the existence of the psychological phenomena of association on the assumption that the subject already has, albeit minimally, a capacity to use universals, i.e. a representative power essentially cognate with the power to use perceptible symbols. An ascription of the most minimal perception of change, or its opposite, entails the use of universals by the subject; since it must involve an awareness of something now *not* being in some respect the *same*, or, on the contrary, its *still* being in some respect the *same*, as it was. Hence initial acquisition of the capacity to use universals cannot be explained satisfactorily in terms of association:

The true doctrine is that, when elements have co-existed, they tend to be connected. What does this mean? It means that if (say) in a perception *A* the elements *β* and *γ* are conjoined the mind gets a tendency to join one to the other whenever either reappears. But what are *β* and *γ*? They are universals (*PL*, pp. 311-12).

Later he says:

We might explain [such an association] by a physiological disposition to a certain cerebral function, which (given the stimulus of a new perception or idea) passes into fact. And against this explanation I will not say one word. I will insist only on this, that *it is not a psychological explanation at all*, and that in the hands of those who know their business it is not offered as such (*PL*, pp. 322-3).

In so far as the triggering stimulus to the physiological disposition is taken to be a certain perception had by the subject, then the psychological capacity to associate universals is presupposed and its existence in the subject remains unexplained. On the other hand, no intelligible explanation of anything psychological could be given if the stimulus were taken to be *not* a perception but itself a mere physiological happening in the subject.

Quine, in his schematic account of how a child initially acquires a language, can be seen as adopting an input–output model which is essentially of the same form as that of the associationists. This is apparent when he says:

We have been reflecting in a general way on how surface irritations generate, through language, one's knowledge of the world. One is taught so to associate words with words and other stimulations that there emerges something recognizable as talk of things, and not to be distinguished from talk about the world.[10]

Again:

We can look upon man as a black box in the physical world, exposed to externally determinate stimulatory forces as input and spouting externally determinable testimony about the external world as output.[11]

The questions arise: what are we to understand as involved in this capacity to *associate* words with words and words with other stimulations? And what kind of things are *stimulations* to be taken to be?

Bradley would no doubt agree that if we take stimulations to be *perceptions* we could make sense of the idea of a person, as a result of a process of operant conditioning, coming to associate the meaning of a symbol with the *universal content* of a repeated stimulation. But since the term 'universal' can only be understood to mean those aspects of sense perception which are in principle formulable symbolically, the schematic model could not then be regarded as capable of providing an *explanation* of the kind that the philosopher seems to demand. As Wittgenstein remarks of St. Augustine's description of the child's initial language learning, it would in effect treat the child as already having a language, but not *this* one.

If, on the other hand, we were to take stimulations, as Quine in his discussion of stimulus meaning suggests we should, to be patterns of irradiation occurring in a person's retinae, Bradley would certainly decline to find intelligible the suggestion that mere repetition of such events could explain the person's acquisition of a capacity to 'spout sentences'.

At this point, however, Quine might refer to his postulation of a 'quality space' that a child must be taken to possess if in the first place it is in a position to begin to learn language through a process of operant conditioning. Quine, with a commitment-withdrawing 'so to speak', says of the child:

He must, so to speak, sense more resemblances between some stimulations than between others.[12]

Postulation of such 'sensings', Bradley would doubtless agree, is essential to the intelligibility of the schematic model. But how are we to construe the status of these sensings? If the child is credited with the capacity to sense varying degrees of resemblance between successively given things then he is already being credited with a capacity to represent things *as* being in some respect either as they are or as they are not. Sensing, therefore, is being construed as proto-perception. The model becomes intelligible again but only by taking the effective stimulations to be the subject's *perceptions* of stimulations (construed, for example, as sensory irradiations occurring at the retinae). In this direction a regress of the worst Rylean sort seems to arise; at any rate we are back with a model which patently cannot supply the kind of explanation which appears to be demanded.

III

Whether one is convinced by them when deployed in relation to Quine, the burden of Bradley's arguments within the context of his philosophy is clear. The metaphysician's attempt to psychologize or naturalize knowledge, mind, and meaning by bringing them within a single *world* identified by reference to one or any group of special sciences is to be rejected. However, it is important to see that Bradley does not intend to legislate as to what the special scientist can legitimately concern himself with. A special science is to be judged by reference to its results; with many sciences he would be the first to admit that the practitioners are the only ones capable of understanding what the results are, and therefore the only ones competent to judge success or the lack of it:

To suppose that the metaphysician should come in, and offer to interfere with the proceedings of the physicist or to criticize his conclusions, is in my judgment to take a most wrong view of metaphysics. It is the same with psychology (*PL*, p. 340).

Bradley's anti-psychologism and anti-naturalism is not an attack on empirical science. It is, at least in part, a matter of placing in question the intelligibility of a certain *a priori* schematic model in terms of which empiricist philosophers have characteristically claimed that the existence of knowledge, meaning, and truth *must* be explicable. As Quine puts it:

Surely one has no choice but to be an empiricist so far as one's theory of linguistic meaning is concerned.[13]

Bradley would not deny that there is *some* sense in which we must be empiricists with respect to meaning. What he would deny is that an intelligible characterization of the sense in which we must be empiricists with respect to meaning is given in terms of the input–output schema adopted, in different forms, by the philosophers of the School of Experience and by Quine.

IV

Bradley is not the only recent philosopher unable to accept the intelligibility of attempts to psychologize or naturalize meaning. It is a continuous theme in both the early and later philosophy of Wittgenstein. However, this theme as manifested in the *Tractatus* takes a form which is in many respects a polar opposite to the form it takes in Bradley's philosophy. For the *Tractatus* the world is the totality of facts or the totality of states of affairs represented as existing by true contingent propositions. The natural scientist can properly aim to have knowledge of the world thus conceived. But the sense that propositions have, and the meanings that their constituent names have, cannot, according to the *Tractatus*, be construed as facts. They cannot be construed to fall within the world of which we have knowledge in sense perception and which is the proper object of natural science.

The *utterance* of a proposition will have perceptible aspects and those aspects could become factual data for the natural scientist. But such an utterance will not be merely a *perceptible* fact. As Bradley puts it, it will be a fact which not only possesses its own *that* and *what* but also has meaning. In the terminology of the *Tractatus* a proposition *is* a propositional sign in its *projective relation* to reality. Thus the *identity* of a proposition will not be accessible independently of a grasp of the rules exercised in its construction. To have a grasp of these will be to understand its sense or know its truth-conditions as opposed to its truth-value.

Likewise, when a subject establishes by sense perception the existence of some state of affairs that has been represented *as* existing by some proposition, and, in Wittgenstein's words, 'the reality that is perceived takes the place of the picture',[14] his sense perception will have aspects which could become factual for the empirical psychologist. But Wittgenstein insists: 'Psychology is no more closely related to philosophy than any other natural science'.[15]

This is so since a sense perception, or a cognitive act of any sort, if it is to have a symbolically formulable content (and surely it must have such a content if it is to be able to bear logical relations to human beliefs), must be construed to have the same kind of relation to reality as does a proposition. Thus essentially the same kind of rules of projection involved in the construction of contingent propositions (true or false) must be construed to have been involved already in the generation of any sense perception whose contents are symbolically formulable. It is the business of philosophy to indicate the existence and nature of such rules; they cannot be discovered by psychology or by any *empirical* science since their possession and exercise by a subject is a condition of his being able to perceive (or, for that matter, to misperceive) any state of affairs whatsoever. Such rules, therefore, must be utterly disparate from the contingent natural laws which the empirical sciences establish inductively by means of sense perception.

In the *Tractatus*, Wittgenstein gives expression in an utterly original way to an idea in the history of modern philosophy which goes back to Leibniz via Kant's 'transcendental deduction' of the categories. This is the idea that there is a 'universal grammar' that must be instantiated in any means of expression, natural or conventional, by which the contingently existent or non-existent can be represented. The nature of this 'faculty', which *is* in essence the knowing subject, cannot be affected by what happens to exist or not to exist in the world. It necessarily stands as the 'limit' of the world *qua* the totality of facts, neither capable of affecting it nor being affected by it.

It is plain that any such view of meaning must place its 'explanation' quite beyond the scope of the natural sciences. Moreover, the kind of understanding that is had in understanding the meaning or sense of a proposition, or piece of 'language impregnated' behaviour, must be totally disparate from the kind of understanding that can be had by means of empirically established natural laws. Here, obviously, is a basis for the kind of distinction that Collingwood drew between what he called 'historical understanding' and the understanding achievable by natural science. It is instructive to see how Bradley's view contrasts with the above conception of meaning. This contrast will allow us to highlight some similarities between Bradley and Quine.

V

The theories of Leibniz, Kant, and Wittgenstein postulate in their different ways the determinateness of sense, and thus rest on different versions of what Quine calls the 'museum myth' of meaning, or a 'mentalistic semantics'. He characterizes this view in the following terms:

> Seen according to the museum myth, the words and sentences of a language have their determinate meanings. To discover the meanings of a native's words we have to observe his behaviour, but still the meanings of the words are supposed to be determinate in the native's *mind*, his mental museum, even in cases where the behavioural criteria are powerless to discover them for us.[16]

For Leibniz, Kant, and Wittgenstein, the mind or subject, construed as the source of the universal rules of synthesis or grammar, is not to be thought of in terms of the Cartesian model of an intrinsically private world of immediately known objects. Leibniz's ultimate genera, Kant's unschematized pure concepts of the understanding, and Wittgenstein's simple objects are in a sense the most *public* of all things. Their identity in different subjects is what makes communication of truth and falsehood (with respect equally to inner and outer things) between them possible. But the point is that they are to be construed as absolutely *determinate*, one and the same in all the more or less imperfect symbolisms and vehicles of truth and falsehood that exist.

On this issue of the determinateness of sense, Bradley stands much closer to Quine than he does to Leibniz, Kant, or Wittgenstein. However Bradley's position does not rest on anything analogous to Quine's concept of *stimulus meaning*.

In the *Principles of Logic*, Bradley, just as surely as Quine, collapses the absolute distinction between questions of meaning and questions of empirical knowledge. Hence he rejects the validity of an absolute distinction of the kind implicit in Kant's division of judgments into analytic and synthetic:

The simple enquiry 'Is the denotation fixed?' leads at once to the result that, here as everywhere, intension and extension fluctuate together. Both are relative to our knowledge. And the perception of this truth is fatal to the well-known Kantian distinction. A judgment is not fixed as 'synthetic' or 'analytic': its character varies with the knowledge possessed by various persons, and at different times. If the meaning of a word were confined to that attribute or group of attributes with which it set out, we could distinguish those judgments which assert within the whole one part of its contents from those which add an element from the outside; and the distinction would remain valid for ever. But in actual practice the meaning itself is enlarged by synthesis. What is added today is implied to-morrow. We may even say that a synthetic judgment, so soon as it is made, is at once analytic (*PL*, p. 185).

In consequence, Bradley's conception of inference as the 'ideal self-development of an object' must be understood to contrast utterly with that conception of logical necessity which received its classic expression in Wittgenstein's *Tractatus*. According to the latter, all complex contingent propositions are truth-functions of logically independent contingent propositions, and all implications between contingent propositions rest on truth-functional tautologies which, so to speak, leave all possibilities open to facts. This conception of the nature of implication and inference rests on the possibility of logically independent contingent propositions. Their possibility rests in turn on the intelligibility of a conception of negation (that involved in the fundamental logical operation of joint negation) which Bradley would characterize as 'bare' negation. He rejects this notion as unintelligible, and with it the intelligibility of the idea that there could be as the ultimate foundations of knowledge a totality of purely positive contingent truths, each, together with its negation, absolutely determinate with respect to its sense. In his view any judgment, affirmative or negative, or any inference, must take place in time within a *given* context of mutually exclusive alternative possibilities. No judgment is merely affirmative and none merely negative. The line between judgment and inference becomes blurred:

Hence in all judgment you have a whole in which you take one feature ('this'), and distinguish it really, though not always formally, from another feature ('that') . . . Hence in asserting 'this', you in effect deny that it is 'that', and you thus affirm a universe in which are two differences, each one of which, you find, excludes the other. Thus every judgment is in essence, though not explicitly, both negative and disjunctive. And disjunction within a whole is the one way in and by which in the end negation becomes intelligible (*PL*, p. 662).

With this view any conception of logic having a 'crystalline purity' independent of an empirically given world of contingently existing facts is rejected. There is no pure form. 'Logic assumes that *implication* exists, and that implication, where genuine, is also real' (*PL*, p. 600). Thus according to Bradley's conception of inference as the ideal self-development of an object, the latter is a given object and the development is a historic one which takes place in time. The inference need not involve an empirically given object, but what Quine describes as recalcitrant experience forcing the redistribution of truth-values within a system of beliefs would be an example of what Bradley means by the ideal self-development of an object.

However, at this point, to come to a proper understanding of Bradley's philosophy it is essential to realize that for him logic is simply a special science and that it can be necessary for particular purposes within logic to work with different and even conflicting conceptions of truths, falsehoods, meanings, etc. Hence Bradley is equally insistent that logic *must* also work with a conception of truth and falsehood which requires a conception of meaning which is inconsistent with the radically 'historic' view just characterized. He expresses the contrary conception:

Wherever you have an object taken as good or beautiful or true, or as the opposite of one of these, you have at once something which reaches and holds beyond time and event. And, if it were otherwise, a truth, true at one moment, might at another moment have become a falsehood; and, if so, obviously the whole notion of truth is destroyed . . . We can say, of course first, 'Now it is light,' and then, 'Now it is dark,' but obviously, with this, the first truth is not falsified. That truth was stated ambiguously and imperfectly, and involved a condition not made explicit. But assuredly, so far as it was true, its truth is eternal . . . Truth qualifies that which is beyond mere succession, and it takes whatever it contains beyond the flux of mere event (*ETR*, pp. 339–40).

Bringing the conflicting viewpoints together, Bradley says:

We must in logic assume that truth, as truth, is itself out of time, and that, as truth, it does not and can not exist; though on the other side (. . .) all truth must 'have' existence (*PL*, p. 704 n.).

And again:

In order to be, truth itself must happen and occur, and must exist as what we call a mental event. Hence, to completely realize itself as truth, truth would have to include this essential aspect of its own being. And yet from this aspect logic, if it means to exist, must abstract (*PL*, p. 612).

Hence he concludes:

Certainly the world of truth is on my view pervaded by inconsistency . . . Hence, though truth claims to be a system where nothing is changed and all is at once actual, it claims no less to be a world in which development holds good, and where partial knowledge and ignorance and possibility must in consequence be found. Nor within logic is there any remedy but to admit and to affirm both sides of this total claim, however inconsistent and however discrepant the one with the other (*PL*, pp. 704-5).

This problem, Bradley maintains, is of great importance, and if it has a solution, it cannot lie outside metaphysics. The bearers of truth and falsity, on the one hand, must lie beyond mere succession. All the arguments against psychologism in logic compel us to consign them to a Fregean third realm. But, on the other hand, we seem equally compelled to treat the bearers of truth and falsity as events, mental and physical, with unique positions in our real spatio-temporal series. It is undeniable that temporally successive waking sense-perceptions provide human beings with their fundamental points of cognitive contact with reality and therefore sense perceptions themselves must be regarded as capable of being bearers of truth to them. Truth, it seems, both must and cannot qualify what is beyond mere succession.

In so far as we are in the grip of the first view, it seems that meanings and senses expressed by our symbols (as well as the contents or objects of our psychological acts), must in themselves be determinate independently of their particular, perhaps imperfect and ambiguous, datable expressions, both mental and physical. However, when the other viewpoint is adopted, it seems that we must admit that we confront reality in our successive sense perceptions with a system of beliefs and knowledge which is continually subject to change as a result of new material which comes to light through our own and others' more or less systematic, active dealings with, and reflections upon, things. Such changes cannot leave the meanings and senses of the words we use unchanged. Nor can it leave any room for the idea that there were hidden, *true* meanings and senses which our more or less imperfect symbolic expressions really had all the time. The meanings and senses of our symbols must gain content in conformity with the new material which continually comes to light. The museum myth of a mentalistic semantics must, as Quine claims, be simply a myth.

Bradley maintains that logicians do and must draw theoretical distinctions which will in various ways enable them for particular purposes to take up one or other of such conflicting and overlapping viewpoints while abstracting from or ignoring the rest. In doing this the logician will be acting like any other scientist. However, Bradley argues that the metaphysician, in his attempt to come to an understanding of reality as a whole, cannot abstract in this way. Nor could the metaphysician's intellect be satisfied if he left disparate viewpoints on reality lying side by side, as if the adoption of one rather than another were a cosmic analogue of the *seeing as* phenomenon discussed by the later Wittgenstein. In fact reality will be represented in the context of human beings' experiences and systems of belief in disparate and conflicting ways. But metaphysics cannot allow that reality itself is self-contradictory. The principle of non-contradiction cannot be denied without inconsistency and Bradley maintains that it must be allowed to rule in any sphere of discursive thought, special or otherwise, which aims at the truth.

If disparate viewpoints cannot be brought together consistently within the context of a more comprehensive viewpoint, then no such viewpoint could, for the purpose of metaphysics, satisfy the intellect. For Bradley this would be so no matter how comprehensive, internally consistent, and practically efficacious in our lives, was the system of discursive thought in which the particular viewpoint came to be articulated. Such a system of thought could at best be allowed to give an *appearance* of reality or *phenomena*. It would simply present us with phenomena merely externally related to other phenomena, accessible by means of systems of thought in which other disparate and conflicting viewpoints had been articulated.

However, at this point Bradley's metaphysical argument can be seen as taking a twist which involves him in an even more thoroughgoing rejection of a mentalistic semantics and the museum myth of meaning than Quine's — at least it is more thoroughgoing than Quine's if we take the latter's notion of a *canonical* notation seriously.

VI

The twist that Bradley's argument takes, stems from his reflection on the nature of our faculty of symbolic or discursive thought itself and his conclusion that it is intrinsically inadequate to reality. He finds himself forced to conclude that the categories, which of necessity we exercise in our discursive thought and which are embedded in our intentional behaviour and conscious experiences of reality, are themselves radically incoherent. With this conclusion comes a rejection of any form of the vision involved in a mentalistic semantics and the notion of determinateness of sense.

This does not involve Bradley in rejecting the principle of non-contradiction as the sole criterion of the nature of reality that metaphysics can have. But it does rule out the postulation by the metaphysician of any kind of structural isomorphism between our categories and the reality which is represented, in terms of those categories, in our conscious experiences, and systems of knowledge. In consequence it entails what might be called a 'profound' scepticism: thought in the nature of the case can only yield *appearances* of reality.

Referring to the criterion of non-contradiction for metaphysics, Bradley says:

It would, of course, not be irrational to take one's stand on this criterion, to use it to produce a conclusion hostile to itself, and to urge that therefore our whole knowledge is self-destructive, since it essentially drives us to what we cannot accept (*AR*, pp. 120-1).

It is in chapters II and III of *Appearance and Reality* that Bradley takes a stand on the criterion, turns it on the categories of substantive and adjective, quality and relation, and finds that it produces a conclusion hostile to itself. In other words he argues that although our 'arrangement of given facts

and relations and qualities may be necessary in practice',
nevertheless our doing so is *theoretically* unintelligible
since 'the very essence of these ideas is infected and contradicts itself' (*AR*, p. 21).

These arguments are undoubtedly quite fundamental in
Bradley's metaphysics and it is essential at the outset to grasp
their precise status. It is certainly not the case, as was once
suggested by Russell, that they rest on a failure to recognize
the distinction that must be drawn within logic between
the predicative use of 'is' and the so-called 'is' of identity. To
believe that would be to misconstrue the status of Bradley's
arguments. In fact in the course of his discussion Bradley
implicitly recognizes that the reversibility of subject and
predicate expressions provides a criterion for distinguishing
the different uses of 'is' in question (cf. *AR*, p. 17). Nor is
Bradley ignorant of the fact that it is 'the business of relations
to relate'.

What Bradley does is to examine a series of putative
theoretical accounts of predication. These accounts stem
from the theoretical dissatisfaction commonly felt by philosophers when they reflect on the subject-predicate form.
Hence his discussion can be seen as taking place at the same
level as, for example, Russell's and Wittgenstein's. They were
concerned to argue (i) that the grammatical form of our
sentences can be misleading as to the logical forms of the
propositions we formulate by means of them, and (ii) that
at the fundamental level at which our thoughts relate to
reality those thoughts cannot be construed as formulable
in propositions which are subject-predicate in logical form.

So there is nothing odd in Bradley finding difficulty with
the notion of predication. Russell himself, in *An Inquiry
into Meaning and Truth*, leaves no room for the predicative
'is' at the atomic level; he introduces a modified category of
simple *quality* according to which the notion of a quality
does not require the notion of something which *possesses*
that quality. Likewise, it is part of the insight involved in
Wittgenstein's picture theory of propositional meaning that
there is no room for the idea that the reference of one part
of a picture can be *true of* or, conversely, *satisfied by*, the
reference of some other part. In other words the picture
theory leaves no room for the idea that an elementary

proposition is true in virtue of its logical subject possessing some quality or relation — the quality or relation designated by an expression playing a logically distinctive role and *predicated of* the logical subject by it. In that direction lay all the difficulties of Frege's account. For the *Tractatus* the distinction between function and argument is present at the elementary level but Wittgenstein supplants Frege's asymmetrical metaphor of saturation by suggesting that simple objects are related to one another in states of affairs 'like the links in a chain'. What is important about this metaphor is that it implies that there are no nameable objects which have the special role of *relating* other objects and which are *incomplete* in a way that other objects are not.

Bradley is thus not alone among philosophers in finding difficulties with the predicative 'is' and the categories of substantive, quality, and relation. However, he differs radically from both the early Wittgenstein and Russell in his conclusion. This is that any search for an ultimately satisfactory account of the 'general propositional form' must fail.

Bradley begins by asking what is meant by 'is' in predicative contexts, for example when we assert of a lump of sugar that it is white or that it is sweet. What we cannot do, he argues, is to understand the assertion as *identifying* the lump of sugar with the quality white, or with any one of its qualities, or even with all its qualities taken severally. The latter would not account for the unity or the particularity possessed by the lump of sugar. However, we cannot take the lump of sugar to be anything apart from its qualities. Nevertheless, implicit in attempts to give accounts of the predicative use of 'is' in terms of the metaphors of inherence or possession is the suggestion that a lump of sugar is something apart from its qualities. These are essentially *relational* metaphors which, if understood as serious attempts at theories, must be taken to entail that the thing (the lump of sugar) that has the qualities has an identity independent of its qualities. Surely that suggestion is absurd.

We seem forced therefore to regard the unity and particularity of the lump of sugar as a function of a specific relation holding between the qualities which (as we would ordinarily say) can be asserted of it. Now it would seem, as Bradley puts it, that properly speaking the qualities themselves are to be regarded as the true logical subjects 'about which we are saying something' (*AR*, p. 17). The logical form of the original assertion would be better expressed, for example, by the sentence: 'White is in relation *R* to sweetness.' However, within this context the question of the meaning of 'is' arises again. Once more it cannot be taken to identify white with 'the relation *R* to sweetness'. If it is suggested that 'is' should be replaced by 'has' or 'possesses', that would be to revert to the unexplained relational metaphor. Moreover, Bradley notes that if a complex object were to be regarded simply as a complex of certain qualities interrelated in a certain way, then any assertion that an object of the sort in question had a certain quality would either be false or add nothing (i.e. in effect be analytic). And that problem is one that in fact faces Leibniz's account of general propositions.

However, to avoid these problems it might be suggested that the relation is in no sense an attribute or predicate of the qualities; it is to be treated simply as another merely *nameable* constituent, co-ordinate with the other constituents of the complex. The relation might, that is, be treated as 'independently real' (*AR*, p. 18). But if the relation is construed in this way and not, so to speak, as a specific order which the other constituents *instantiate*, then the specific unity which the constituents have, for example *qua* a particular lump of sugar, will no longer have been explained. In order to account for that unity it will be necessary to postulate another order which the constituents (including the original relation) instantiate. But given that *ex hypothesi* all relations are to be treated as independently real then Bradley's famous regress arises.

Now it is clear that Bradley does not regard the failure in the above kinds of account, kinds which are easily identifiable in the history of philosophy, to be a function of philosophers' stupidity. He regards the contradictions which occur in such accounts to be the result of an intrinsic incoherence in the categories of quality and relation. In Chapter III of *Appearance and Reality* Bradley proceeds to argue independently that 'the very essence of these ideas is infected and contradicts itself' (*AR*, p. 21).

VII

Bradley's argument is quite general. It is to the effect that quality and relation 'each can be something neither together with, nor apart from, the other; and the vicious circle in which they turn is not the truth about reality' (ibid.). However, the argument can be placed in the historical context of the debate concerning the determinateness of sense, and this perhaps makes it easier to appreciate.

If we think about the nature of our discursive thought, and reflect on how it is possible for us to think what is true and what is false of a given reality, we can, under pressure of the idea that the possibility of communicating *the* truth requires us to have as a vehicle of truth, expressions which have quite determinate senses, be driven to postulate one or other version of what Quine would describe as a 'mentalistic semantics'. There are many different versions of such semantics identifiable in the history of philosophy; for present purposes it will be convenient to concentrate attention on the Leibnizian version. His 'ultimate genera' are construed as a plurality of attributes proper which, unlike Russell's postulated qualities, do presuppose the existence of that which possesses them. Moreover, they are construed to be in some sense simple and to be what they are independently of relations. They would, it seems, constitute paradigm examples of what Bradley refers to as 'original and independent qualities' (*AR*, p. 22).

Bradley maintains that if we reflect on the nature of truth from a given viewpoint we must conclude that truth 'qualifies that which is beyond mere succession' (*ETR*, pp. 339–40), and that, equally necessarily, we will be driven to postulate the determinateness of sense and some kind of mentalistic semantics, i.e. a semantics which, in one way or another, rests on the idea of there being a plurality of 'original and independent qualities'. However, he also argues that the idea of there being a plurality of simple qualities or attributes, each being what it is independently of relations, is contradictory:

For consider, the qualities *A* and *B* are to be different from each other; and, if so, that difference must fall somewhere. If it falls, in any degree or to any extent, outside *A* or *B*, we have relation at once. But, on the other hand, how can difference and otherness fall inside? If we have in

A any such otherness, then inside *A* we must distinguish its own quality and its otherness (*AR*, p. 24).

So, taking the second leg of the argument first, we could take *A* to be different from *B* in virtue of being, so to speak, *B* plus some quality. But then *A* would not be simple nor an original and independent quality. It would be at best a complex possessing, or made up of, two such qualities in a certain relation. On the other hand, taking the first leg, *A* could be taken to be different from *B* in virtue of being at a different location in one and the same 'quality space'. In other words, *A* could be different from *B* in virtue of each being a different determination of one and the same attribute. Such a difference would then 'lie outside' each quality and would not be inimical to their remaining in some sense simple. However, in being taken to be located at different positions in the same quality space, the qualities would thereby have been taken to be *related* to one another, and to other positions, in that space.

Thus if we take Leibniz's 'ultimate genera' to be a series of simple, logically independent attributes (each individual, actual, and possible, possessing a precise determination of each attribute), then Bradley's argument is that no sense could be given to the idea of there being a *plurality* or *series* of such attributes. Each attribute, on the Leibnizian view, is taken to generate a logically independent dimension of predication, or quality space, each space containing an infinity of mutually exclusive positions which are orderable as more or less distant from the perfection of the attribute. Bradley's argument, then, amounts to the contention that the only way to give sense to the idea of there being a plurality of different quality spaces (which is compatible with the idea that the attribute generating each space is simple) is to construe them as all interrelated within a single, comprehensive, space. However, to do this would be incompatible with the attributes being, as *ex hypothesi* they are, originally generative of logically independent dimensions of predication. Hence there could not be a plurality of original and independent qualities.

No sense can be given to the idea of there being qualities independent of relations. But on the other hand, Bradley asks, can we make sense of qualities together with relations?

He argues that a negative answer must be given to this question also. If we assert a relation to hold between two terms or qualities, and our assertion is to be true, it seems that our assertion must have a 'real substantial foundation' within those terms or qualities (cf. *AR*, p. 18). Or in other words, the relation must hold 'somehow at the expense of the terms' (ibid.). Hence if *A* bears the relation *R* to *B* then it seems that it must be, so to speak, in *virtue* of the natures that the two qualities *A* and *B* possess independently. However, the thought arises: can we make sense of a quality having any nature at all independently of its having a determinate set of interrelationships to other positions which define its position within a given quality space? Then far from the natures of the qualities having to provide the real substantial foundation for the relations, we seem compelled to think that it must be the 'relation which somehow precipitates terms which were not there before' (*AR*, p. 27). Any given colour, so to speak, has the nature it has *simply* in virtue of the interrelationships that it has to other positions in colour space. Here again, we might think in terms of the mentalistic semantics of Wittgenstein's *Tractatus*, where the simple objects must be construed to be 'in a manner of speaking, colourless'.[17] As such, simple objects have no material properties, merely formal or internal ones. These must be simply their possibilities of combination with other objects in states of affairs. To adopt Bradley's words (probably used in relation to Leibniz's monads) such things would be 'simple beyond belief' (*AR*, p. 25). We are driven to conclude that the nature of qualities (simple objects) cannot be constituted *merely* by their relations (possibilities of relation) to one another. It seems therefore that qualities must be construed to have a dual nature which is partly the foundation of their relations to one another and partly a result of those relations. But this would be tantamount to treating each quality as a pair of qualities in a certain relation to one another, each of which, in turn, we would be compelled to think of as a pair of qualities in a certain relation, and so on *ad infinitum*. As Bradley spells it out:

A is both made, and is not made, what it is by relation; and these different aspects are not each other, nor again is either *A*. If we call its diverse aspects *a* and *α*, then *A* is partly each of these. As *a* it is the difference on which distinction is based, while as α it is the distinctness that results from connexion. *A* is really both somehow together as *A* (*a* − α). But (as we saw . . .) *without* the use of a relation it is impossible to predicate this variety of *A*. And, on the other hand, *with* an internal relation *A*'s unity disappears, and its contents are dissipated in an endless process of distinction (*AR*, p. 26).

Thus Bradley is driven to a position even more hostile to a mentalistic semantics and a notion of determinateness of sense than is Quine's:

The conclusion to which I am brought is that a relational way of thought — any one that moves by the machinery of terms and relations — must give appearance, and not truth. It is a makeshift, a device, a mere practical compromise, most necessary, but in the end most indefensible (*AR*, p. 28).

So since any body of knowledge or truth accessible to human beings must of necessity be formulated in a symbolism which moves by the machinery of terms and relations, no body of knowledge, no matter how comprehensive and practically useful it might prove to be in our lives, could for the purpose of metaphysics be taken to be capable of yielding more than an *appearance* of reality. Hence if natural science were taken as doing more than this, as it is by a naturalist metaphysics, then it would become thereby straightforwardly false. If, on the other hand, it is seen for what it is, namely a special science which must abstract from and ignore most aspects of human life, then it can be admitted as one of the most impressive bodies of truth that human beings have come to possess.

VIII

At this point a philosopher (who, perhaps, did not take naturalism in metaphysics very seriously anyway) might well complain that we surely need not wait on a complex argument that shows that the categories of relation and quality are self-contradictory in order to be convinced that symbolic thought is inadequate to the nature of reality. Surely immediate experience, accompanied by pleasure and pain, is an undeniable feature of human and animal life, yet it is something to which discursive thought is patently inadequate? In a way Bradley would be the first to agree with this sentiment. However, it must be remembered that Bradley is arguing as a metaphysician confronting a history of philosophy containing rationalist and realist philosophers in the Leibnizian tradition who did maintain that our faculty of thought was in principle adequate to reality. In the following passage Bradley gives expression to the sentiment contained in the above question but postulates, for the purpose of delineating his own contrasting position, a view of the relation between thought and reality which is realist in the Leibnizian sense.

Let us then suppose that the dualism inherent in thought has been transcended. Let us assume that existence is no longer different from truth, and let us see where this takes us. It takes us straight to thought's suicide. A system of content is going to swallow up our reality; but in our reality we have the fact of sensible experience, immediate presentation with its colouring of pleasure and pain. Now I presume there is no question of conjuring this fact away; but how it is to be exhibited as an element in a system of thought-content, is a problem not soluble. Thought is relational and discursive, and, if it ceases to be this, it commits suicide; and yet, if it remains thus, how does it contain immediate presentation? Let us suppose the impossible accomplished; let us imagine a harmonious system of ideal contents united in relations, and reflecting itself in self-conscious harmony. This is to be reality, all reality; and there is nothing outside it (*AR*, p. 150).

In supposing the dualism inherent in thought to have been transcended Bradley is postulating a position which, on a certain construal, is equivalent to Leibniz's. For Leibniz, sensibility was not to be construed, as Kant came to argue it must be, as a totally passive faculty for causal contact with reality, yielding, through sensations received, 'matter' on which the subject's active representative faculty is exercised. According to Leibniz's epistemology a subject's sensibility was simply a consequence of a determinate degree of imperfection in an essentially active representative faculty — a faculty which is in its essence identical in all subjects actual or possible. This faculty would yield in its perfected form, in a purely active being, omniscience with respect to the reality, represented more or less confusedly in our conscious sense perceptions and in the systems of symbolic knowledge derived therefrom. Of course, finite subjects like ourselves need to master the use of linguistic symbols if we are to be in a position to have anything approaching clear and distinct knowledge of items represented in our sense perceptions. A perfect being would not need to do this. His cognition would be unlike ours since it would be non-symbolic or *intuitive*; he would know with total adequacy all that exists in the act of creating it. However, what is crucial to Leibniz's epistemology, and what marks off his transcendental realism from Kant's transcendental idealism, is the contention that sensibility is to be construed simply as a consequence of a degree of imperfection in an essentially active representative faculty which *in principle could yield omniscience*. Thus, according to Leibniz's realist view of knowledge, the grammars of our languages, in terms of which we formulate the contents of our perceptions and theorize therefrom, yield us an explicit but more or less imperfect grasp of the ultimate genera which (a) operate spontaneously in the generation of subjects' sense perceptions, and (b) were exercised in the act of creation of the universe represented in these perceptions.

So it follows, according to Leibniz, in the case of the Absolute or perfect being, that, to use Bradley's expression, 'the dualism inherent in thought is transcended'. In other words, the symbolic or 'intentional' character of our thought, in virtue of which thought necessarily points to something (= x) beyond its own datable psychical or physical existence, is gone. Yet nevertheless, in the Absolute, thought for Leibniz is supposedly still in its essence identical with our necessarily symbolic faculty of thought. And moreover, nothing can be lost in the Absolute. Somehow all that there is to finite subjects' suffering, all that there is to evil, error, and so on is known with complete adequacy in thinking the precise degree of imperfection which each subject possesses in the scale of being and which individuates it from all other subjects, actual and possible. Given that the ultimate genera exercised in thinking are the attributes possessed in perfect form by the Absolute itself, we arrive, it seems, at something very close to what Bradley enjoins us to imagine when he says: 'let us imagine a harmonious system of ideal contents united by relations, and reflecting itself in self-conscious harmony [with] ... nothing outside it' (*AR*, p. 150).

Of course, it is at this point that Kant claims Leibniz's system falls into incoherence. Kant had argued that by 'transcendental reflection' on our cognitive faculties we can see that our symbolic thought is essentially discursive and intrinsically *general*. Therefore Leibniz in treating sensibility simply as a consequence of a degree of imperfection in such a faculty, had, in effect, and with obvious absurdity, treated reality (the universe) itself as a system of abstract objects or mere *intelligibilia*.[18] Kant concluded that reality must, after all, be regarded as something (= x) which is the causal source of a subject's sensations. *Ex hypothesi*, these manifold sensations, received subject to 'pure forms' determined by the specific nature of the subject's totally passive sensible faculty, were construed to provide the matter of the objective, or 'intentional', experiences generated in the subject's consciousness by a spontaneous exercise of a totally active symbolic faculty. Kant followed Leibniz in maintaining that the latter faculty is in essence necessarily identical in all finite subjects capable of representing what is the case or not the case in regard to sensibly given objects. However, for Kant, it was to be construed as a *merely* discursive faculty, no matter how perfect an instance of it might be, intrinsically unable by itself, so to speak, to determine the *individual*.

Bradley will not accept Leibniz's realism with its contention that our thought could retain its essential nature in the Absolute, or in principle be adequate to the ultimate nature of reality. However, he is, if anything, more unwilling to follow Kant into the even worse contradiction of his radical causal theory of sensation, with its dualism of sensibility and understanding, and postulation of a reality of noumenal subjects and objects which are *ex hypothesi* thinkable but unknowable. He says with devastating effect:

It would be much as if we said, 'Since all my faculties are totally confined to my garden, I cannot tell if the roses next door are in flower.' . . . If the theory really were true, then it must be impossible. There is no reconciling our knowledge of its truth with that general condition which exists if it is true (*AR*, p. 111).

Bradley's own position, with a profound scepticism in respect to discursive thought latent in it, can scarcely be expressed in anything but his own words.

Without a metaphor, feeling belongs to perfect thought or it does not. If it does not, there is at once a side of existence beyond thought. But if it does belong, then thought is different from thought discursive and

relational. To make it include immediate experience, its character must
be transformed. It must cease to predicate, it must get beyond mere
relations, it must reach something other than truth. Thought, in a
word, must have been absorbed into a fuller experience. Now such an
experience may be called thought, if you choose to use the word. But
if any one else prefers another term, such as feeling or will, he would be
equally justified. For the result is a whole state which both includes
and goes beyond each element; and to speak of it as simply one of them
seems to be playing with phrases. For (I must repeat it) when thought
begins to be more than relational, it ceases to be mere thinking . . .
Thus, in reaching a whole which can contain every aspect within it,
thought must absorb what divides it from feeling and will. But when
these all have come together, then, since none of them can perish, they
must be merged in a whole in which they are harmonious. But that
whole assuredly is not simply *one* of its aspects. And the question is
not whether the universe is in any sense intelligible. The question is
whether, if you thought it and understood it, there would be no difference left between your thought and the thing. And, supposing that to
have happened, the question is then whether thought has not changed
its nature (*AR*, p. 151).

To return to Quine; his postulated Absolute is Nature. And
Nature is for him identified as that which is given in terms of
that single system of discursive thought which has natural
science etc. at its centre and confronts experience via 'occasion'
sentences (keyed directly into causally given stimuli) at its
periphery. Nothing can be left to perish outside the scope of
this single system. Thought, immediate experience, with its
colouring of pleasure and pain, will, etc. must all somehow
be contained within its scope: a single 'inanimate' reality,
so to speak, striving to reflect itself through the categories
of the canonical notation of natural science in self-conscious
harmony.

Bradley would agree with Quine that the metaphysician
must allow that immediate experience, will, and all the
phenomena available to human beings in terms of their
disparate and conflicting systems of thought must somehow
come together harmoniously in the Absolute. But he maintains that no system of relational thought could in the
nature of the case enable us to see in the end how this is
possible. Moreover, Bradley would decline to accept the
validity of any pragmatic justification, in terms of its power
to enable us to predict and control the occurrence of events
in this world of things in space and time, for giving a privileged
metaphysical status to one rather than another of our systems

of thought. What relevance has such predictability got, for example, to the reality available to human beings in terms of their systems of moral, aesthetic, and religious thought? The 'bloodless categories' of natural science are patently inadequate to the concrete human activities and experiences in which such thought is embedded.

NOTES

1. *Language, Truth and Logic*, London, 1950, p. 36.
2. *F. H. Bradley*, Harmondsworth, 1959, p. 18.
3. *Ontological Relativity and Other Essays*, New York, 1969, chap. II, p. 27.
4. *From a Logical Point of View*, London, 1961, p. 42 ff.
5. *From a Logical Point of View*, p. 38 ff.
6. *Mind and Language*, ed. S. Guttenplan, Oxford, 1975, pp. 94-5.
7. *Word and Object*, Cambridge, Mass., 1964, p. 3.
8. For example *PL*, p. 309; *Ontological Relativity*, p. 156.
9. 'Mental Events' in *Experience and Theory*, ed. L. Foster and J. Swanson, London, 1971, pp. 91-2.
10. *Word and Object*, p. 26.
11. *Experience and Theory*, pp. 2-3; see also *Ontological Relativity*, p. 81.
12. *Word and Object*, p. 83.
13. *Ontological Relativity*, p. 81.
14. *Philosophical Remarks*, Oxford, 1975, para. 43.
15. *Tractatus Logico-Philosophicus*, London, 1961, 4.1121.
16. *Ontological Relativity*, pp. 28-9.
17. *Tractatus Logico-Philosophicus*, 2.0232.
18. *Critique of Pure Reason*, A264/B320.

CHAPTER 2

Bradley and Critical History

W. H. Walsh

The Presuppositions of Critical History,[1] Bradley's first philosophical publication, appeared in 1874 when its author was twenty-eight. A pamphlet of only fifty pages, fitted out with a self-conscious preface, a portentous introduction, and no less than five appended 'Notes', it was apparently not successful in causing a stir even among the zealots and is passed over in silence in Bradley's later writings. Part of its failure must be put down to its style which, while giving some foretaste of the splendours that were to come, was too ornate for the occasion. Whereas in *The Principles of Logic*, especially in the crucial opening chapters, Bradley used his considerable rhetorical powers to sharpen and point his argument, here rhetoric tends to lie heavy on the thought and at times almost obscures it. Bradley has obviously taken trouble to find the proper way of expressing his ideas, but leaves the impression of having polished his sentences too long. Victorian readers no doubt saw as embellishing what now strikes us as embarrassing, but even when allowance is made for that, the work is not quite all it should be from the literary point of view.

As a piece of philosophical argument, however, the essay calls for a different judgment. True, there are defects in substance as well as in manner, in so far as topics are not explored in the detail they need and objections are overlooked or not fully answered. Bradley himself was conscious of points whose treatment needed improvement; he mentioned in the preface 'the whole subject of probability and certainty' as one which 'ought to have been investigated'. Yet when we reread the work today we can hardly fail to appreciate the vigour and penetration of the thought which lies behind the stiff exterior; whether he got the answers right or wrong Bradley raises here a series of lively questions which were not only interesting in his own time, but remain interesting today. *The Presuppositions of Critical History* is in fact something of a pioneer work: it is, so far as I know, the first serious piece of writing in English on truth and fact in history, the first to argue that historical facts are 'constructions' or 'constitutions', along the lines later followed by Collingwood, Oakeshott, and Leon Goldstein. If only for that reason it deserves renewed study. It also puts forward an account of historical thought which, surprisingly, does justice to empiricist as well as to Hegelian ideas. Bradley is already severe in his criticisms of the empiricist theory of knowledge, particularly as he takes it to apply to history; it turns out, however, that he shares certain important empiricist views, perhaps more by chance than through deliberate adherence.

Bradley's case against empiricism in this pamphlet is closely linked with that for his own view that historical facts are constructs. Declaring at the outset (p. 8) that the history he is to investigate is history as it is for historians, which implies a 'union' of 'the past in fact' and 'the present in record', he proceeds to examine a simple account, 'natural to the uncritical mind' (p. 9), according to which history can provide fact without activity on the historian's part and without the need for any presuppositions in his thinking. The story is that historical truth is possible thanks to the circumstance that reliable eyewitnesses report things as they actually are or were, and that their reports are transmitted to subsequent generations as faithful transcripts of fact. The conscientious witness knows he must reproduce and not garnish; when he does so he gives us access to past reality in an unadulterated form. Against this view Bradley adduces the facts of historical practice. Instead of a single agreed account of the past we find ourselves confronted with 'divergent accounts' produced by 'a host of jarring witnesses' (p. 9); if we try to sort this 'chaos of disjoined and discrepant narrations' under the headings 'true' and 'false' we are compelled to abandon the attitude of pure passivity which was to guarantee access to reality and to bring the critical mind into play. The critical mind stands in need of a criterion, which it will use, but of which it will not necessarily be conscious, in deciding what to believe. But the activity of the historian is not confined to the task of harmonizing records or distinguishing what is fabricated from what is authentic: once the records are agreed, he has still to comprehend them, in order to get at the underlying truth of what occurred. The problem is recurrent since 'with every fresh standing-ground gained by the growth of experience, with every rise of the spirit to a fuller life, comes another view of the far-lying past from a higher and a new level, and a fresh and corresponding change in the features of the object recognized' (p. 10). Thus, so far from being presented with truth about the past without effort on his part, the historian has to get at it by an activity which is at once critical and unceasing. It is the central features of this activity that Bradley proposes to lay bare.

Bradley adds further points to this criticism of the copy theory of historical truth in the comparison of historical tradition with a fresco which forms the subject of his Note A (pp. 54-9), insisting in particular that the material on which the historian has to work is not only divergent but also incomplete: the drawings which constitute the fresco have great gaps in them. But it is less important to pursue this now than to say something about Bradley's alternative view. If a historical fact is not a past reality mysteriously preserved in testimony, what is it? Bradley's answer is that it is the product of critical inference and judgment. Whatever the strength of our conviction that past conditions were what they were without regard to what anyone thinks of them now (a conviction which Bradley himself shares), the fact remains that the past as we know it stands and must stand in relation to the present. The past as it actually unfolded is not available for our inspection now, and our only chance of reconstructing it is through critical scrutiny of the evidence for it that we possess in the way of narratives, records, accepted or disputed interpretations, and the like. We must conclude what happened after considering such evidence against the background of our accepted beliefs, i.e. in the light of what we presently take to be true.

It may be remarked in passing that Bradley's conception of historical evidence would hardly satisfy a modern historian. He speaks throughout as if explicit descriptions of what was said to have occurred ('testimony') constituted the historian's main, perhaps his sole, material, and in one passage (p. 35) goes so far as to rule out as not properly historical 'evidence from excavations, and evidence from language', on the ground that 'they do not essentially lie within the period of human records'. Even if that is true it would only preclude their use in prehistory, not their supplementing other forms of evidence in periods for which human records exist. What Bradley failed to appreciate was the importance of material that testifies *indirectly* to the human past — parish registers, tax records, legal documents, coins, monuments, traditional ceremonial procedures, among others. But though this was a defect, it was not perhaps a fatal one.

There are two immediate difficulties about the view that historical facts are not so much discovered as (in Goldstein's term) 'constituted' in historical thought. One is quite simply our conviction, mentioned already, that there was a real past quite independent of present thought, and that history must promise us knowledge of this if it is to be taken seriously. Reflection on the present evidence, with or without presuppositions, provides us with a relative past, whereas what we want is a past which existed absolutely. I regret to say that Bradley does nothing to remove this difficulty. The second problem is that if historical facts are constituted, that comes dangerously close to saying that they are made up. Bradley appears to be especially open to this objection, in so far as he stresses not just the relation between past fact and present experience, but that between past fact and *personal* experience (cf. p. 18). The historian, he tells us, must decide what he is to take as being fact for himself. As the last paragraph of Note E puts it (p. 70), there are 'no facts but my facts'. I shall return to this puzzling topic later, in the mean time remarking that, this point aside, Bradley's theory of historical judgment does not represent that activity as arbitrary. In the first place historical thought is directed on an object: it starts from history as a going concern, with its mass of data, problems, and proffered solutions, and its task is to bring order to this confusion. Unless there were a given element in history there would be nothing objective about it, nothing to differentiate it from mere fiction. No part of the given need be absolute, in the sense of having to be accepted just as it stands; even without this, however, it imposes powerful restraints on what historians can conclude.

And there is a second feature of historical thought which makes it for Bradley the reverse of arbitrary, namely that it proceeds on principles which are essentially rational. History as explained above stands in need of a criterion by which to assess its evidence; it must make use of that criterion but has no need to defend it. The defence falls to philosophy, which both makes the criterion explicit and shows its acceptance to be reasonable, thus demonstrating that historical judgment is reputable after all.

Bradley employs much of his space in *The Presuppositions of Critical History* in spelling out and defending his criterion, which turns out to be more complex than at first appears (hence the reference to 'principles' above). His first formulation speaks of it in terms which recall Hume and Mill, but could conceivably have been taken from Kant: 'the universality of law, and what loosely may be termed causal connexion, is the condition which makes history possible' (p. 21). The assumption is one common to history and natural science, since both are agreed that 'a fact which asserts itself as (loosely speaking) without a cause, or without a consequence, is no fact at all' (p. 23). No discovery made in natural science could invalidate this principle, since it underlies all scientific enquiry: I have to presume the 'absolute stability' of relations in things in order to conclude 'that a false judgement is the result of a false inference in me, and not of a shifting connexion in the world' (p. 22). If anything could happen, coherent thought about nature would be impossible. But what about events in the human world? Do not men have free will, and does not this mean that their volitions are uncaused? To say that there are no events without causes is to imply that causes operate in a constant way. Yet may not history surprise us by recording actions, reactions, ways of thinking and behaving which are remote from those we see around us? However constant physical nature may be, is it not one of the lessons of history that man is indefinitely various, that past persons were not so much like ourselves as unlike, and of interest just because of that fact?

Bradley's treatment of these questions is not wholly satisfactory. As in *Ethical Studies* he begins by declaring himself out of sympathy with libertarian views. If the freedom of the will (which in some sense he does not dispute) means 'that the actions of men are subject to no law, and in this sense irrational' (p. 23), the possibility of history disappears. We are precluded in these circumstances 'from counting on human nature', which means that 'our hold upon tradition is gone, and with it well nigh our only basis for historical judgement' (ibid.). Bradley backs this up with the claim that 'the contrary is every day assumed as certain' in the criminal courts, where people are 'executed in many cases by right of what comes to a construction from the laws of human action' (p. 23–4). But what are these 'laws of human action'? Do they record true causal uniformities found to hold between (to speak vaguely) circumstances and behaviour? Or are they laws in a different sense, principles of rational activity, on which agents may, perhaps will, but do not invariably, act? When a prosecuting counsel purports to reconstruct criminal behaviour to which testimony is incomplete, does he do it by invoking causes which necessarily affected the alleged criminal, or by producing what he says is the rationale of the latter's actions? I do not wish to rule out the first alternative, but would suggest that the second is more often the proper account. If it is, talk about 'counting on human nature' becomes more difficult. For ideas about what should be done in this sort of situation or that notoriously vary from society to society, group to group, age to age: what could be counted on as normal (and therefore as a clue to probable behaviour) at one time cannot necessarily be presumed at another. Bradley's comparison with what goes on in the courts is defective just for this reason: accused, judge, and jury belong to the same society, and there is accordingly reason to think that they will be at one in their reactions to specified contingencies. A defending counsel does not often feel it necessary to demonstrate that his client was actuated by strange principles, though he may be concerned to establish that he saw his situation in an unusual way. But when we move from the law to history, we have to reckon not just with unfamiliar ways of seeing the world, but with unexpected views about how to deal with it as well.

When he talked about 'counting on human nature' Bradley seemed to be echoing Hume, an author he presumably studied when preparing his work but did not mention in the published text.[2] Hume declares[3] that 'the common distinction between *moral* and *physical* necessity is without any foundation'; Bradley probably disagreed (he refers at one point (p. 23) to the question 'whether, strictly speaking, causation retains a meaning when applied to the will'), but made no clear pronouncement on the subject in this essay. Hume again speaks of 'the regular springs of human action and behaviour', which he specifies as 'ambition, avarice, self-love, vanity, friendship, generosity, public spirit'.[4] It looks as if Hume thought that these 'passions' function as constantly operating causes determining what men do, though he allowed that their effects can vary from case to case thanks to 'the diversity of characters, prejudices and opinions' (op. cit., p. 85). In view of what he was to say in *Ethical Studies* only two years later Bradley could hardly have accepted that view either, though once more he fails to formulate any clear alternative. Yet it seems that he must accept *some* story about the springs of human action being unchanging if he is to justify his claim that present experience is the final test of what is historically credible. He must presume that men in the past were *ultimately* like ourselves, however differently we and they behave in situations which are apparently similar.

What *should* Bradley have said on this topic? In a previous discussion of the subject[5] I tried to argue that the only thing a historian need hold to be constant in human nature is the form of practical thinking itself. People in the past need not have seen the world as we do nor have reacted to it as we do, but they must have seen things in a more or less coherent way, have had what we should call principles for dealing with situations of different types, and possessed the ability to put them together in a practical syllogism issuing in action. On this view we can understand an act if we can construct its rationale, and to do that we need only to *enter into* another's point of view, not to *embrace* or *share* it. However, I had to admit at the end of my discussion that there are imaginable cases where this condition is satisfied, but which we should still regard as unintelligible, on the ground that the principles of action concerned were bizarre: we could not see how anyone could find them appealing. In order to reduce their alien character we must seek to connect them with basic impulses we take the persons concerned to share with ourselves. This appears to resurrect Hume's regular springs of human action. But it is not necessary to suppose that these are simple causes exerting an unchanging or nearly unchanging effect on everything we do. No doubt, as Hume argued, every human being experiences the passions of love and hate and has some sense of himself, together with a certain fellow-feeling, however faint and restricted in application, for others; these give rise to pride and shame on the one hand and to moral feeling on the other. But it does not follow from this that there are constant or near constant laws of human action, if only because the objects of love and hate, pride and shame, moral approval and disapproval, can and do vary from society to society, if not so much within particular societies. The same motives are at work in modern times as were operative in the ancient world, but modern man and ancient man need not for that reason be materially the same. The important thing to emphasize here is that Hume's list is a list of motives, and that motives make themselves apparent in a context of free action, not of causal necessity. In particular contexts, knowledge of an agent's principles, with a presumption of his motives, is enough to make reliable predictions possible, as in Bradley's case of the law. But the uniformities to which appeal is made here are local uniformities only.

The contention that 'present experience' is the touchstone of what is historically credible is thus seriously misleading. Certainly we have to presume that men in the past were like ourselves in some degree if we are to make sense of what they did. But the likeness is far from being total. If I am correct it amounts to no more than possession of (a) a shared apparatus for deliberation and decision, one which is formally identical in all human agents though capable of infinite variety in content, and (b) a set of basic impulses or, better, motives which are common to all human beings in name, though again widely different in their operation. And whether I am correct or not it is clear that Bradley should have said more on the subject than he did.

That he treated it so lightly can perhaps be explained through his own historical interests at the time. The only historians to get a mention in *The Presuppositions of Critical*

History are Herodotus, Gibbon, and a group of German church historians of the earlier part of the nineteenth century. Herodotus and Gibbon get only passing mentions, both in connection with their attitudes to alleged physical facts (having the sun rise on one's right when circumnavigating Africa, speaking without tongues). Bradley's interest in D. F. Strauss, F. C. Baur, and C. Holsten, all of whom wrote about the beginnings of Christianity, was more serious. He was concerned above all with Baur, who wrote in the first volume of his *Geschichte der christlichen Kirche*[6] that though for the believer the history of Christianity begins with 'the most stupendous of miracles', the task of 'those who are interested in the scientific study of history' is 'to show how the miracle of the absolute beginning may itself be regarded as a link in the chain of history, and to resolve it, so far as the case admits, into its natural elements' (*English trans.*, pp. 1–2). After mentioning and analysing some factors in the contemporary world which, as it were, prepared the ground for the Christian religion, Baur went on (op. cit., pp. 22–3):

On what grounds can we regard Christianity itself as a phenomenon purely supernatural, as an absolute miracle introduced into the world's history without the operation of any natural causes, and therefore incapable of any historical connection, when we find in every direction, wherever we turn, numerous points of connection and affinity in which it is linked with the most intimate bonds to the whole history of the development of mankind? It contains nothing that was not conditioned by a series of causes and effects going before, nothing that had not been long prepared in different ways.

Baur was far from denying that, for the believer, the Resurrection and the conversion of St Paul were evident miracles; his contention was only that the historian is in no position to stop at that point *qua* historian. The history that historians write is necessarily secular, for though historians have to recognize *belief in* the miraculous, doing their job means showing that developments which at first sight have no natural antecedents do not in the end answer this description. It is this conception of history, with its background of theological problems, that Bradley set out to examine. By 'critical history' he meant history as practised by Baur and others of the same way of thinking, who were committed to extruding from history those events with no causes, or with only supernatural causes. Not surprisingly, in view of the period with which Baur and Bradley were primarily concerned, this brought to the fore questions about physical possibilities or impossibilities, water turning into wine, dead men rising from the grave, a person who had died reappearing and ascending into heaven. Bradley need not have concentrated on such cases, and indeed gave some attention to a different one, that of the conversion of St Paul, where psychological as opposed to physical possibility is at stake (see pp. 51-2 n., especially point (ii)). But he does not seem to have taken note of the difference, and accordingly ended up with a position not unlike that of Hume. The latter wanted to ban the miraculous altogether, whereas Bradley's argument bans it only from history, leaving 'a higher form of knowledge' (p. 51 n.), with the possibility of bringing it back. But despite this difference both contend that what cannot be accounted for in natural terms cannot be taken as part of the reality under investigation.

It is clear from this that, despite the hostility Bradley shows in the early part of his essay towards the copy theory of truth and a sensationalist account of knowledge, his own philosophy at the time shared an important element with empiricism. Indeed, a cynic might describe Bradley as having positively strengthened empiricist theory, though hardly as having aimed at that result. He strengthened it in two ways: first, by making clear, as has just been shown, that what Hume asserts without qualification and with seeming dogmatism is borne out in respectable historical practice, second, by pointing to certain differences between history and natural science which both confirm the empiricist doctrine that science is empirical knowledge *par excellence* and bring out a special way in which history is dependent on experience.

He begins by conceding that in favourable circumstances we are prepared to accept scientific testimony to the occurrence of phenomena which bear no analogy to anything that has fallen within our experience; the question is whether we should be prepared to accept corresponding historical testimony. Bradley answers this with the firmest of negatives. The propositions of science, he tells us without argument, are and must be matters of theoretical demonstration, those of history, although sometimes beyond practical doubt, admit only of probability, not proof. Scientific inference thus proceeds on a firm foundation, historical inference on an uncertain one. Again, in the scientific case I can assure myself of the competence and integrity of a witness, so much so that I can take his testimony to be equal to my own 'most careful observation' (p. 29), while the same is not true in history. The world of the scientist is, in a sense, a limited world, one which can be shared by different persons and whose mastery is comparatively easy, thanks to the fact that many differences in those concerned can be set aside as irrelevant: nationality and religion, for example, can mostly be neglected when it comes to assessing scientific reports. But 'historical testimony not only is *to* history, but is also *in* history. This addition prevents the identification of our minds with the minds of the witnesses' (p. 39). The historical witness is and has to be 'the son of his time' (p. 41), which means that his point of view cannot be taken as identical with our own. History is progressive; the knowledge of itself which humanity has at an earlier stage must be 'partial and false' when compared with what it has at a later stage (p. 40). Further, history is concerned with the fortunes of particular persons and societies, individuals which as it were exist in the round and are hard to comprehend just because of that fact. Those who bear witness to historical happenings themselves belong to such concrete wholes and reflect their idiosyncrasies.

It follows that the historian can never 'succeed in exhibiting identity of standpoint' (p. 42) in himself and his witnesses. But even if he could, reconstruction of what happened can never be complete enough to take him beyond mere probabilities. In addition to the difficulties already mentioned, historical events are unique, perishable, and unrepeatable, historical witnesses for the most part incapable of being questioned. Accordingly the only prudent course is to give credence at most to such part of their reports as can be borne out in present experience. We must dismiss as unacceptable all testimony to the non-analogous. Bradley maintains that his result is anything but sceptical:

The present experience, which is open to our research, is so wide in its extent, is so infinitely rich in its manifold details, that to expect an event in the past to which nothing analogous now corresponds may fairly be considered a mere extravagance (p. 43).

Existing historical practice here bears out philosophical theory, and if it is said that things will be different when history becomes a science, as Buckle and Mill said it would, Bradley treats that possibility with a scepticism that is barely polite.[7]

How good are these arguments? An immediate objection could be found in the point made already, that Bradley has a defective idea of historical evidence, believing it to consist wholly or almost wholly in the testimony of witnesses. A marriage certificate or the contents of a grave can provide evidence of past practices, circumstances, and beliefs, but do not testify as straightforward narratives do. However, we had perhaps best set this objection aside and take Bradley in his own terms. Here it must be said first that the general contrast between science and history over 'exhibiting identity of standpoint' is worth careful consideration. If we are to put our trust in a witness and accept his testimony as true, we must believe that his standards of observation and reporting are at least as high as our own. We can find grounds for the belief in the scientific case, precisely because, as Bradley says, science is a restricted activity which does not involve man in the full range of his capacities. On any account it is harder to achieve the same confidence in history; in some cases, those where we deal with witnesses who have strange beliefs, powerful imaginations, or little or nothing in the way of a critical sense, it may well be impossible to achieve.

Unfortunately Bradley spoils an interesting case by producing arguments in its favour that are either dubious or unsupported. He does nothing to elucidate his basic contrast between science as certain and history as merely probable. He fails to ask whether the difficulty of identifying with an historical witness is logical or empirical. The indications are that he thought it was logical, and that the references made to the unique character of historical events and the holistic features of historical inquiry are intended to reinforce the point. But if they are, they do not succeed. That an event in history is unique does not prevent its being given a general description; it can be comprehended and made intelligible under that description. And that different aspects of individual and social life go together in a special way, so that nothing about them can be fully understood until everything is understood, does not imply that, failing that, nothing about them is understood. Nor is the argument about progress in history entirely worthy of its author, who might have been the first to point out in a different context that though earlier stages of consciousness are false when compared with that into which they develop, the latter does not merely cancel them but preserves them as part of itself.

It appears from this that to enter into the mind of a historical witness or (we may add) a historical agent is difficult but not logically impossible, at least as far as Bradley's arguments are concerned. But the chief problem for his theory turns on his phrase 'present experience'. As already mentioned, he says at an early stage in the essay that not only is it true that all knowledge comes from experience, but also that all experience is personal experience. The experience which the critical historian must bring into play as a check on his wilder judgments has to be essentially his own; it will not do for him to appeal to 'mere common experience' (p. 26), where that signifies something taken over without examination. However, we need not conclude that he must rely exclusively on himself and the experiences he has had as a particular individual. The critical thinker must indeed authenticate each item for himself, recognize it as part of the world which is constituted in judgment. But there is no reason why, in doing this, he should not profit from the experience of others, provided he does not treat their claims uncritically.

In an interesting passage (pp. 26–7) with strong Hegelian overtones, Bradley explains how the contents of consciousness, 'consisting as they do of our individual experiences blended into one substance inextricably with the experiences of others', exist first in a 'confused and unsystematized' way and are then transformed by 'the critical intelligence' into something more rational and systematic. That which 'has sentence of life and death' in this transformation is 'the world of critical observation' which is 'constituted by that which has been, or can be, personally verified in our own external or internal critical observation'. 'It is thus', he concludes, 'our immediate personal (though that need not mean our individual) experience, on which, by many steps

or by few, all our certainty depends.' But even if it is true
that each individual must decide for himself what is really the
case, it does not follow that what is the case has any special
relation to my consciousness as opposed to yours. The experience I bring to bear in judgment represents the conclusions
of previous judgments, and judgment itself is an impersonal
activity. Bradley himself sees this clearly at an early stage
of the essay when he writes:

The facts which exist for critical history are events and recorded
events. They are recorded, and that is to say that, although the work
of the mind, they now at any rate are no mere feelings, nor generally
the private contents of this or that man's consciousness, but are fixed
and made outward, permanent, and accessible to the minds of all
men (p. 13).

After this the only excuse he could offer for saying that
there are 'no facts but my facts' (already quoted from p. 70)
is that the impersonal subject of judgment is an abstraction
which has to be realized, so far as it is to exist at all, in
concrete individuals, among them myself. I am, as it were,
the temporary spokesman for consciousness as such. But it
does not follow that I come on the scene in any objectionable
personal capacity, nor that the experience which I at once
constitute and invoke is mine in any exclusive sense.

'Present experience' is thus neither merely present nor
merely mine. What now of its content? I have spoken so far
as if this covered all the items, particular and general, which
the critical intelligence is prepared to authenticate, on the
strength of appropriate evidence and in accordance with the
principles Bradley has set out. Bradley gives us the more
general principle of the universality of causal law, which is
common to history and natural science, and the narrower
principle of accepting only the analogical which is peculiar
to history.[8] There is a potential problem about circularity
here, but I shall assume that Bradley solved it in the passage
on pp. 26-7 from which I have already quoted. What I
wish to point out now is that the statement makes Bradley's
position simpler than it in fact is. Although he nowhere
embarks on anything like a full discussion of what is involved
in historical consciousness, he offers a few hints in passing
of the view to which he inclines. One passage which is particularly illuminating in this connection is the one in which he

contrasts 'the interest of science' with 'the interest of history' (p. 36). Science, he tells us, is concerned with the individual case only for the sake of the universal it illustrates: 'The concretion of life is worth having solely for the sake of the abstract relations it contains' (loc. cit.). By contrast history is interested in the individual, if not quite for its own sake, then as embodying the story of humanity. 'Our interest in the past is our feeling of oneness with it, is our interest in our own progression; and because this human nature to exist must be individual, the object of historical record is the world of human individuality, and the course of its development in time. For scientific testimony the man is a mere example, for historical never: he is a new incarnation of the same felt substance, the manifest individualization, it may be, at highest, of a stage in progress.'

Bradley adds in parentheses 'but on this point we wish to express no opinion'. Three pages later (pp. 39-40) he had grown bolder. 'History (we assume it) is progressive, is a progress not only in the sense of that which increases in quantity, but in the sense of that which develops or evolves itself, is essentially the same in stages of growth which are diverse in quality.' What is it that thus evolves or progresses? The answer is man, or rather the mind of man. History records the stages of the development of human consciousness from crudity to sophistication, seeing the later members of the progression as the goal to which the earlier are tending. That history should be conceived on these lines is, Bradley argues, essential to its having any interest for us. If the various episodes of which it consists were merely different from one another, 'the possibility of history is inconceivable'; if history revealed a humanity which was fundamentally static and whose changes were in consequence merely accidental, its interest would be no higher than that of 'an ordinary novel'.

These doctrines perhaps explain Bradley's opaque dictum that while the individuals of science are 'limited to be abstracted', those of history 'are incorporated to be realized' (p. 36). What is incorporated and given (at least partial) realization is what might be called the spirit of man, or perhaps Spirit more generally. The absence of this Hegelian term from Bradley's text can scarcely disguise the Hegelian affinities of the whole set of ideas; the connection with

Hegel becomes even plainer in the near quotation from the *Phenomenology* toward the top of p. 40 ('this illustration is borrowed'). Despite what was said earlier about Bradley's thought in this work being in certain respects close to empiricism, the general cast of his mind was of a very different order. Bradley was prepared to propound doctrines which commanded empiricist support, though not under that description, for certain limited purposes; he drew attention in the final paragraph of his essay (p. 53) to the restricted character of what had been attempted. The upshot of the last sentence of the work, more than usually clouded by the rhetorical language, seems to be that critical history can proceed on its path 'subject to no intrusion and oppressed by no authority'. What might intrude or threaten oppression would be 'that which beyond her realm may be or may call itself religion and philosophy'. Yet it seems that critical history as Bradley believes it must operate has to invoke not just the principles on whose discussion he spends so much effort, but also a further principle taken over from metaphysics. If that is correct, the world which the critical historian helps to construct may well be different in vital respects from the world as seen by empiricists.

Was Bradley correct in saying that, without some doctrine of progress, history is 'inconceivable'? The only alternative that he saw was to acquiesce in the Mill/Buckle idea of history as a generalizing science (cf. pp. 43–5). Against that he has many objections: we lack evidence of the proper degree of scientific certainty in the historical field, and if it is said that statistics (cliometrics?) will remedy the defect, serious problems remain. It may be possible to formulate some generalizations in the area of social statics; when it comes to social dynamics and the task of divining the 'eternal laws' which are alleged to explain historical change, we need to know where history is going before we can make a start. Apart from that difficulty, our laws will explain only general features, not individual developments. Bradley was helped in making these comments by the fact that Mill too was a believer in historical progress, and had conveniently said that a science of history could only be a 'science of tendencies'. Even so, it is hard to deny that Bradley's criticism assumes the correctness of his own point of view.

Is there a further alternative? Many present-day writers on the philosophy of history echo Bradley's contrast of history and science so far as to say that science essentially deals in generalities, paying attention to the particular only as exemplifying something universal, whilst history is concerned with individual happenings and states of affairs without regard to anything general that can be abstracted from them. The contrast is not wholly clear, since of course history uses general terms to describe its subject-matter ('the *battle* of Waterloo'), and historians affix general labels to whole periods ('the end of the feudal era', 'the age of reform'). It is not true that history has no interest in generalities, but it is true that it is not concerned with what Hegelians called 'the abstract universal' for its own sake. The question is whether this commits it to 'the concrete universal', in the way Bradley supposed. Modern philosophers say that history studies individual events for their own sake; Bradley asks what possible interest they can have unless we can see them as part of the continuing story of mankind, a story which naturally concerns us for the light it throws on ourselves. As Collingwood was never tired of saying, history fascinates us because it provides self-knowledge. But it may do this without our having to go all the way with Bradley.

That history grips us because the deeds and sufferings it narrates are those of men like ourselves could certainly not be denied. We cannot ignore or be quite indifferent to the human past just because it is human. It is true also that the past contains many developments or retrogressions which bear witness to our forebears' aspirations, achievements, and failures; it is entirely natural that we should want to know about these for the light they throw on the variety of human life and the possibilities of human nature. Even in the most primitive societies the way in which the mind of man grapples with its problems must and does stir our interest: the simplest of institutions, the least sophisticated beliefs, demand attention because we can see them, for all their strangeness, as the product of ourselves. But all this could be true without our having to believe that the human past makes up a single development, the steady maturing of the mind of man. Social life can indeed be seen as the mind of man writ large, and history is concerned with the fortunes of men in society. Further, we find it difficult to resist the thought that what mind achieves in some ages is superior to what it achieves in others; in making such judgments we take our own values as the norm. What makes it impossible to proceed from this to a straight theory of progress is first, that declines sometimes succeed advances in human achievement (Rome after Greece), and second, that history shows how norms themselves are subject to change. It is possible to organize historical happenings inside the kind of framework that Bradley believed to be indispensable: Hegel did this in his lectures on world history in a way which remains impressive despite the fact that the empirical detail is now mostly out of date. It could be that the Hegelian view of history still embodies the standard Western way of looking at the human past; it is significant that in this respect it was not challenged by Marx. But clearly it is not a view which is compulsive. We might very well argue that history is not a single process but an affair of separate starts and stops, some of which proceed entirely independently of others, the rest with varying degrees of interdependence. Followers of Vico, for instance, would see events as displaying a repeated pattern which certainly depends on a connected series of mental changes but does not add up to a single development; the mind of man is here supposed to go through a sort of life cycle, without the presumption that any one stage is superior to another and with a denial that the cycle occurs just once. Someone who took this view would not be debarred from finding what history narrates of human interest. Nor would more sceptical thinkers who are prepared to see movements and trends in history, but discern neither overall movements nor repeated trends.

I represented Bradley above as having argued that history operates with the concrete universal, the idea of a self-developing individual. The truth is, however, that he does not confine himself to this claim in a general form, but wants to say that historical thought involves the application of a particular example of the species, the evolution of humanity, to the human past as a whole. Reflection on the points just made suggests that to describe what has occurred as the evolution of humanity, at best sits loosely to the facts and may indeed be quite improper. But we need not conclude from this that concrete universals are irrelevant to history. As I have tried to show elsewhere,[9] concepts of this kind play a distinctive part in historical thinking, in so far as part of the task of the latter is to pick out and characterize certain processes, movements, and 'developments'. The important thing to notice about these now is, however, that they are in normal cases limited in spatial and temporal spread; an attempt might be made to find one that applied to the entire course of events, but in practice we do not observe much interest in that possibility among working historians. They tend to think it enough if they can illuminate particular stretches of history, without embarking on the difficult task of making sense of history as a whole. And it is enough for the wider purpose Bradley had in view, namely to show that the study of history has a particular appeal to the human mind.

NOTES

1. Quoted as it appears in F. H. Bradley, *Collected Essays*, Oxford, 1969, pp. 1-70. Numbers in the text refer to pages of this version. I should like to acknowledge my debt to the work of Pierre Fruchon, *Francis Herbert Bradley, Les Présupposés de l'histoire critique, étude et traduction*, Paris, 1965, especially for its elucidation of Bradley's relations to Baur on the one hand and Hegel on the other.
2. Bradley was obviously concerned with Paley, who in turn was concerned with Hume.
3. *Treatise of Human Nature*, I, iii, 14, p. 171 in Selby-Bigge edn., Oxford, 1888.
4. *Enquiry concerning Human Understanding*, viii, p. 83 in Selby-Bigge edn., Oxford, 1894.
5. See my essay 'The Constancy of Human Nature', in *Contemporary British Philosophy*, 4th series, ed. H. D. Lewis, London, 1976.
6. Bradley used the third edition, Tübingen, 1863. There is an English translation of this first volume by Allan Menzies, London and Edinburgh, 1878, under the title *Church History*.
7. For some discussion of this point, see below, pp. 48-9.
8. Cf. p. 48, where Bradley makes clear that candidate events which satisfy his two principles cannot be affirmed as fact by the critical intelligence until 'mediated with the real' by a 'sufficient connexion' — presumably through some properly attested universal law.
9. 'Colligatory Concepts in History', originally published in *Studies in the Nature and Teaching of History*, ed. W. H. Burston and D. Thompson, London, 1967; reprinted in *The Philosophy of History*, Oxford Readings in Philosophy, ed. Patrick Gardiner, London, 1974.

CHAPTER 3

The Insufficiency of Ethics

David Bell

He who would do good to another must do it in Minute Particulars,
General Good is the plea of the scoundrel, hypocrite, and flatterer.[1]

I

The subject of moral philosophy is amongst the sub-subjects
of philosophy perhaps the most susceptible of merely fashionable interest. The reason is not far to seek: the world of
which the moral philosopher tries to make sense is not set
over him as something with its own laws and being, to which
theory, philosophical or scientific, must answer. Rather, that
to which it has to answer is a part of itself, namely our moral
intuitions, values, interests, and sense of coherence of the
moral world. Hence the appearance which ethical justification
often takes on, of ingenious dialectical trickery, mirror-
gazing, or the mere imposition by fiat of consistency upon
our values. Hence also, the current popularity of 'non-
cognitivist meta-ethics' allied none the less with great fervour
to large and important 'first-order' ethical debates.

In the light of this, the reader might well ask one hundred
years after the appearance of *Ethical Studies* whether the
work is more than a historical curiosity. A second edition,
together with notes intended for a revised version, appeared
posthumously in 1927, a time when it might fairly be said
that some interest in idealist ethics was still shown by profes-
sional philosophers. The modern reader imbued as he is with
notions of progress both within and without the philosophical
world will tend to the view that a reconsideration of Bradley's
work in moral philosophy can hold little more than antiquarian interest. Idealism, it will be said, is dead or discredited,
surviving only with the benefit of modern logic in refined

modern versions. The distinct religious tinge to be found in the work of the British Idealists, and not entirely absent from Bradley's contributions, would nowadays be held by many to have no place within philosophy at all. The project of a first philosophy transcending synoptically and synthetically the more particular projects of the natural sciences, the nascent sciences of society (of which we may count economics the most advanced), and the first-order plethora of moral debates, seems either outdated or to smack of a metaphysical hubris which the characteristically modest temper of post-Wittgensteinian philosophy has eschewed. Comprehensive theoretical monism is not the temper of contemporary debate.

It is not only from the side of modesty in philosophical pretension that Bradley may nowadays suffer; the naturalistic tendencies in modern philosophy, the view that the sciences of nature provide the content and methodological data for the philosopher to mull over, sits ill with the partly deserved reputation of idealism for relegating natural science and its modes of thought to an inferior level of the understanding. Furthermore, it cannot be denied that Bradley makes use in the exposition of his ethical views of a technical vocabulary which has fallen entirely out of fashion: concrete universals, identity-in-difference, the idea that all relations are internal and that there is no such thing as mere externality — these and other notions are not part of the contemporary philosopher's terms of art.

In addition to these shortcomings there is a methodological issue within philosophy itself. Both the marvellous burgeoning of the formal sciences and the anti-systematic tendencies stemming from the later philosophy of Wittgenstein seem to guarantee eclipse for a philosophy as closely associated with the dialectical method of Hegel as Bradley's seems to be. Not even the recent revival of interest in the origins of Marxist thought and in Hegel's philosophy has succeeded in restoring respectability to dialectical thought. The will towards system, so reprehensibly dominant in Hegel, has been associated also with his supposed disciple Bradley, to the neglect of the unsystematic and sceptical tendencies prominent in Bradley's work. As he himself said:

We want no system-making or systems home-grown or imported. This life-breath of persons who write about philosophy is not the atmosphere where philosophy is. (*PL*, p. x)

There is some justice but much injustice in these points. Bradley is nothing if not his own man, a distinctive voice aware of its distinctiveness. 'As for the "Hegelian school" which exists in our reviews, I know no one who has met with it anywhere else' (*PL*, p. x), he was prompted to say in response to charges of undue influence from Hegelian sources. As other essays in this work will testify, it can even be argued that Bradley made distinctive contributions to the revival of modern logic, some of which closely parallel Frege's polemic against naturalism in logic, and others which are to be found reflected in the early work of the Bradleian apostate Bertrand Russell. In the light of these points it may be that the charge of merely antiquarian value will be felt to lie most heavily against Bradley's work in ethics.

None the less, in reviewing recent work on utilitarianism the discerning reader of Bradley's *Ethical Studies* is forcibly struck by the resurrection in the work of contemporary utilitarians and their critics of points made long ago by Bradley, something which makes even more puzzling the omission of Bradley's name from the widely read, recently republished, discussion of utilitarianism by Smart and Williams.[2] It is perhaps for this reason that Bradley's attack on what he took to be a prevalent and harmful orthodoxy of his own period may be singled out as the putatively classical element in his ethical writings. This however would be a further injustice. Magnificent and trenchant as Bradley's attack on the philistine Mills may be, it is, as he himself emphasizes, a merely negative moment which in saving us from error does little to furnish the practical and positive insight which the reader has the right to expect from moral reflection. Much the same goes for the brusque dismissal of Kant's moral philosophy as mere formalism. The true focus of *Ethical Studies* is to be found rather in the reflections of 'My Station and its Duties'. Furthermore, this view if sustainable should provide some basis for a claim upon present interest in Bradley. A doctrine of the nature of moral right and wrong which fixes so closely upon the objective institutionalizations of moral practices in a society cannot but be of interest to a generation of philosophers who face, in the guise of the discipline of sociology, a rival to their own accounts of moral practices.

II

Disposing of the doctrine of pleasure for pleasure's sake is for Bradley more than an eristic exercise and a clearance of the ground for the presentation of his own views. The doctrine attacked is a living social reality within the polity he addresses:

... modern Utilitarianism which may be called, I suppose, our most fashionable moral philosophy (*ES*, p. 103).

It is for him an influential system of thought, having the status of a dogma or revealed, and hence unexamined, truth. Bradley, for all his individuality, belongs in his attack upon utilitarianism to a reaction (one almost says, 'a conservative reaction') of opinion against what had become widely accepted as the touchstone of advanced and enlightened thinking on political and social matters in mid-nineteenth-century England. The central figure is John Stuart Mill who fell heir, despite his own doubts and qualifications, to the legacy of reforming empiricism of Bentham and his father. Other figures of advanced thought such as Matthew Arnold and Herbert Spencer do not escape the sharp edge of Bradley's dialectical sword but the prize target remains Mill. It is Mill, the scholastic systematizer, qualifier, and popularizer of the utilitarian philosophy who, for all the generality of Bradley's account, is the implicit exemplar of the doctrine. Bradley in some ways revives and systematizes the attitudes to the grinding of the philistine Mills earlier expressed by the ageing Wordsworth, by Coleridge, and by Carlyle.

Nowhere are these attitudes more trenchantly expressed than in his discussion of what happiness is. He concedes that it is something which all men seek but insists that to be told to seek happiness as an end is to be given no practical directive at all. Conceptions of happiness are as variable as mankind itself, though he is prepared to concede that there may be some broad measures of agreement upon what happiness is not. This last point might well be accounted an anticipation of negative utilitarianism. The accommodating, tolerant, not to say liberal, nature of positive utilitarianism, particularly in its modern versions as they appear in discussions of welfare economics, is often held by its defenders to be one of its cardinal virtues. Maximization of social utility by compounding individual utility schedules, where these are constructed in turn from preferential behaviour, the existence of wants in great variety, myriad satisfactions sought by myriad agents — all prove acceptable grist to the mill of the social welfare function. Thus there is conferred upon modern utilitarianism an apparent liberality in its attitude to human wants. I say 'apparent' because of course the crunch comes when personal utility schedules are compounded together in some formula by the expert advisers of the rulers in order to form the social utility function from which, when implemented, guidance in social coercion, subject to its own arbitrariness, will be derived. What is so liberally allowed when compounding the input to the function may in various and unforeseeable ways be illiberally curtailed after the machinery of the welfare function has ground out its optimizing answer in the form of actual legislation. One uses here the language of *possibility* in part because what is involved are the probabilities concerning the compounding of the personal schedules to reach the total outcome. One may be lucky in the sense that the personal happiness schedules prove to be only weakly various as between agents; but given a strongly various differentiation in personally held conceptions of happiness the utilitarian legislator may not be so lucky. The chances of this last situation coming about may be maximized if we are considering a community of persons who are not themselves convinced utilitarians and whose adherence to personal utility schedules is not deeply motivated (if at all) by the utilitarian notion of rationality. It is this possibility which I take to be inherent in Bradley's insistence upon the failure of utilitarian proposals to accord with the intuitions of the ordinary man.

The exegetical point is reinforced when one turns to the account of 'My Station and Its Duties'. There Bradley insists that to the extent that a community has a continuing life, then one already has *in concreto* a myriad of interlocking projects variously and in complex ways conditioned by history, psychology, and the natural basis of life. Furthermore, and this is the main point, this life of the community is not one which is the result of application of the characteristically utilitarian calculative criterion of the best. Maybe, surveying such a society from on high, the utilitarian can show that according to his criterion all is for the best in the actual world. But he could scarcely claim that this was because of the operation of his principle in the world. If there is anything in this line of reflection I take it as narrowly and exegetically showing that one cannot properly assess Bradley's repudiation of utilitarianism without reference to what he takes to be at least the partial solution to the myriad problems of practical life which the utilitarian philosopher addresses. When he says of utilitarianism that its heart is in the right place but its head is wanting, he is in part saying that like the rest of us the utilitarian wants the best and thus far we may agree; but to the extent that the theorist has little grasp except at a very abstract level of what the reality is in which and through which the best must be sought and found, then utilitarianism's contribution to understanding that best and perhaps making it better is likely to be practically dangerous or transcendentally negligible. I take this to be at least part of Bernard Williams's charge against utilitarianism that it fails to pick up very much of the world's moral baggage.

Furthermore, there is a psychological point to be added to the difficulty of definition: there is a wealth of testimony suggesting that to want happiness and to have reasonable hope of that want being satisfied will mean that one should *not* seek happiness as an end. One hopes, one may even pray, that immersion in particular projects of marriage, work, philanthropy, aesthetic creation, and so forth will result in happiness. But to pursue such things with more than an occasional and weather eye upon happiness is likely to doom or frustrate the very projects through which whatever happiness coming to one will arrive. It is these difficulties which lure the utilitarian. He wishes to propose an end which is palpable and such that 'when we have it we know it'. Despite the proverbial literature decrying the very possibility of finding satisfaction in the pursuit of pleasure the utilitarian none the less proposes pleasure as the end. The reality of pleasurable feeling and its nature as self-proclaiming presence serve to solve at one fell swoop the problem not only of the end but also of knowledge of that end.

It is not merely one's own pleasure which is proposed as the end but rather the pleasure and the maximum of pleasure of all sentient beings. Hence, traditional rejections of hedonism on the grounds that it erects selfish libertinism into a system cannot prevail against such a high-minded view. Who, it might be asked, can possibly reject such a laudable proposal? Certainly Bradley does not argue that common opinion rejects it. Rather his strategy is the indirect one of trying to show that, proposed as an end, the utilitarian ideal is neither practicable nor explanatory of 'the moral world'.

Bradley's argument goes from the non-explanatory nature of such hedonism to its rejection at least by common opinion. The respect in which such a doctrine lacks explanatory power is, according to Bradley, its inability to connect with and hence to explain what men do. Many, if not most, men believe that there are things which ought to be done and of some moral relevance which we should do even if they bring no pleasure. So as far as common opinion is concerned, morality cannot be encompassed and explained only by the proposal that the supreme moral end is the maximum of pleasure for all sentient creatures. There are occasions upon which the injunction, 'Do it because it will maximize the pleasure of all sentient beings!' will seem not to connect at all with anything which might seem to the agent a good and relevant reason for doing or not doing the action in question. But, it will be familiarly said, this is only because we are already sunk in the habituations of the race, one deposit of which has been to condition us to be disposed towards the performance of those actions which the experience of mankind has shown to be causally efficacious in securing the maximum degree of pleasure for all sentient beings. It none the less remains the case that the utilitarian end constitutes the final appeal court which will judge of the morality of an action, whatever might psychologically be the case concerning the motive or end for which it is performed.

This reply raises amongst other important issues that of rule- and act-utilitarianism, one which Mill was responsible for broaching and which Bradley in taking up helped to make a central issue in the critical discussion of utilitarianism. However, before turning to what Bradley has to say about that, let us complete his case against the practicability and explanatory power of the doctrine. The case is not that vulgar opinion rejects hedonism in its high-minded utilitarian forms as an end but rather that the fact of vulgar opinion's periodic separation of the question of hedonic consequence from that of good moral reason implies that there is an issue about what the essence of morality may be. There are, if common opinion is any guide, at least some occasions when, at the very least, moral justification seems independent of hedonic grounds even though it may be the case that on many occasions it would be admitted that the morally right act is also one which serves the utilitarian end. There is, we might say, the possibility of an extensional equivalence of non-utilitarian and utilitarian judgments; but Bradley challenges the utilitarian theorist to show that this is more than accidental. It would therefore be a mistake to see the appeal to common opinion here as of only psychological consequence. It raises also the question of how one is to demonstrate that all and only those acts which are moral are necessarily also those which produce the maximum of pleasure for all sentient creatures.

Here Bradley pauses to point out that it is not sufficient to disprove the validity of alternative criteria of moral action. One also has to prove that the theories considered constitute an exhaustive division of the field of possible theories. Hence, Mill's simple dichotomy of moral theories into the hedonistic and the intuitive is wanting this vital additional premiss.

We adverted above, in suggesting why one cannot separate Bradley's critique of utilitarianism from his views in 'My Station and Its Duties', to the accommodating nature of the utilitarian end. It should also be noted that one element in Bradley's argument rests upon taking the end proposed more narrowly than this. He rejects versions of the theory which place the end simply in those feelings arising as states of the self as a consequence of the satisfaction of desire. Modern utilitarians have been perhaps more circumspect in this regard, preferring, as we have already said, to couch their theory in terms of satisfactions, preferences, and other apparent entities which do not present the difficulties of the Protean concept of feeling. It may be thought therefore that Bradley's concentration upon cruder versions of the doctrine of utility renders some of his argument beside the point as far as more recent versions are concerned. His view certainly is that in so far as the end at which to aim is conceived as mere pleasurable feeling and the maximum of pleasurable feeling either in the community or the individual is no more than the aggregate of such feelings, then utility presents the agent with a chimerical end impossible of attainment. As an aggregate of feeling states, maximum pleasure is held to be a contradiction and hence the search for such an aggregate futile. Pleasures he holds are 'a perishing series' such that though such a series may have a beginning it has no end except in communal or personal death. As a series without end it has no determinate sum and, having no determinate sum, can furnish no determinate end. The agent, we may assume, has at any point in his life the satisfactions, i.e. pleasures, which he has been able to obtain. But equally he knows there are more to come if only he can get them and at these he is to aim, and so on down the 'perishing series'. At no point has he the maximum; he only has more than he had, with more to come. If at any point he is held to be happy, then happy he may be, but not through having obtained the greatest pleasure possible. Bradley concedes that on this view it may be said that one can only *approximate* the greatest sum of pleasurable feeling. But, he asks, does it make sense to suppose that one can approximate to a fiction? Even if this were to be conceded one is still left with the dilemma: either happiness on this view is never reached or, at any given point on the perishing series, one has the greatest happiness attainable.

It is these and other related difficulties of the 'classical' view which account for the attempt of utilitarians, especially Mill, to place the end in some qualification of the classical standpoint. Notoriously, in Mill's case this took the form of (1) the introduction of qualitative as well as quantitative distinctions between pleasures; and (2) an explicit introduction of the closely related idea that utility may be pursued indirectly (and this is most prominent in Mill's discussion of the virtue of justice) through adherence to some system of ends which, while not pursued because they bring pleasure but for other reasons unrelated to pleasure, none the less turn out to yield the optimific consequences demanded by the utilitarian standard. By these two routes one arrives at the idea that:

we have got interests and these are objects of desire not thought of as means to pleasure. We have adopted happiness in the vulgar sense, and really have given up Hedonism, as the consistent hunt after pleasure for pleasure's sake (*ES*, p. 100).

This appeal to the vulgar consciousness is reinforced by a characteristic Bradleian point of more strictly philosophical significance. The abandonment of the 'classical' view implicit in Mill's introduction of a qualitative criterion of pleasure is reinforced by a logical consideration. Just as Bradley was to insist against the naturalist logicians (for example Bain and the associationist school) that for the purposes of logic ideas must be regarded as possessing a representational content, so to espouse practical ends is to espouse something having representational content. It is to espouse something which is more than mere feeling. While not here wishing to enter into the vexed question of objective idealism it is worth noting that this twofold insistence upon what nowadays we should call intentionality places Bradley in the camp of those thinkers who were subsequently to revolt against naturalism. On customary readings of Bradley it may seem odd to put him in the camp of Frege, Russell, Moore, and Husserl. None the less, there is ample evidence both in his ethics and still more in *The Principles of Logic* that Bradley is to be counted as at least on the fringes of the revolt against naturalism and subjective idealism. The importance of the point in the present context is that it is in terms of the representational content of ends that grounds of justification are to be found and not in something as extrinsic as mere pleasurable feeling.

The move beyond the classical position to be found in Mill's introduction of a qualitative criterion of pleasure is not unwelcome to Bradley. What he is intent on pointing out is that it is not consistent with either utility or hedonism. Further, he discerns in it elements of elitism, of clerisy, and of 'Platonic aristocracy', hardly consonant with that accommodating and demotic acceptance of ends characteristic of the classical position and summed up in Bentham's dictum that push-pin is as good as poetry. The introduction of a lexicographical ordering of pleasures on grounds of quality is not only inconsistent with the classical position but raises difficulties of its own over who decides the ordering to hold sway:

. . . I, e.g., know the alphabet of pleasures, always or sometimes, up to M. 'Immoral man to choose M, when you should have chosen P or R or even X' (*ES*, p. 121).

We are familiar now with the solution of Mill: the prize must go to the man who is acquainted with the pleasures of Pythagoras as well as those of the pot. Indeed, Mill seems confident that the rule-utilitarian aspects of his teaching will also turn out to be those endorsed by persons of hedonic versatility, or at least by philosophers. But what, Bradley asks, is the ground of the title of such persons:

> Are we (as proposed for the franchise) to have an examination, passing in which shall entitle a man to try 'experiments in living'? Or shall we leave it to private judgement? Then I should like to know in these days of 'advanced thinking' who would *not* be a 'philosopher', and how many would be left in the 'multitude' (*ES*, p. 111 n.).

Such references represent an implicit opposition on Bradley's part to what he takes to be fashionable advanced thinking in his day. It is not merely Mill and his 'pitiable sophism' which Bradley has in mind. Matthew Arnold, Herbert Spencer, and Sidgwick, the most painstaking defender of Utilitarianism, all come in for some measure of harsh if not contemptuous criticism. While in detail the criticisms vary, what they all may be said to have in common is something closely akin to the chief burden of Burke's polemic against Paine and the rights of man: namely an objection to abstract theorizing.

There is some irony in the fact that a doctrine set on the path of popularity by Bentham as a ground of opposition to the philosophy of natural rights as derived from natural law — 'nonsense upon stilts' — should by the time at which Bradley is writing find itself open to the same charges of abstract moralizing which Burke had levelled at the radical versions of the doctrine of natural rights. But there is perhaps in the irony a lesson. It teaches us that with the radical improving spirit there is necessary association neither with the would-be 'scientific tendencies' of classical utilitarianism nor with the Platonizing tendencies of doctrines of natural right. Taken in itself the radical improving spirit is mere sentiment and carries in itself no necessary relationship to any theoretical stance, still less any justified theoretical stance.

The charge of abstract moralizing is for Bradley rooted ultimately in a point of metaphysics. It may thus prove easy to dismiss in so far as one is inclined to reject the metaphysics. To put the point briefly: the critique of the individualism implicit in the utilitarian creed is a particular application of the doctrine of the concrete universal. The positive assertion of the morality of my station and its duties is yet another application of this doctrine. It is for this reason that no assessment of Bradley's views in either respect can afford to neglect some critical consideration of the metaphysical doctrine. The necessity for this is not removed by Bradley's own assertions that the assertion of *mere* individuality by the utilitarian need only be met by the counter-denial. In one way *Ethical Studies* is a curious work in that Bradley says over and over again that crucial issues which arise in ethics cannot be entirely settled within ethics. In this sense he denies the autonomy of ethics. Problems will inevitably arise in ethics in that it is the reflective consideration of moral life and experience, which will require for their solution not only metaphysical but also religious enquiry. Bradley does little but hint at these enquiries. One such problem is the inevitability of conflict of duties on any system; another is the position of the agent who cannot find himself in the morality of his particular station and social system. It may thus be thought that the position developed by Bradley is in essential respects incomplete and unworked out. To this charge he would plead guilty. But in so far as we are taken up with these problems with which he does not deal, it is through the application of a metaphysical thesis. It is to some examination of this thesis which we must now turn.

III

The critique of utilitarian doctrine is admitted by Bradley to be of negative significance. The most it has revealed by contrast is the importance of self-realization. The examination of hedonism has revealed the impossibility of the self realizing its happiness in the endless perishing series of moments of satisfaction. Equally the examination of duty for the sake of duty has revealed that the self cannot find itself in the mere universality of the moral law either. Put another way: utilitarianism supplies an arbitrary content to morality while deontologism supplies no content at all. What both doctrines have in common is that in their own ways they fail to connect with the real individual's actual projects, involvements, and motives. The anti-Platonizing spirit of classical utility cleaves to the mere accidental particularities of this or that feeling; the assertion of abstract universality in the form of the moral law leaves an agent at the mercy of a form of law to which obedience will result in a denial and abnegation of his actual self.

I have said that Bradley's solution has a metaphysical basis and that this basis is the doctrine of the concrete universal. I have hinted further that this doctrine may be open to serious question on metaphysical and logical grounds. The serious question I have in mind arises from an assumption characteristic of modern logic that whatever may be concluded about the existence of abstract entities, should they none the less be admitted to exist they will exist as abstract entities. Indeed, the very posing of the question as one concerning the existence of abstract entities invites a response which will dispose of the existence of concrete, i.e. non-abstract, universals. In short, concrete universals appear to be a contradiction in terms, at least so far as deliverances of contemporary philosophical logic are concerned. Furthermore, one should beware of confusing nominalism with the doctrine of the concrete universal. As the attempt to dispense with merely abstract entities and hence abstract universals, nominalism may seem to be a step towards the doctrine of the concrete universal, for it presumably leaves us with nothing existing except concrete entities. But, characteristically, nominalism will deny that any of these existences are universals. However, one is tempted to argue thus: in so far as nominalism insists upon, for example, the existence of brute resemblances between existences, thus far it seems to admit the existence of concrete universals. If two concrete entities may be seen to resemble each other in colour or shape, then it would seem that what is here seen, is one and the same and concrete in both the sharers.

It is something like this 'brute' resemblance which Bradley requires in order to get the metaphysical aspects of his ethical doctrine off the ground. He wishes to argue that there exist in any actual self and its projects both particular and universal existences. Further, the universal existences present in the essence of any self may be present also in the essences of other selves. It is precisely this sharing of one and the same concrete but nevertheless universal entity that constitutes the objectivity of morality as far as any individual self is concerned. As universal it cannot be merely particular and hence subject to the whim of those mere particulars we call individual persons. It resides concretely as the common feature of a plurality of persons. There also seems to be a hierarchy of such pluralities of which examples would be the family, the village, the town, the region, the nation, etc., successively more embracing as far as the number of individuals is concerned.

On to this doctrine there are grafted further metaphysical assumptions. The most notable of these are:

(1) the doctrine of identity in difference
(2) the doctrine of the internality of relations between individuals.

The first of these doctrines may be regarded as another way of expressing the doctrine of the concrete universal. What it emphasizes is that plurality and diversity are not intended to exclude identity, that is that a number of numerically different and self-identical individuals may none the less be held to share one and the same characteristic or characteristics. The second of these doctrines is unlikely to recommend itself to contemporary philosophers. To say that a relation is internal is to say that it is part of the nature or essence of that which it relates. Since Bradley thinks of a relation as relating at least two things, that is as at least dyadic, then one may also regard this doctrine as an instance of the doctrine of the concrete universal. (He seems not to consider the case of relations which things may have to themselves.) The two entities thus related both have as parts of their nature one and the same thing.

Of course it is true that Bradley considered relational propositions as in the last analysis incoherent, and I do not propose to rehearse his arguments here nor the counter-arguments and assertions of Frege, Russell, Moore, and Wittgenstein. That Bradley on occasion presents relations as kinds of things alongside their *relata* rather than stumbling upon the Fregean insight that they are unsaturated concepts, is undeniable.[3] Rather than unjustly regard him as being some kind of semantic primitive, we should give him credit for having developed the incoherences of the traditional view. But it is important to point out in the present context that if the denial of the doctrine of internal relations is sustained then it would seem that an important prop is removed from the doctrine of my station and its duties. One implication of insisting upon the externality of relations is that entities related retain their own natures when their relations to other entities cease to obtain or when they enter into new relations. With the retention of the entity's own nature there goes along the retention of the identity of that entity and of the related criterion for such identity. Thus what is *quietly* excluded here is that the properties constituting something's nature and hence the ground of its identity are or could be relational properties. Another way to put this would be to say that the only class of properties relevant to the application of a Leibnizian criterion of identity are non-relational properties.

The use to which Bradley wishes to put this doctrine in 'My Station and Its Duties' is to provide a metaphysical and hence final basis to dispose of 'mere' individuality, that is to dispose of the doctrine that a person apart from his relations could be the same person as that person in those relations. For example, he holds that what is wrong with contractual views of the origins of the state and society (and for this we might substitute that agreement which is supposed to take place amongst Rawls's people in the original position) is the supposition that apart from social and political relations there are in any recognizable sense identifiable persons to deliberate and enter into such agreements. The story told in such theories implicitly supposes that the relations constitutive of persons in society obtain when, either in reality or for the purposes of some thought-experiment, we suppose such persons out of society and thus bereft of all those social relations constitutive of their natures. (The argument incidentally has close analogies with Hume's argument against contract theory.)

The 'individual' man, the man into whose essence his community with others does not enter, who does not include relations to others in his very being, is, we say, a fiction . . . (*ES*, p. 168).

The argument is a counterpart of the critique of those epistemologies which suppose a *tabula rasa* theory of the mind. It may even be suggested that such epistemologies tend to provide support for those doctrines in social and political theory which make essential use of attentuated individuals from whom have been stripped accumulations and accretions of society and state in the interests of performing some thought-experiment like that under criticism here. There are clearly conceptual limits to the application of impartial abstraction to my own case. At a certain point in my exercise of impartially stripping myself of all the particularities of my own existence, I am likely to harbour the reflection that what I conjure up in this way is a phantom and only *myself* in a sense satisfied by the mere requirement of numerical identity. The matter becomes even more fraught with difficulty when, having constituted myself for the purposes of theory as such a mere individual, I am then invited to make an exercise of practical judgment. How then to prevent, despite my exercise of discursive powers of abstraction, the flooding back into the determination of that choice of some at least of what goes to make up my nature? In Bradley's critique of abstract individualism the problem appears as one of determining the sense in which an agent whose description meets the requirement of such abstraction may be considered an agent at all. Further, one may question whether such a conception of self would make any sense to the agent himself. It is akin to the counter-identicals problem as it may appear in those theories of welfare which require comparisons of my own utility with that of others in the sense that I make myself possess their preferences and desires rather than my own. In so doing I cease to be myself at all and hence it becomes quite unclear who or what is making the comparison. No amount of theorizing about the powers of the imagination or of capacities for 'empathy' can get round this essentially logical point.

The point I wish to make about this excursion into metaphysics as the apparent basis of the doctrine of 'My Station and its Duties' is that what Bradley is concerned to emphasize may be highlighted without the logico-metaphysical apparatus which he invokes. This should not be surprising to students of political thought; the same points can be found in Burke without the quasi-Hegelian apparatus just described. What I am about to argue is that in so far as one accepts such an apparatus then it may serve as vehicle and prop of the Bradleian claims, but in so far as one does not then there is the alternative 'appeal to fact' which may be made independently of those claims.

What then are the facts in question? The first is the extreme difficulty of finding human agents whose behaviour is not characterized by patterns essentially deriving from the social context in which they have been raised. Another way to put this would be to say that it is rare to find individuals (except perhaps in the academies) whose behaviour is wholly or in large part a function of theory, rather than of a myriad of influences ranging from the natural genetic and evolutionary basis of life (explicitly recognized by Bradley) to historical factors bearing upon the life of the community and family of which they are a part. The second is that once the first point has been admitted these historical factors are then seen to be the real and practical basis of the life of the individual, and the area in which both understanding and explanation of the agent's behaviour are to be found. The third point is that, bearing these facts in mind, an important part of the nature of any individual will consist in relational facts which are true of him and especially of relational facts in which the *relata* are persons and the relations concerned are mediated by understanding and awareness of those relations. So much ought to be commonplace, and I suspect is commonplace amongst students of history, some sociologists, and those who take the discipline of anthropology seriously. Fourthly, and here we come to the specifically moral aspects of the question, some part of this complex of relations and the behaviour to which they lead and to which they respond consists in what may be called moral traditions and moral habits. For the most part they are followed blindly; or at least this will be so where, as we say, such traditions are deeply rooted and are subject only piecemeal to the onslaughts of theory and critical reason. That this is so constitutes a certain kind of objectivity for morality in the sense that in some communities or nations there simply do exist such patterns and traditions of behaviour. Of course, to the extent that a Durkheimian anomic state may be widespread in a given community, then such phenomena will not seem in any sense governing or dominant as explanatory factors for the appropriate range of behaviour. To this matter (recently argued for contemporary Western culture in general by A. MacIntyre) we shall come in a moment. All this and more seems not to require the support of metaphysics.

However, the attack upon it may come not from a rejection of metaphysical doctrine but rather from the invoking of what broadly would be called a logical point, namely some version of the distinction between fact and value. 'All this', it will be said, 'is indeed fact. As fact it has no bearing upon morality. Morality requires the consideration in a practical deliberative context of practical principle. We do not deny the blind following of moral traditions nor their explanatory power nor still their incarnation in the individual. But what concerns morality is precisely the distinction between assertions that some pattern of behaviour obtains or some rule is followed and a *moral* justification of such behaviour or such a rule.'

Bradley does not and would not attempt to deny some force to this point, even though he does not explicitly consider it in the rather more contemporary form in which I have just stated it. Furthermore, from what he does say the point can be explicitly accommodated in a variety of ways. Most notable perhaps is his insistence that moral philosophy is *not* a practical science. Nowadays we are accustomed to drawing the distinction between first and second order moral questions. This distinction, I suppose, amounts to that between a deliberative and justificatory debate concerning some substantive moral issue (for example abortion, environmental protection, the morality of nuclear war, etc., etc.), and an analytical attempt to understand some widespread pattern of moral behaviour. Bradley is insistent that the role of a philosophy of morals is to understand moral experience. In this he is characteristically Hegelian. The owl of moral philosophy flies only at dusk and the grey in grey painted by philosophy has as its object understanding rather than justification. Part of his case against utilitarianism, which figures prominently in the exposition of the morality of 'My Station and Its Duties', is the practical danger and tedium of the cultivation of 'an incessant practical casuistry' which would seem to be demanded by an act-utilitarian ethic. The encouragement of such an attitude would be likely, he believes, to debauch the sound practical understanding of the common man. It has also as consequence a kind of absurdity typified in the consideration of such questions as whether or not some contemplated adultery would seriously diminish or enhance the sum total of pleasure in the universe. He thus stands opposed to a tradition of moral reflection which takes the primary object of moral philosophy to be practical. It is not, as we shall see, that he does not recognize the existence of practical questions requiring perhaps for their clarification and answer skills which may be supposed (with some optimism) present in the philosopher, or, as Quine has recently put it, demanding *sophia* rather than *philosophia*. However, even on this last count Bradley has some doubts of an Aristotelian kind, seeming to take the view that for most people faced with a practical dilemma it is not a method completely without merit to consider what some practically wise man of one's acquaintance would do about it. Possibly such deference to the *phronimos* will not appeal in this more democratic age. Bradley does not believe that even within the ambit of my station and its duties a conflict of duties can be avoided, and hence occasions of great practical perplexity will arise from time to time for all agents where the resources of tradition and unthinking habit will fail. Then indeed we may have recourse to theory and even to those abstract considerations of optimific consequence characteristic of utilitarianism both hedonic and ideal. But for the most part he seems to think that such occasions will be rare. If one is to hold him foolishly optimistic in this respect it is not easy to see that such optimism is any more foolish than the utopian assumptions made from time to time (though not invariably by Mill) about the ultimate removal of all obstacles to the realization of the general happiness by the application of utilitarian reason.

It would seem that Bradley supposes the possible existence of a working moral consensus from within which it is only sporadically necessary to resort to theory and high-level reflection for the solution of moral conundrums. This seems a sensible attitude if only because the theoretical attitude to practical questions is itself a tradition not found in every time and place. It may be that we obtain the illusion of the possibility of a total and comprehensive theoretical attitude to practical questions from a number of sources, amongst which we might instance the ambition of a Newtonian picture of the moral world (cf. Bentham) and also the prevalence in nations with popular representative institutions of government of public debate upon practical issues. Such historically conditioned phenomena suggest models for the moral life which may be very misleading, at least to the extent to which they seem to propose the existence of a general anomic situation. Thus such models misconstrue a particular ethic belonging to what may be called the tradition of republican virtue as a general state of rulelessness. Emphasis upon my station and its duties is not only a corrective to such misconstrual but also a possibly stabilizing element in a world sometimes rendered chaotic by revolutionary pretension and its pale academic reflection of perpetual practical theorizing.

These considerations then are a part of Bradley's answer to the objection from fact and value. It amounts to the assertion that a good deal of morality is factual, i.e. objective, and that the appearance of morality as in general a dubious demand standing in need of incessant practical casuistry on the part of every moral agent is a distortion of fact. This is not the place to enter into the very large issue of what the fact/value distinction amounts to in logic. Here it is perhaps sufficient to observe in relation to Bradley's idea of the objectivity of morality that intuitively there is nothing to be said against the idea that statements involving the modal auxiliary 'ought' are true or false and hence have truth-conditions statable in some suitable theory. To hold this is not to commit the 'naturalistic fallacy' or anything like it, but is rather to place in a suitable theoretical context an undeniable, and in the first instance grammatical, intuition. A good deal of obscurity still surrounds the question of the semantic and syntactic behaviour of 'ought', despite, for example, the many attempts to construct and to refine deontic modal logics. I emphasize here that it is about the modal auxiliary that I write. Its susceptibility to alethic qualifications is not paralleled by that of the simple order or command. It may be the case, as Hare and others have argued, that such modalities imply or entail simple imperatives, but I suspect that all such accounts of this relationship are too simplistic, especially when it comes to some theory defensible in the dimensions of syntax, semantics, and pragmatics. All I claim here is that Bradley's own claim of objectivity for the morality of my station and its duties certainly fits within a theoretical framework which in turn is designed to accommodate the obvious fact that, despite all talk of prescriptivity and imperative meaning, it is no solecism either in grammar or logic to regard utterances involving the modal auxiliary 'ought' as true or false.

None the less, there is a form in which Bradley does seriously consider and accommodate within his system a world appearing thus to the moral agent. Failure to recognize this and to see its relevance to the objection from fact and value canvassed above, may stem from something as simple as a failure to turn over the page from the chapter. 'My Station and Its Duties' to that on 'Ideal Morality'.

I have noted above that Bradley insists that the doctrine of 'My Station and Its Duties', while of positive significance for morality, cannot be a comprehensive understanding of morality. At the philosophical level it is part of the answer, but at the level of agency and especially that of the Cartesian do-it-yourself moralist beloved of contemporary theory it may seem no part of the solution at all. It is towards the problem of the agent in this condition that Bradley's account of ideal morality is aimed. In short, the problem of what to do in a situation where through chance or choice a man cannot make the morality of his immediate world his own, where he finds himself in a genuine state of *anomie* in relation to that world. The occurrence of such cases is clearly possible. Their actuality may have many sources and we may mention two species: a man may reach such a stage from a genuine repugnance with features of his moral environment which are fact. Alternatively, such repugnance may be self-engendered and bear no important relationship to features of the moral environment. Clearly also a state of anomie may be a mixture of these two.

For all the curious Hegelian rhetoric of the concrete universal with which Bradley surrounds the idea of the moral organism (tricked out, it may be said, with its due meed of post-Darwinian emphasis on evolutionary change), he is at pains to insist that the morality of my station and its duties is no final solution. He is careful to specify in some detail the respects in which the solution falls short. The attempt to overcome the opposition of 'ought' and 'is' not only fails but must fail and for the following reasons.

(1) The 'bad' self which is suppressed in meeting the demands of objective morality is none the less a reality and as such a source of discontent to the agent.

(2) Furthermore, the community in which an agent is expected to find himself may be 'in a confused or rotten condition'. There are degrees of such shortcoming but no visible community can in every detail satisfy every agent by ensuring the perfect and comprehensive coincidence of might and right.

(3) There are afflictions affecting agents 'for which no moral organism has balm or physician' though, he is careful to add, a community may have alleviation for such conditions.

(4) The individual may have to be sacrificed to the community even to the point of loss of life in defence of the values of that community (*ES*, pp. 202 ff.).

To these fairly obvious points Bradley adds some others of less obviousness. One thing he notes is the growth of cosmopolitan ethics, of the idea of a moral agent whose morality and moral status owe nothing to social and historical particularities. An agent thus convinced will have little relish, at least in theory, for the relative demands of the local tribe or nation. Perhaps more importantly, there are values which seem to owe little or nothing to the morality of the community in which they may be found. Principal amongst these are the various forms of the pursuit of the realization of truth and beauty.

For all these reasons the moral world because in constant change and evolution cannot constitute a self-consistent and complete whole. Furthermore, from the standpoint of the agent this predicament appears not only, if at all, as an incoherence in the theory and science of morality; but it also appears as a predicament:

cases of collision of duties are not scientific but practical questions ... this can be dealt with solely by practical insight, not by abstract conceptions and discursive reasoning (*ES*, p. 225).

To put this otherwise, and in the jargon of another period, we cope with moral incoherence by the exercise of a practical capacity, of a knowing how rather than a knowing that. The need of a solution amongst the myriad details of practical life is met only by the often discursively dismissed and practically fragile reliance upon a supposed skill. No doubt the extent of this fragility will have much to do with the surrounding society and its ingrained habits, with the degree of education, with the quirks of personality, and with the ineluctable differences between the practical capacities of non-cloned individuals. But even given some uniformity of these surrounding conditions it none the less remains the case that the fragility of the skill involved is often manifest in the outcomes of its exercise. Hence, the retrospections of guilt coupled with memories of the best of intentions at the time generate despair at the partial realization of the good. It remains in its perfection but an ideal which mocks the theoretical fantasies of the rational and ideal moralist.

I referred at the start of this essay to a number of respects in which the cast of Bradley's thought might be held repugnant to the contemporary thinker with leanings towards naturalism. Nowhere is that repugnance likely to be more keenly felt than in Bradley's rejection of the self-sufficiency of the moral standpoint as expressed either in the partial doctrine of my station and its duties or in the headier reaches of ideal morality. The autonomy of ethics has been much debated since Bradley. The Moorean charge of commission of naturalistic and non-naturalistic fallacies in traditional moral philosophy has been widely taken to show the *irreducibility* of morality to something not obviously moral. Such irreducibility has been in turn taken to herald some sort of 'logical' gap between characteristically practical and other kinds of language and thought. Nothing of this, however true, seems to me to amount to what Bradley is pointing to in his insistence upon the limited nature of the moral standpoint, however construed. Rather we would incline to the view that he is here best compared to Kierkegaard in his insistence upon the necessity and possibility of transcending the moral point of view towards something else.

The sphere to which the shortcomings of even ideal morality points to is, of course, that of religion. The possibility of such transcendence and our reconciliation in it to the incoherencies of the world of agents would be today widely rejected if canvassed at all. The characteristic symptom of this is, so to speak, to read back into morality its short-comings and, in the different versions of non-cognitivism in ethics, to make these limitations part of the essence of morality itself. These views may even be found combined with a none the less unflagging zeal for the production of 'arguments' upon practical questions, of a kind of higher casuistry, whose impression on the casual reader can only be to convince him of their author's disregard for the 'meta-ethical' non-cognitivism which in their more theoretical moments they espouse. Perhaps such incoherence is due to '. . . irrelevant appeals to practical results' which are allowed to make themselves heard in philosophical enquiry and of which Bradley complained with such force.

The task of the metaphysician is to inquire into ultimate truth, and he cannot be called on to consider anything else, however important it may be. We have but little notion in England of freedom either in art or in science (*AR*, p. 398-9).

and again:

We may note here that our country, the chosen land of Moral Philosophy, has the reputation abroad of being the chief home of hypocrisy and cant (*AR*, p. 386 n.).

It is in his sense of the partiality and one-sidedness of the moral point of view that Bradley has most to teach us today. Whether it is a partiality and one-sidedness with which we can live as agents without hope of transcendence is a large and unclear question for another occasion.

NOTES

1. William Blake, *Jerusalem*, pl. 55.
2. *Utilitarianism: For and Against*, Cambridge, 1973.
3. The difficulty here is that Bradley, for the purposes of a sceptical argument against the self-subsistence of relations and qualities, accepts in *ad hominen* style his opponents' assumption that relations may be separated from their terms. He thus deduces the unintelligibility of the assumption made (*AR*, p. 25 ff.). But he also asserts the unintelligibility of the contrary assumption (*AR*, p. 25). In the passages referred to, the assertions of unintelligibility come so thick and fast that it is not easy to make out the settled view. One may here sympathize with Russell's breaking of the Gordian knot (see especially *AR*, p. 27 n.).

CHAPTER 4

The Moral Organism*

Crispin Wright

I

The general orientation of Bradley's moral philosophy is, as is familiar, broadly Hegelian. Like Hegel, he sees the fundamental dilemma of the moral philosopher as that of steering a course between the Scylla of the 'abstract universality' of Kantian ethics — the futile attempt to elicit substantial moral norms from the idea of a purely rational will[1] — and the Charybdis of 'Modern Utilitarianism' (that is, for Bradley, the views of J. S. Mill).[2] Bradley sees both the problem, and at least the beginnings of its solution, in Hegelian terms: what is wanted is a *synthesis* — a basis for morality which has both the objectivity and the universality to which the Kantian account aspired, and at the same time, like the utilitarian view, sees morality as something essentially subservient to human needs, and the moral life as something in which a man may find happiness and fulfilment. He writes:

What we have left then (to resume it) is this — the end is the realization of the good will which is superior to ourselves; and again the end is self-realization. Bringing these together, we see the end is the realization of ourselves as the will which is above ourselves. And this will (if morality exists) we saw must be 'objective', because not dependent on 'subjective' liking; and 'universal', because not identifiable with any particular, but standing above all actual and possible particulars. Further, though universal, it is not abstract, since it belongs to its essence that it should be realized, and it has no real existence except in and through its particulars. The good will (for morality) is meaningless, if, whatever else it be, it be not the will of living finite beings. It is a concrete universal, becaue it not only is above but is within and throughout its details, and is so far only as they are. It is the life which can live only in and by them, as they are dead unless within it; it is the whole soul which lives so far as the body lives, which makes the body a living

*I should like to thank Anthony Ellis, Gordon Graham, and Lanning Sowden for helpful comments on an earlier draft of this paper.

body, and which without the body is as unreal an abstraction as the body without it. It is an organism and a moral organism; and it is conscious self-realization, because only by the will of its self-conscious members can the moral organism give itself reality. It is the self-realization of the whole body, because it is one and the same will which lives and acts in the life and action of each. It is the self-realization of each member, because each member can not find the function, which makes him himself, apart from the whole to which he belongs; to be himself he must go beyond himself, to live his life he must live a life which is not *merely* his own, but which, none the less, but on the contrary all the more, is intensely and emphatically his own individuality. Here, and here first, are the contradictions which have beset us solved — here is a universal which can confront our wandering desires with a fixed and stern imperative, but which yet is no unreal form of the mind, but a living soul that penetrates and stands fast in the detail of actual existence. It is real, and real for me. It is in its affirmation that I affirm myself, for I am but as a 'heart-beat in its system'. And I am real in it; for, when I give myself to it, it gives me the fruition of my own personal activity, the accomplished ideal of my life which is happiness. In the realized idea which, superior to me, and yet here and now in and by me, affirms itself in a continuous process, we have found the end, we have found self-realization, duty, and happiness in one — yes, we have found ourselves, when we have found our station and its duties, our function as an organ in the social organism (*ES*, pp. 162-3).

Bradley does not care, in 'My Station and Its Duties', to be too explicit about the social identity — family, immediate community, state, mankind — of the moral or social 'organism'. But two things are completely clear. First, it is no mere metaphor that is intended:

The state is not put together, but it lives; it is not a heap nor a machine; it is no mere extravagance when a poet talks of a nation's soul. It is the objective mind which is subjective and self-conscious in its citizens: it feels and knows itself in the heart of each (*ES*, p. 184).

Further:

The belief in this real moral organism is the one solution of ethical problems (*ES*, p. 187).

That Bradley is in literal earnest is perhaps clearest in his response to the well-known passage in which he gives expression to the opposing point of view.

The family, society, the state, and generally every community of men, consists of individuals, and there is nothing in them real except the individuals. Individuals have made them, and make them, by placing themselves and by standing in certain relations. The individuals are real by themselves, and it is because of them that the relations are real. They make them, they are real *in* them, not because of them, and they would be just as real *out* of them. The whole is the mere sum of the parts, and the parts are as real away from the whole as they are within the whole ... Everything is in the organism what it is out, and the universal is a name, the existing fact answering to which is particular persons in such and such relations. To put the matter shortly, the community is the sum of its parts, is made by the addition of parts; and the parts are as real before the addition as after; the relations they stand in do not make them what they are, but are accidental, not essential, to their being; and, as to the whole, if it is not a name for the individuals that compose it, it is a name of nothing actual (*ES*, pp. 163-4).

If the 'moral organism' had been a mere metaphor, Bradley need not have contested the *substance* of this opposing point of view. It would have been enough to contest its moral significance: to make a case that, if one wishes to understand the character of moral concepts and the cogency of moral reasoning, any standpoint which considers a man in abstraction from the social structure in which he is an agent — whether by seeing morality as the servant of pre-social human needs or as the expression of supra-social rational constraints — is certain to fail. It would have been enough to stress that, while society is not *literally* an organic structure of the institutions and, ultimately, individuals who compose it, morality is nevertheless a social phenomenon; and this not just in the sense — which many would not dispute — that it is only by entering into social relations that human beings incur moral obligations, but also in so far as the detail of those obligations cannot be understood simply by adverting to needs which all men or women have in common just because they are human. The detail of our needs, and hence of our rights, cannot be understood without adverting to what society, and our places in society, have made of us.

This is evidently true of such interrelated needs as that for self-expression, for self-esteem, and for respectful treatment: people have such needs only *because* they are social creatures and the specific form which these needs take depends, loosely, on one's specific place in the relevant social (sub-) structure. No doubt there are basic human needs, shared by most other animals; and probably they are best served by living in the sort of communal co-operatives

in which most of us live our lives. But it is an obvious fact —
and no less fundamental for that — that it is society itself
which creates many of the needs which we feel most keenly;
and that the detail of our moral thinking cannot be understood without paying attention to the detail of these needs,
our wish to satisfy them in ourselves, and our respect for
them in others. If this is an obvious fact, however, it is a fact
of which there is no prospect of explanation within the
Kantian strait-jacket; and which the strict utilitarian can
accommodate only by Procrustean contortions of the notions
of pleasure and pain.

Had Bradley's 'moral organism' been a metaphor, it is
along these lines that one would have expected him to
elaborate his criticisms and positive point of view. But it is
evident that he wishes to assert far more; specifically, that in
a certain sense people have no *reality* outside society. Bradley
is setting himself against the view that social entities like the
family, or the state, are — in a more modern, though already
archaic-sounding terminology — 'logical constructs' out of
the human individuals which participate in them. Admittedly,
Bradley's own formulations of the opposition are almost
entirely unhelpful; the issue is presented as whether or not
the state, say, can be seen as the 'sum of its parts', or as
whether it is the state, or the individual in isolation from the
state, who is a 'mere abstraction'. So expressed, there is no
obvious way of addressing the issue squarely; nor does
Bradley attempt any clear account of what it is that is
distinctive about organic unities in contrast with those which
are, whatever it means to say so, 'sums' of their constituents.
But he is explicit (*ES*, pp. 165-6) that he is making a serious
metaphysical claim: there are social, organic entities in which
men are constituents; in some sense men have no existence
outside these entities; and it is impossible to understand the
character and function of our moral thinking unless one pays
due heed to the fact.

The second evident point is that Bradley succeeds in
developing absolutely nothing by way of substantial argument for this point of view. It is difficult to say whether he
was under any illusions on this score. He writes:

But we are not going to enter on a metaphysical question to which we
are not equal; we meet the metaphysical assertion of the 'individualist'

with a mere denial; and, turning to facts, we will try to show that they lead us in another direction (*ES*, p. 166).

The question is what, having ducked the metaphysical issue, Bradley believes that the 'facts' which he is about to adduce are apt to show. He expresses his intention like this:

> We say that, out of theory, no such individual men exist; and we will try to show from fact that, in fact, what we call an individual man is what he is because of and by virtue of community, and that communities are thus not mere names but something real, and can be regarded (if we mean to keep to facts) only as the one in the many (*ES*, p. 166).

This certainly makes it seem as if Bradley believed that he could corroborate the metaphysical point by the adduction of (empirical) fact. And certainly, if there are uncontroversial cases of causal influence exerted by communities on individual men, then at least the autonomy of communities, if not yet their organic character, would have to be granted; for no 'mere abstraction' can be the initiator of change. But, naturally, prior to a resolution of the metaphysical issue, there are no *uncontroversial* cases of causality of that sort. The facts to which Bradley calls attention (*ES*, pp. 168–74) are essentially three. First, our inheritance at birth is an aptitude for socialization:

> It is the opinion of those best qualified to speak on the subject, that civilization is to some not inconsiderable extent hereditary; that aptitudes are developed, and are latent in the child at birth; and that it is a very different thing, even apart from education, to be born of civilized and of uncivilized ancestors. These 'civilized tendencies' . . . are part of the essence of the child: he would only partly (if at all) be himself without them; he owes them to his ancestors, and his ancestors owe them to society (*ES*, p. 170).

Second there is the inheritance of the communal language. The child learns:

> . . . to speak, and here he appropriates the common heritage of his race, the tongue that he makes his own is his country's language, it is (or it should be) the same that others speak, and it carries into his mind the ideas and sentiments of the race . . . and stamps them in indelibly (*ES*, p. 172).

Third, Bradley emphasizes (*ES*, pp. 172–3), following Hegel, the role of ethical training in forming the character of the individual and in supplying him with the network of goals and standards, which, while giving his life purpose and value, do so only because they are recognized as communal currency.

Now each of the three considerations illustrates a respect in which it would normally be thought quite natural to say that the community exerts an influence on the individual; more than that, we can agree with Bradley that it is not wild hyperbole to say that the community makes the individual what he is. But to grant Bradley's facts would seem to be consistent with holding that a full account of the causal relations involved could ultimately omit reference to the *community* altogether; that the ultimate initiators of the changes which constitute the socialization of an individual are actual and historical human beings. And unless that combination of views is inconsistent, Bradley's facts merely emphasize what I stressed above, that as a metaphor the notion of the moral organism would have a great deal of point.

It is important to realize that there is a good deal at stake in the question whether Bradley's notion should be taken as merely a metaphor or as something more substantial. So long as its legitimate content is exhausted by appropriate stress on the socialized character of mens' needs and goals, it can require at most a gloss on the utilitarian point of view. The good for the individual can still be seen as residing purely in the satisfaction of his desires; and the good in general as a maximal satisfaction of the desires of maximally many individuals. It is just that we must recognize that a substantial core of the desires of the individual are desires which are possible to him only because he lives in society, only because he estimates himself and others by communally acknowledged standards, only because social life has nourished in him expectations and ambitions of a quite different order to those associated with his purely physical capacities for pleasure and suffering. So we should have a corrective to the very crude philosophical psychology with which classical formulations of utilitarianism were encumbered; but we should have no corrective to the overriding utilitarian *motif*.

The situation would be quite different, however, if it could be established that there is in reality a social, or moral, organism in which people are organs. For any constituent in an organism is subject to certain modes of appraisal just in virtue of being such a constituent: a kidney, for example, is subject to appraisal according to how well it performs the defining function of a kidney, that of preservation of the chemical composition of the blood by filtration of certain substances from it. Kidneys are better or worse according to how well they perform this function, — it can even perfectly properly be said of a diseased kidney that it is not functioning as it *ought*. More generally: an organ functioning within an organic structure can, quite unmysteriously, be seen as having an *essence* — its essence will be the function by which it is defined — by reference to which what it is *actually* may be evaluated. That men have such an essence, indeed, that it is in some sense to be *free*, is common to both the leading philosophical schools which have their roots in Hegel's writings: the Marxists and the existentialists. But it is an idea which has found little sympathy among moral philosophers of the Analytic school. If, however, the notion of the social organism can be sustained as a metaphysical thesis, the acceptability of such an idea becomes the merest formality: in explaining the character of the organism, we shall have explained what men essentially are; and thereby elucidated a dimension for appraisal of their character and conduct which has exactly the (kind of) objectivity that is possessed by the manner in which we appraise the functioning of a kidney in a human body. This is exactly what Bradley means when he speaks of the good for the individual as consisting in *self-realization*: that is, realization of the essential nature of the self, the nature which it derives from the role which it plays in the social organism.

Plainly there would be no immediate connection of this good with the utilitarian good, the maximal satisfaction of the individual's desires. What is in prospect here, as far as utilitarianism is concerned, is, at best, an explanation of why it is that evaluation by utilitarian criteria very often gives acceptable-seeming results — whereas from the utilitarian point of view, such an *explanation* is out of the question — and, at worst, the uncovering of a deep basis for moral judgment which cuts across utilitarian criteria and reveals their inadequacy.

It is, then, the metaphysical issue which needs to be tackled if 'My Station and Its Duties' is to be seen as presenting a viable objectivist alternative view of morality to that of classical utilitarianism and its modern descendants. But Bradley, to repeat, does not tackle it; and neither, I venture to suggest, did Hegel.[3]

II

What is an organism? — what makes for *organic unity*? An evident necessary condition is hierarchical structure: no entity can constitute an organic unity unless it divides into parts, which in turn divide into parts, . . . , etc., in a way that is characteristic of its being an instance of the *kind* — tree, toadstool, human body, for example — which it exemplifies. Thus the human body divides in the first instance into various major systems: the central nervous system, the cardio-vascular system, the digestive system, the lymphatic system, and so on; these in turn are distinctively structured out of various organs; some of these organs have, for their part, their own substructure of constituent organs, and all are constituted by an organized system of cells of appropriate sorts. Prescinding from complications occasioned by the possibility of integrating artificial organs within the body, it is fair to say that for something to be a living human body just *is* for it to be a functioning system of this structure and composition. An analogous claim could plausibly be made for the State, universities, business corporations, and the family. But the parallel is of no great consequence in the present context, since such a structure is also exemplified by many entities whose unity we should not regard as organic; for example, a molecule of sulphuric acid, or a token inscription of 'The Walrus and the Carpenter'. (Of course, what is crucial for our present purpose is that the distinctive structure of these latter types of entity seems to carry with it no basis for *evaluation* of their constituents.)

A second evident necessary condition for organic unity is that the unity should in some way depend upon a certain causal interdependence of the constitutents: the proper functioning of the human body, for instance, depends upon the proper functioning of each of its vital organs, and the proper functioning of each of these organs requires that of all the others. But this, too, is only a necessary condition. No such interdependence is manifest among the constituents of a token inscription of 'The Walrus and the Carpenter', but something of the kind *is* presumably true of the atomic constituents of a molecule of sulphuric acid — and of a great many other commonplace physical objects which we should not normally regard as constituting organic unities (for example, an archway which would collapse if any one of its constituent trapeziform bricks were removed; or a Rubik Cube). Nor do we get a significant strengthening of the condition by specifying that the requisite interdependence is to be *functional*. For that had better mean no more than that the state (in relevant respects) of any one of the constituents is determined as the value of some (complex) function of the states of the other constituents; and that is already the situation in the sorts of example which we are trying to discount.

One wants to reply, however, that this is to interpret 'functional' too narrowly; that what is 'functional' about organic unities is not merely that there is a functional interdependence between states of their constituents but, more, that the constituents each *have* a function, determined by their role in the promotion of some state, or objective, of the whole. With organic unities, explanation of the behaviour of the constituents has to be, at least in part, *teleological*: there are questions about the characteristics and behaviour of the constituents which can only be answered if we pay due heed both to the fact that they are constituents in a larger unity and to the characteristics and behaviour of the other constituents. There is no understanding the structure of a kidney, for instance, unless one knows what it is that kidneys do; and there is no knowing what kidneys do unless one knows a good deal about the chemistry of the blood and the role of the blood supply in maintaining the function of vital organs in the body.

Care is needed with the formulation of this point. It is not merely that, with organic unities, a full understanding of the nature of the constituents will need to take account of the role which they are playing in the whole: that is no more than the condition of functional interdependence which we have already seen to be insufficient. The present thought is rather that, where organic unities are concerned, certain sorts of questions are appropriate about the constituents which are not appropriate elsewhere, and which can be answered only by, among other things, adverting to the role which that constituent plays in the organism as a whole. Roughly: these are questions which call for explanation of characteristics of the constituents not in terms of the background causal ancestry of those characteristics but in terms of what possession of those characteristics enables the constituents to do. Thus it is perfectly true that a full understanding, in one reasonable sense of the phrase, of the characteristics of a hydrogen atom, which when bonded together with other atoms of hydrogen, oxygen, and sulphur forms a molecule of sulphuric acid, will need to involve knowledge of properties which explain the amenability of such atoms to that particular mode of bonding. But there is no *telos* in the offing: it is no explanation of *why* a hydrogen atom possesses those properties to call attention to the way in which they facilitate its participation in molecules of sulphuric acid. Whereas it is, or is felt to be, an explanation of the cell-structure of the kidney that it enables the kidney to act as a filter. More generally: we conceive a structure as an organic unity only if we suppose not merely that there is a functional interdependence between certain of the characteristics of its constituents but more, that explanations of at least some of those characteristics will be teleological, will proceed by making it clear how it is that possession of those characteristics enables the constituent to carry out its distinctive function in the whole.

To avoid misunderstanding: the foregoing is intended only as a characterization of one aspect of the concept of an organism which we actually use. It is no part of my purpose to take sides on the question whether or not teleological explanations are, in some sense, irreducible; or whether, if they can be reduced to non-teleological ones, it would be proper to draw the conclusion that the notion of organic unity is an empty one. Of course, if that conclusion were correct, Bradley's metaphysical claim would have to be empty as well; but our present goal is merely to assess that claim from a standpoint which accepts that some structures do exhibit an organic unity, and that there is a coherent account to be given of their distinctive features.

Bradley himself appears to have kept this teleological aspect of organic unities in view only episodically. In particular, even if we granted that the above 'facts' which he adduces can be taken straightforwardly as evidence of causal interaction between the community and the individual, they anyway appear — at least if the objective is to reveal the community as an organic structure — to be of the wrong kind. If the community, or a social substructure within the community, is to be shown to be an organic structure of the people who compose it, it will not do merely to argue that the individual is 'made what he is' by his social environment, that 'the soul within him' is saturated by 'the universal life' (*ES*, p. 172). Rather Bradley needs to call attention to characteristics of individuals whose explanation would have to advert to their functional role in the social organism. It is only if there are such characteristics that it can make sense to conceive at all of organic social structures whose constituents are individual persons.

There is a connection, of course, between the teleological aspect of the notion of an organism and the capacity of Bradley's metaphysical thesis to subserve the intended moral view. Simply: what makes teleological explanations of the characteristics of an organ appropriate is the conception that it has an essential role to play; and it is our understanding of this essential role which supplies, in the manner adumbrated earlier, the standard whereby its actual performance may be evaluated. So it really is vital that Bradley draws the analogy in the relevant respect, i.e. that there be a range of human characteristics the explanation of which is teleological and proceeds in terms of social roles played by the individuals exemplifying them.

Evidently, though, it would not have been difficult for him to do so, if only for the trivial reason that any well-organized social institution is liable to employ people in ways that take account of their special strengths and limitations. There will thus be explanations of the athleticism and co-ordination of footballers, the perfect pitch and manual dexterity of orchestral violinists, and the wisdom of university administrators, of just the sorts that Bradley's thesis requires.

Viewed in the light of these considerations, Bradley's view is apt to strike us as much more reasonable than its detractors over the years have made it seem. There is no question but that it is part of our ordinary moral thinking that if someone takes on a role in a certain organized activity, he thereby incurs certain determinate obligations, the details of which depend upon a conception, perhaps vague, which we have of *ideal* performance of that particular role. The use of evaluative adjectives as *attributives* in concatenation with role-descriptions — 'good farmer', 'able administrator', 'bad doctor', etc. — is intelligible because and only because of this. If this was the whole content of the moral philosophy of 'My Station and Its Duties' then we could give Bradley the point and wonder that he needed over fifty pages to make it. But, of course, the claim is much larger: it is a claim about the fundamental nature of the *truth-conditions* of moral judgments. If someone really supposed — a position from which Bradley in the end recoils — that 'My Station and Its Duties' represented a wholly adequate moral theory, his thesis would have to be that the legitimate meaning of moral adjectives is *exhausted* by the kind of attributive function illustrated, and that any contexts in which we appear to judge a man's conduct in isolation from the social role or roles which he plays must be understood as involving ellipsis of some such attributive use. Where we are concerned with a genuine organism, the only basis — other than aesthetic — for evaluation of the performance of its constituents is in terms of the roles which the organism requires them to play.

To conceive of this kind of evaluation as constitutive of all legitimate moral judgment would seem less rebarbative if, like Bradley, we took it that fulfilment of our 'essence' would *eo ipso* make us happy — indeed, only if that is supposed can Bradley see himself as having retained what he views as correct in the utilitarian standpoint. But, however that may be, the salient point is that Bradley will seem merely to have blown up one aspect of our moral thinking out of all proportion, unless the thesis of the organic nature of social structures can be sustained in a more robust sense than any so far indicated. It is not enough merely to observe that there is *some* scope for teleological explanation, in relation to the objectives of the corporations of which they are members, of characteristics and behaviour-patterns which people display.

In fact the propriety of teleological explanations of aspects of its constituents is evidently insufficient to characterize a structure as an organic unity in any case. Just such explanations could be given of the characteristics of many parts of a clock, or motor car, for example; and indeed of the shape of the bricks that make up the arch (supposing that they were designed for such a job). So what further conditions ought to be imposed? One obvious consideration which we have so far ignored is that organisms are typically *live* in the biological sense: they have, that is to say, a natural cycle of development and decay, certain capacities for self-regeneration and growth, certain capacities of adaptation to change in environmental conditions, and the ability to reproduce their kind. Such a conception of nations, or states, at the level of metaphor is commonplace and is displayed in familiar imagery like that of 'development' or 'decadence'. Should Bradley really be taken to mean, more, that certain social wholes really are living entities, whose study would thus be a province of biology? Sometimes it appears so. He writes, for example:

> The universal to be realised is no abstraction, but an organic whole; a system where many spheres are subordinated to one sphere, and particular actions to spheres. This sytem is real in the detail of its functions, not out of them, and lives in its vital processes, not away from them. The organs are always at work for the whole, the whole is at work in the organs. And I am one of the organs (*ES*, p. 176).

The conception of social wholes as living, regenerative, historical individuals is, of course, more explicit in Hegel; indeed it is the focal point of his entire philosophy of history. Had Bradley, in effect, committed himself to it, or is there some stance, intermediate between the Hegelian view and the admission as appropriate of certain types of teleological explanation, which will nevertheless sustain the moral philosophy of 'My Station and Its Duties'?

It would be of considerable interest to examine the Hegelian view in its own right (of course, we would expect to find against it), if only because we should be forced to make progress on the question concerning what constitutes a living whole, one cardinal problem of the philosophy of biology. But I shall not try to take on that issue here. For Bradley is clearly making certain demands on the notion of a *person* which we can appraise independently of making progress on that issue, and indeed independently of deciding whether there is any stance available to him of the intermediate sort just mentioned. It is, as noted, characteristic of organisms, and of many mechanisms, that the sortal concepts under which their constituents fall — concepts like kidney, heart, stomach, root, stalk, gill, spring, cog, transistor, etc. — classify those constituents in accordance with functional role. Our conception of the sort of thing a kidney, or cog-wheel, essentially is, thus carries with it an implicit reference to the type of task it is suitable to perform and the sort of larger entity in which it is apt to perform it. This is not to deny that somebody could learn to classify such objects without knowing anything about their function: the point is merely that such a classificatory ability would not be enough for an understanding of the sortal concepts involved, whatever precise further knowledge we would want to regard as sufficient for understanding.[4]

There is thus a clear sense in which to attempt to conceive of a functional constituent of an organism, or mechanism, in isolation from the role which it plays is to entertain, as Bradley puts it, a mere 'abstraction'. For, to stress this, the functional roles of such entities are *essential* characteristics of them; hence they cannot survive the *loss* of such a role — or, at least, loss of the capacity to play it. I believe that Bradley means to assert something precisely analogous when he claims that individuals are real only in the social organism. At any rate, precisely this analogy is what is wanted if the moral theory of 'My Station and Its Duties' is to aspire to comprehensiveness. But in that case, the following specific, and assessable, demand is being made on the notion of a person: Bradley is demanding that the attempt to conceive of an individual person in abstraction from the social whole, or wholes, into which he is integrated, is, correspondingly, to attempt to abstract away from characteristics essential to his being a *person* at all. If the person outside society is to be a mere 'delusion of theory' (*ES*, p. 174), then the concept of a person must contain the same sort of tacit reference to larger social structures that the concept of a kidney contains to animal bodies. Can such a demand possibly be sustained?

One's instinctive response is that it cannot; that the concept of person is simply that of one *natural kind* of autonomous entity, and that Bradley's demand is quite misplaced. On reflection, however, it emerges that, on the contrary, Bradley has the support of a substantial insight. To explain, persons are essentially *rational*, as Aristotle saw, not in the sense that they are predominantly cool-headed, logical, and resistant to superstition, but in the sense that at least a large part of their behaviour is susceptible to explanation in terms of systematic theories of their beliefs and desires. Persons are also essentially *self-conscious* in the sense that they possess a conception of themselves as continuants, with a determinate legacy of previous experience, and the prospect of future experience which they can anticipate at least in broad outline. Putting rationality and self-consciousness together, we have that a person, whatever else it is, is a subject aware of its possession of determinate future objectives for itself and of scenarios of how they may be achieved. No creature could satisfy us that it deserved to be viewed in this light unless it was capable, in its behaviour, of manifesting the various relevant conceptions: a grasp of the distinction between itself and other things, knowledge of its own history, an awareness of possible future states which it is within its power to promote and beliefs about the appropriate means for promoting them, the capacity to modify such beliefs in the face of changing circumstances, and a self-consciously entertained framework of desires and goals. If, and only if, a creature presented us with full-blooded behavioural grounds for attributing such concepts and abilities to it, would it then be reasonable to regard ourselves as confronting a person, irrespective of its appearance or constitution; so persons are *not* a natural kind.

Now it is, I think, evident that no behaviour which was not *linguistic* could possibly be rich enough to warrant such a view of an agent. Only linguistic behaviour can manifest a conception of the self; only linguistic behaviour can manifest a conception of various future possibilites. And while it is true that we sometimes apply the belief/desire scheme of explanation to the behaviour of more intelligent non-human animals, there is a significant indeterminacy about the *content* of beliefs attributed to languageless creatures, since — in contrast to the situation which prevails with persons — intersubstitution of coextensive expressions within the formulation of a belief attributed to a dog, say, will not jeopardize the explanatory power of the attribution.[5] Since to be a person is to be able to behave, *ceteris paribus*, in a way distinctive of being a person, and such behaviour must — if the foregoing is cogent — be linguistic, it follows that to be a person is to be master of an (appropriately rich) language.

We are now close to the Bradleian insight. To clinch it, however, we need to borrow one of the later Wittgenstein's. One way of expressing a leading corollary of his thought about rule-following,[6] is that language is an essentially social activity in the sense that only in a community of speakers are certain conditions met whose satisfaction is necessary for a justified belief that the language exists at all. This thesis, and its celebrated application to the Cartesian conception of language concerning those of a subject's mental states about which he is normally granted a special authority — sensations, intentions, etc. — is not universally accepted by philosophers; and it would take us too far afield to review the grounds for it. Let me merely record both my own belief that they are extremely powerful; and the thought that Bradley would likely as not have had little time for the strong realism to which, I believe, an opponent of Wittgenstein's thesis must commit himself.

Now some interpreters of Wittgenstein have held that the corollary about private language would extend to exclusion of a language used by a Robinson Crusoe to describe the physical surroundings on his island. If that is correct, and language-mastery can thus be exercised only in the context of an actual society of language-users, then, in the light of our above reflections, that someone is a person at all can be manifest only in behaviour which is uniquely possible in the society of other persons. But only in behaviour which manifests his personhood did an agent function distinctively *as* a person: it would appear to follow that in order to function as a person, one must function (in a reciprocally intelligible way) among the members of a social group.

It is important to see, however, that we can forgo this relatively controversial interpretation of Wittgenstein, yet still make out a close analogy between person *vis-à-vis* society and kidney *vis-à-vis* human body.[7] First, define 'x functions as a ϕ' as: x behaves in a way in which *necessarily*[8] all and only ϕs can (unless prevented) behave. Thus for x to function as a kidney is for x to filter the blood (in a certain way) and, by our earlier reflections, for x to function as a person is for x to deploy a (sufficiently rich) language. Now a kidney can survive excision from its parent body just so long as its capacity to function as a kidney survives; so too, *mutatis mutandis*, for Crusoe's social 'excision' on his island. What, then, does Wittgenstein, less controversially interpreted, have to say about Crusoe's purported solitary linguistic behaviour? Just that its capacity correctly to be regarded *as* language-use is conceptually dependent upon its capacity to admit of intelligible integration into a community of language-users. So Crusoe can 'function as a person' in solitude; but the claim that he is doing so is answerable to what would happen if he were to be reincorporated within a normal linguistic community. But then the parallel with a kidney is evident. For, in the relevant sense, a kidney too can function as such in isolation: we can pump blood from a blood bank through a disembodied kidney and monitor its performance. Yet the claim that it is functioning as a kidney is conceptually answerable to what would happen if it were to be (appropriately) reincorporated within an otherwise normal, living human body.

The analogy is thus:

(a) Kidney and person are both sortal concepts.

(b) Necessarily: to be a kidney/person is to be able (unless prevented) to do certain things which all and only kidneys/persons can do (unless prevented).

(c) The relevant kinds of activity are standardly performed in the context of integration within a larger whole, but can, abnormally, be performed in isolation.

(d) The claim that a particular performance in isolation constitutes one of the relevant kinds of activity is conceptually answerable to its capacity to pass tests associated with (re-) integration into an appropriate larger whole.

It hence is arguable that there is indeed a sense in which the notion of person points to the notion of a larger social entity in which persons are constituents; and in which the attempt to conceive of a person in isolation from the capacity to function in such a larger entity is a futile attempt to conceive of him in abstraction from certain essential characteristics. So Bradley is, arguably, right.

III

If this is an insight, it would nevertheless be a confusion to attempt to rest the theoretical stance of 'My Station and Its Duties' upon it. The explanation is simple. The notion of 'functioning as a person' appealed to in the construction of the analogy has been associated with no *telos* for the relevant whole. The parallel is that for an entity to function as, and indeed *be* a person, or kidney, is, for purely conceptual reasons, possible only if that entity could function in just that way as a successful constituent in an appropriate larger totality. But that is as far as the parallel goes — not far enough for Bradley's purpose. For it remains that to function as a kidney is to play a certain part in promotion of a *telos* of the whole; whereas, although 'functioning as a person' is answerable to integration within a community, it is not, or need not be, a matter of playing a part, after integration, in the achievement of some goal — if only the 'proper functioning' — of the community as a whole. So the sense in which the very notion of a person adverts to a larger totality is not the sense that was wanted.

This is only to point out a lacuna. I do not pretend to *know* that a deeper analysis of the notion of a person could not construct the more thoroughgoing parallel which Bradley needs (and hence overthrow the above suggestion that mastery of a sufficiently rich language is sufficient to constitute personhood). But it is natural to be very sceptical about the prospect. Evidently it would be necessary to be specific about the *telos* of the social organism, in order to verify that the notion of a person does indeed have an appropriate teleological aspect; but all that Bradley has to offer is that the end of the whole is self-realization of its constituent organs — and that is just as circular, though just as correct, as saying that the *telos* of the human body is the proper functioning of its organs.[9]

As noted, Bradley himself is not in the end content with the theory of 'My Station and Its Duties'. At the end of his essay (*ES*, pp. 203–6) he introduces and sustains a number of objections to it, including its inability to account for 'cosmopolitan' aspects of morality and certain sorts of (what Bradley sees as) duties to oneself — in particular, in so far as one is capable, the production of truth and beauty. He does not make fully explicit, however, what is likely to strike anyone, irrespective of his views on Bradley's 'metaphysical question', as the most serious objection of all: that the theory provides no basis for what is evidently possible, viz. significant evaluation of the morality of the social whole in which one's 'station' is defined. Failing the elucidation of some larger totality in which such wholes are themselves constituent organs,[10] the strict consequence of 'My Station and Its Duties' has to be that moral categories are simply inapplicable to the conduct of such institutions. This is a repulsive consequence; as is the ease with which it comes to those whose political thinking is dominated by the notion of 'social organism' to engage in such conceptions as that of political dissidence as a form of *disease*.

Still, for all that 'My Station and Its Duties' is unacceptable both as morality and as moral theory, it arguably rests upon a conceptual insight; but an insight which Bradley grasped only dimly and which, unless developed in ways I cannot foresee, is inadequate to sustain it.[11]

NOTES

1. See in particular Hegel, *Philosophy of Right*, Oxford, 1942, tr. Knox para. 135. A good synopsis of Hegel's criticisms is given by chap. IV of W. H. Walsh, *Hegelian Ethics*, Macmillan, 1969. Bradley's objections are concentrated in chap. IV of *Ethical Studies*, Oxford, 2nd edn., 1927.

2. Bradley's dissatisfactions with utilitarianism are various. See *Ethical Studies*, Essay III, 'Pleasure for Pleasure's Sake'. First, the pursuit of pleasure for its own sake, which he sees as the essential motif of the utilitarian standpoint, is simply impractical: 'the world has learnt that, if pleasure is the end, it is an end which must not be made one, and is found there most where it is not sought . . . if you want to be happy in the sense of pleased, you must not think of pleasure, but, taking up some accredited form of living, must make that your end, and in that case, with moderately good fortune, you will be happy' (*ES*, p. 87).

   Second, utilitarianism, however careful its formulation, is enormously counterintuitive: 'When moral persons without a theory on the matter are told that the moral end for the individual and the race is the getting a maximum surplusage of pleasurable feeling, and that there is nothing in the whole world which has the smallest moral value except this end and the means to it, there is no gainsaying that they repudiate such a result. They feel that there are things "we should choose even if no pleasure came from them"; and that if we choose these things, being good, for ourselves, then we must choose them also for the race, if we care for the race as we do for ourselves' (*ES*, p. 88).

   But Bradley's main theoretical objection is to the hedonism on which he believes utilitarianism must ultimately rest, viz. that it leaves morality with *no realizable objective*. For Bradley, the moral life is essentially a life in which the self is fully *realized*; and whatever the correct account of this notion of realization, it must, on pain of the pointlessness of moral conduct, supply a practical, feasible objective. But the pursuit of pleasure, for Bradley, even the maximum pleasure for the maximum number of people, is the pursuit of a state which, in the nature of the case, is transitory: 'And pleasure (as pain) we find to be nothing but a name which stands for a series of this, that, and the other feelings, which are not except in the moment or moments that they are felt, which have as a series neither limitation of number, beginning nor end, nor in themselves any reference at all, any of them, beyond themselves. To realize, as such, the self which feels pleasure and pain, means to realize this infinite perishing series. And it is clear at once that this is not what is required for a practical end' (*ES*, p. 95). In short, as Bradley sees it, utilitarianism renders the moral task *incompletable*. The objection is apt to seem odd to anyone accustomed to think of the moral life as one in which practical decisions are habitually informed by the application of moral principles rather than as one in which a certain *task* is achieved — a task in something akin to the sense in which we think of someone's life's work as a task, and judge, for example, that W. H. Auden and Bertrand Russell completed their respective tasks while Dylan Thomas and F. P. Ramsey did not. But it is, of course, this very conception of morality that Bradley wishes to challenge.

3. In view of the arcane character of Hegel's *Logic*, such a claim must, of course, be tentative!

4. People identified the kidneys, for example, long before their function was understood (perhaps as we now identify the vermiform appendix); but it is characteristic of this type of concept that once the function is understood, it comes to dominate other, original bases of classification. We can make perfect sense of the possibility of people who had a quite different *type* of kidney to ours: kidneys which looked different, worked on a different mechanical principle, and were situated, say, adjacent to the heart.

5. Another way of putting the point would be that any attribution of belief to a dog may equivalently be recast so as to give wide scope with respect to the belief-operator, and hence extensional intersubstitutivity, to any of the constituent expressions in the that-clause. Hence a description of a dog's belief has neither characteristic — indifference to existence or non-substitutivity — which Brentano regarded as the essential features of *intentionality*, the hallmark, as he supposed, of the mental.

6. See in particular *Philosophical Investigations*, Oxford, 1953, paras. 185–242; and *Remarks on the Foundations of Mathematics*, Oxford, 1978 (especially I, paras. 113–18, and VI, paras. 15–49). Recent commentary on this aspect of Wittgenstein's thought includes S. Kripke, 'Wittgenstein on Rules and Private Language', in *Perspectives on the Philosophy of Wittgenstein*, ed. I. Block, 1981, and my own *Wittgenstein on the Foundations of Mathematics*, London, 1980.

7. The 'relatively controversial interpretation' (see, for example, Rush Rhees, 'Can there be a Private Language? ', *Proceedings of the Aristotelian Society*, supp. vol. 28, 1954) is in any case — unlike the milder interpretation which I am about to suggest — at odds with Bradley's apparent willingness to admit the possibility of the unsocialized *acquisition* of language. See, for example, *Essays on Truth and Reality*, Oxford, 1944, chap. XII, p. 357.

8. i.e. it is to be non-contingently true that all and only ϕs can behave in the relevant fashion.

9. If the *telos* of the human body is healthy life, say, it is true that its healthy life consists in the proper functioning of its organs. But it must be possible to explain what 'healthy' life is *independently* of identifying the vital organs and their proper functions if there is to be any basis for regarding the body with its organs as an organic unity at all; for, failing such explanation, how could *teleological* questions about the organs be properly motivated?

10. As Hegel attempted to do.

11. Robert Nozick has recently given extensive space to a theory of value based on organic unity in his *Philosophical Explanations*, Oxford, 1981. Perhaps it is worth remarking that his starting-point is quite different to that of Bradley. For Bradley, integration within an organic whole is the basis of evaluation: value is in proportion to effective discharge of role. For Nozick, it is, crudely, organization itself that is of value; the value of an entity is generated by its own degree and manner of organization rather than its role as an organ in something else. (It will be interesting to see whether Nozick's ideas achieve a more popular reception than Bradley's, and whether they have the effect of revitalizing interest in the latter.)

CHAPTER 5

Bradley and the Nature of Punishment

Peter Johnson

Much of the value of Bradley's philosophical writings is to be found in their unorthodoxy.[1] They are characterized by a determination not to allow convention or sentimentality to interfere with the logic of an argument. The ways by which he disposes of his philosophical enemies in epistemology and metaphysics are repeated in his works on the nature and justification of punishment. He recognizes the impossibility of an examination of the concept of punishment without discussion of its presuppositions. Of these the most imporant are human agency and the form of understanding appropriate to it, the nature of human freedom and the self. His examination of ethical and social life depends upon logical doctrines and cannot be properly understood apart from them. Thus, a philosophical discussion of punishment requires that it make its position plain on the meaning of many other concepts presupposed by, but not uniquely connected with, punishment itself.

Punishment is a concept marked by considerable complexity, found in a variety of contexts. We speak of divine punishment, of military punishment, of punishment in education, within the family, in games, and so on. It is not clear that punishment has an identical meaning in all the social practices in which it operates, or that if it were possible to distil such a meaning it would be the most significant. What is clear, however, is that when we speak of the punishment of the individual by the State we are speaking of one of the starkest expressions of the coercive authority of the State. In the main tradition of political philosophy the theoretical and practical seriousness of this has been recognized. The accounts which have been offered have been based on the assumption that there is a symmetry between the justification of punishment and of political obligation. In other words, questions concerning the nature of the legitimacy of the state, the nature of law, and the demarcation of the rights and duties of citizens need to be answered in order to provide a basis for the justification of punishment. Within political philosophy the justification of punishment is inextricably bound up with the nature of rights and the notions of consent, justice, and equality. This has led to the attempt to take a more refined view of the rivalry between the various standard justifications of punishment — the retributive, the deterrent, and the reformist. It has been suggested that the justification of punishment as a social practice must take a logically different form from the justification of particular acts of punishment within the practice, and that whereas utilitarian considerations are appropriate in the former case, in the latter the retributive emphasis on guilt is a precondition of punishment being just.

Whatever merits this refinement may have, some of Bradley's remarks on punishment serve to highlight its weaknesses, in particular, the failure to investigate the idea of guilt from the perspective of the person who is punished. If punishment is seen externally rather than internally, then a whole cluster of connections between punishment and a range of moral concepts is lost sight of. Here it is necessary to stress the relation between punishment and the criminal's own understanding of his crime. This may involve an examination of the relation between punishment and remorse, or of the sense in which punishment is a necessary condition of atonement or of the expiation of the crime. Thus the refinement under discussion through over-concentration on the establishment of legal guilt fails to see the complexity of the moral issues involved in a person's recognizing that his punishment was deserved. Here a familiar problem recurs in the discussion of the concept of punishment. For we seem to be drawn away from the precise concept towards those broader features with which it shares the conceptual map. In this case the question is of the similarities and differences between political and moral understandings and justifications — and very often the view of punishment we hold will depend on the answer we give to this general question.

One view, however, is indifferent to such subtleties, and discussion of this raises further dimensions and interrelations between the concept of punishment and that of crime. On the basis of the assumption that human activities need to be explained scientifically it is argued that any account of criminal behaviour must involve the isolation of its antecedent causes. The search for a causal nexus necessarily undermines the concepts of intentionality and responsibility central to an understanding of human agency as autonomous. More importantly, however, it entails the replacement of the idea of crime by that of disease, and consequently the replacement of the idea of punishment by that of treatment. Much of the force of Bradley's discussion of Darwinism is directed towards these implications.

Understanding Bradley's characteristic modes of expression is as important as understanding the ideas he expresses. They are two sides of the same coin. The most damaging weapon in his armoury is irony. It is employed rigorously and imaginatively on many occasions, the technique being to take over the argument under discussion with the aim of expanding its scope and so revealing its logical flaws and transforming it into an object of ridicule. Bradley's prose is often marked, as Eliot notices, by 'a sort of solemn banter', itself an expression of irony, and in its critical, dismissive side, by a mischievous teasing with the arguments of his opponents, which is the expression of his sceptical view of the limitations of philosophical reasoning. The love of paradox is often concealed in prose of direct and passionate commitment. But in Bradley's writing not all is as it appears. Nevertheless, there are many passages where Bradley's delight in rhetoric is difficult to halt, and where argument is replaced by oratory of a hectoring and mannered kind. To say simply that Bradley means what he says is merely to assume that all alternative lines of interpretation are closed. This would be inconsistent with his general deployment of irony, and would result in understanding his reflections on punishment either as personal beliefs of a rather extreme kind or as a bland distillation of general theories. Bradley pursues truth obliquely.

This is manifest in Bradley's view of the nature of philosophical argument. For him the purpose of moral philosophy is not to provide a theory of moral conduct by establishing a yardstick against which moral actions can be identified and assessed. Discussing the view 'that there must be some existing theory which is a sufficient account of morals', which Bradley describes as 'an unproved assumption', he says:

If we wished to cross an unknown bog, and two men came to us, of whom the one said, 'Some one must know the way over this bog, for there must be a way, and you see there is no one here beside us two, and therefore one of us two must be able to guide you. And the other man does not know the way, as you can soon see; therefore I must' — should we answer, 'Lead on, I follow'? Philosophy would indeed be the easiest of studies, if we might arrive at truth by assuming that one of two accounts must be true, and prove the one by disproving the other; but in philosophy this is just what can not be done (*ES*, p. 90 n).

In his discussion of the nature of moral beliefs Bradley clearly distinguishes their logical character from that of theories; discursive reasoning plays a limited part in moral conduct.

Thus, after a recommendation to 'give up the harbouring of theories of what should be and is not', Bradley describes the value of the concrete ethics of 'My Station and Its Duties':

It holds and will hold its own against the worship of the 'individual', whatever form that may take. It is strong against frantic theories and vehement passions, and in the end it triumphs over the fact, and can smile at the literature, even of sentimentalism, however fulsome in its impulsive setting out, or sour in its disappointed end. It laughs at its frenzied apotheosis of the yet unsatisfied passion it calls love, and at that embitterment too which has lost its illusions, and yet can not let them go — with its kindness for the genius too clever in general to do anything in particular, and its adoration of star-gazing virgins with souls above their spheres, whose wish to be something in the world takes the form of wanting to do something with it, and who in the end do badly what they might have done in the beginning well; and, worse than all, its cynical contempt for what deserves only pity, sacrifice of a life for work to the best of one's lights, a sacrifice despised not simply because it has failed, but because it is stupid, and uninteresting, and altogether unsentimental (*ES*, pp. 201–2).

This passage contains the kernel of Bradley's view that the proper method in moral philosophy is not to be found by transcending the ordinary language of moral experience.

Moral philosophy articulates moral experience in the sense of elucidating its logical presuppositions, without which it would not be what it is, and it reveals the inconsistencies present in those views which falsify it. The revealing of inconsistencies is a central part of the method of argument in *Ethical Studies*.

Here the predominant influence is his scepticism. This leads Bradley to adopt a method whereby successive accounts of moral experience are shown to be inconsistent and finally discarded. This is most evidently the case in *Ethical Studies* where the doctrine of social ethics articulated in Essay V, is shown to be defective in terms of ideal morality, which in turn yields to religion by virtue of its own internal inconsistencies. Hence we should not be surprised to discover gaps in the argument, and this is most noticeable where Bradley denies the connection between philosophy and practice, a denial important for the proper understanding of his views on punishment:

Who would go to a learned theologian, as such, in a practical religious difficulty; to a system of aesthetic for suggestions on the handling of an artistic theme; to a physiologist, as such, for a diagnosis and prescription; to a political philosopher in practical politics; or to a psychologist in an intrigue of any kind? All these persons no doubt *might* be the best to go to, but that would not be because they were the best theorists, but because they were more. In short, the view which thinks moral philosophy is to supply us with particular moral prescriptions confuses science with art, and confuses, besides, reflective with intuitive judgement. That which tells us what in particular is right and wrong is not reflection but intuition (*ES*, pp. 193–4).

Later, Bradley applies this to the problem of the collision of duties or ethical dilemmas. He argues that moral philosophy has nothing to do with their solution, that being a matter for experience and insight. In the essay on punishment, too, he argues that 'in an ethical discussion . . . practical proposals are out of place'. To that extent, at least, the moral philosopher resembles the theorist.

We must now draw together the implications of the previous argument for the interpretation of Bradley's remarks on punishment. It is necessary to resist the assumption that he means to stand for one theory of punishment rather than another. This assumption lies behind the view that Bradley moves from a retributive theory of punishment in 1876 to a primarily utilitarian theory in the essay on punishment of 1894. This view is over-simplified because first, it neglects Bradley's explicit rejection of theory as a mode of understanding appropriate to philosophy, and second, it ignores his refusal to engage in discussion of the practical consequences of his views, a discussion which a utilitarian account of punishment surely requires. Further, it underestimates Bradley's slashing attack on utilitarianism in Essay III of

Ethical Studies, and so fails to realize that there may be other kinds of interpretation which provide a more accurate account of the development of his views. Part of the difficulty is that Bradley's manner of philosophical writing may deceive us into thinking that the views he appears to hold *are* actually held by him, and are not rejected at a later stage in the argument.

There are serious difficulties standing in the way of the utilitarian interpretation of Bradley's account of punishment. It also does not follow that we can interpret his views as an expression of minimal retributivism, that is the belief that punishment necessarily presupposes guilt. The interpretation flies in the face of his own criticism of aspects of the retributivist thesis in the 1894 essay. As the unambitious title suggests, his object is the more unsystematic but no less vigorous Socratic one of stinging us into a recognition of the fundamental incompatibilities in our justification of punishment. Understandings of punishment are examined, and their implications and inconsistencies revealed. Bradley's analysis of the idea of 'social surgery' in the essay therefore arises as a consequence of his philosophical scepticism, and is not to be understood as the expression of some personal preferences.

His initial account of punishment in *Ethical Studies* is connected with his examination of the idea of responsibility, and his criticism of determinism. It is retributive in character, but not exclusively so in the manner of Kant, who attempted to make guilt both a necessary and sufficient condition of punishment. Bradley does allow non-retributive considerations to enter into its justification. Indeed, he says that 'we are fools and worse, if we fail to do so'. But these considerations are 'external to the matter, they can not give us a right to punish, and nothing can do that but criminal desert'. The logical implications of both impure and pure retributivism are very much the subject of his analysis in the essay on punishment, but at this stage it is necessary to point out only that the presence of non-retributive considerations is not a proof that Bradley intended his account of punishment to be utilitarian. Indeed, in *Ethical Studies* the familiar features of retributivism are present. Punishment can only be elucidated and justified by reference to an agent's past conduct, and, more importantly, it is an end in itself and its own justification in that it is what the criminal deserves. Bradley associates responsibility with liability to punishment; he lists the conditions he considers necessary in order for the idea of responsibility to be rendered intelligible:

A man must act himself, be now the same man who acted, have been himself at the time of the act, have had sense enough to know what he was doing, and to know good from bad. In addition, where ignorance is wrong, not to have known does not remove accountability, though the degree of it may be doubtful. And everything said of commission applies equally well to omission or negligence (*ES*, p. 9).

Responsibility is a presupposition of the attribution of guilt, and guilt is in its turn a presupposition of punishment being deserved.

Bradley talks in a manner reminiscent of Hegel's account of punishment as annulment. 'Punishment is the denial of wrong by the assertion of right', and is 'an end in itself'. By means of these arguments Bradley claims to have avoided the weaknesses inherent in the utilitarian account of punishment with its emphasis on consequences. To treat the criminal as a means is to deny him the status of a rational and responsible being. It does not rule out the punishment of the innocent, should social utility require it. It may involve the manipulation of sentencing in such a way as to achieve what are thought to be desirable social consequences. All this entails a weakening of the connection between punishment and desert, but in behavioural accounts of criminality the connection is obliterated altogether. In *Ethical Studies*, and in a manner which anticipates parts of his discussion of the implications of Darwinism for punishment in the essay, Bradley says that when punishment is severed from desert it becomes 'medicine' or 'training'.

In *Ethical Studies*, Bradley defended a variety of retributivism. But it was not an unequivocal defence, because there he drew a distinction between matters external to the right to punish and matters internal to it. Matters external to punishment are those considerations of social benefit or utility which have only a contingent connection with the consciousness of the individual punished. If this is the case, then by matters internal to punishment Bradley means the cluster of concepts which enter into the criminal's relation with his guilt; in other words, his awareness of his guilt. This contrast between external and internal considerations may itself be elucidated in terms of the distinction between the political and the moral dimensions of punishment. This is an important, and neglected, theme in the later essay, and one which has been the subject of attention by some contemporary philosophers. Peter Winch, for example, writes:

Philosophers have tended to concentrate on questions about the 'justification' of punishment ... One consequence of this ... has been a concentration on the position of an observer contemplating the infliction of punishment by an authority on a third person ... Much less attention has been paid to the way in which the concept of punishment may enter into the understanding of what is happening to him of a person being punished.[2]

These themes and contrasts will be analysed further, but at present it is necessary to offer an interpretation of Bradley's developed views on the nature of punishment as in the essay. His general concern is with the impact of Darwinism on our moral ideas, and his initial view is that although it does not affect our conception of the end, it may lead 'to a different way of regarding the relative importance of the means' (*CE*, p. 149). The moral end remains and is not modified by Darwinism. It is 'the welfare of the community realised in its members' (*CE*, p. 150). Bradley understands social Darwinism to mean natural selection within an antagonistic existence in which the unfit are progressively eliminated. In the past this process has been unconscious, but it is now possible for the community to interfere consciously. Is it possible to establish a rational principle on the basis of which such interference may take place? This is the supreme political question:

We do not deny that progress has been made largely by natural selection, and we must admit that in this process the extinction of worse varieties is essential. It is clear again that with this struggle and this extinction the community now interferes. Thus the method which in the past *has* succeeded is more or less modified. But if we ask on what principle it is changed, and what is to serve in its place, we find no rational answer (*CE*, p. 151).

Bradley argues that Darwinism requires that our familiar understanding of punishment, in terms of education, deterrence, and retribution, must be in part superseded. Darwinism, however, has its most radical impact on the retributive view, because it breaks the relation between punishment and guilt. He examines retributivism 'under two forms, a normal and a diseased growth' (*GE*, p. 153). In the normal form, he distinguishes two aspects, a positive and a negative.

The first of these declares punishment to be essentially the supplement of guilt, while the second asserts that apart from guilt individuals are sacred (*CE*, p. 153).

The positive side of the retributive principle was the view of *Ethical Studies*, but in the essay he is more sceptical. To begin with, both the object and the standard of moral evaluation are doubtful:

If you are to estimate morally, then, in proportion as the moral standard grows more inward, the genuine facts become inaccessible. And it becomes less and less possible anywhere to measure exactly moral responsibility. But with a more external standard again you are threatened from the other side. You are left in doubt if your estimate is genuinely moral (*CE*, p. 154).

These difficulties are internal to the logic of retributivism:

If you can acquire the right to punish only by proving moral crime, it seems hard to be sure that this right is really secured. Thus the principle is good, but its application is seriously embarrassed (*CE*, p. 154).

Utilitarian considerations unavoidably enter the practical dimension of punishment. If this is the case then the retributive principle that punishment presupposes guilt is abandoned as an absolute:

Punishment has ceased to be essentially an affair of justice, and we have been forced to recognize a superior duty to be unjust (*CE*, p. 154).

If these criticisms of retributivism hold, justice is secondary to the needs of social welfare. Now if justice as fairness, and everything that implies, is lost in the negative aspect of retribution, it is also lost on its positive side. If it is no longer unjust to punish for the consequentialist aim of securing the social welfare then it is by the same token no longer unjust to allow absence of guilt to form a barrier to punishment:

We cannot, in short, play fast-and-loose with the supremacy of justice. And having once set that down to be an inferior and subordinate principle, we cannot then attempt on any point to take it as absolute (*CE*, pp. 154–5).

Justice becomes a conditional and secondary consideration; it cannot provide a satisfactory account of punishment. If this is so there can be no obstacle to the state punishing whenever and to whatever degree it considers necessary.

Bradley next turns to an examination of what he calls the diseased growth of the normal retributive principle. On this view, crime is to be understood as a disease; it is therefore a matter for cure, rehabilitation, and therapy. Supporters of this view attempt to derive the best of both worlds:

> Justice on its positive side is restricted, but on its negative side is to retain unlimited sovereignty. Criminals, some or all, are diseased, and are therefore innocent, and the innocent, of course, are by justice proclaimed to be sacred. They are to enjoy therefore that treatment which was assigned to mere disease, when mere disease was not taken to include and cover crime. And surely such an attitude and such a claim are most inconsistent. This insane murderer, we may hear it said, is not to be destroyed. Justice is the assignment of benefit and injury according to desert; but this man is not a moral agent, and hence it is unjust to injure him. But, if he is not a moral agent, I reply, surely what follows is that justice is indifferent to his case (*CE*, p. 156).

He concludes that 'justice (as it must be) is dethroned', and that only what he calls 'the principle of social surgery' can account for the nature and operation of punishment. The objections he considers are derived from humanitarianism and Christianity, and he dismisses them both. He argues that the ideas of the former cannot hold once it is accepted that justice is no longer an absolute moral principle. And the Christian assertion of the value of the individual is weakened by its equivocation between this world and the next. Thus when all other moral objections have been shown to be inconsistent, we are left with the view that punishment is social surgery, to remove what Bradley calls 'diseased growths'. If social surgery is the only coherent understanding of punishment, then it should be put into practice with the maximum efficiency. But, Bradley argues, our present condition is vitiated by hopeless sentimentality and moral confusion. What are we to make of those who oppose the death penalty, a 'terrible necessity', but who do not shrink from condemning someone to lifelong imprisonment in which they are 'buried alive'? Bradley argues there is no presumption in favour of humanitarianism on the question of the avoidance of suffering. 'Too often we drape with the clothes of mercy the detestable idol of stupid cruelty'. He concludes with a defence of the necessity of 'social amputation' with the object of progressively removing the unfit. With the demolition of the principle of justice, Bradley sees eugenics as the only coherent alternative to a chaotic mixture of sentiment and pragmatism as the criterion of social interference.

In assessing Bradley's conclusions it is important to be clear as to how he arrives at them. His argument would surely require us to see punishment in the retributive sense as a piece of lumber to be superseded by the new language of social surgery. It would become one aspect of the process of 'cutting out' the undesirable and the unfit from the social organism. The central idea of Darwinism that the social organism is prior to its individual members cannot be elucidated in utilitarian terms. For Bradley to have attempted this, given his earlier rejection of utilitarianism, would be extremely odd, but the utilitarian requires that individual and communal welfare be balanced one against the other in a way which a Darwinian could not allow.

Earlier it was argued that it is necessary to understand Bradley's process of reasoning if conceptual weaknesses in it are to be detected. It is no use baldly asserting the absolute value of the individual against Bradley's conclusions when the coherence of such notions is at issue. The key area of Bradley's argument is his criticism of normal retributivism. Because he misconstrues this criticism he makes the wrong deductions from it. Although his conclusions and the idea of social surgery illustrate what punishment would look like in a world devoid of guilt or desert, they do not follow. It is possible to agree that normal retributivism contains weaknesses, but that criticism of it can be so construed as to arrive at an account of punishment which is neither utilitarian nor contractual.

Justice understood as the distribution of benefits and burdens on the basis of desert will not serve, Bradley argues, as the foundation of an account of punishment. This view, which would seriously undermine liberal democratic assumptions on the subject, is defended by the argument that retributivism is self-contradictory. In *Ethical Studies*, matters external to punishment — pragmatic considerations of various kinds, and matters internal to punishment — desert, and the cluster of moral notions surrounding guilt, were in the main regarded as supplementary. But even there Bradley wrote:

If, on the one side, punishment is always an end in itself, whatever else it may be, and if, on the other, whatever else it is, it *never* can be an end in itself, one may take it for granted that between the two there is no agreement (*ES*, p. 31).

In the more sceptical essay this absence of agreement is seen as a straightforward contradiction, which demands to be overcome. If retributivism is internally defective, at best, equivocal, at worst, vacuous, then the only alternative is the behaviouralist world of social surgery. It may be argued that Bradley, if we try to visualize the argument in reverse, is employing polemical irony in order to indicate the radical consequences of Darwinism for ideas held to be basic to the idea of human agency. If this is so, or indeed if it is true that he means what he says, then it still does not mean that we are taken to the centre of the problem. Bradley is led to the idea of social surgery because he considers that *however* retributivism is construed it will involve inconsistency. We may, for example, in order to overcome the difficulties in the retributivist idea that the criminal wills his own punishment, postulate some hypothetical situation in which individuals rationally agree to the laws which are to govern them, and to the punishments necessary if those laws are to be effectively enforced. But even with this revision Bradley's criticism would still appear to hold. The contradiction between internal and external considerations would remain, and so the idea of justice would still not provide a satisfactory basis for the justification of punishment. If, as a result, both utilitarian and contractualist elucidations of punishment are ruled out, then it would seem that social surgery must replace the inconsistencies of retributivism.

Bradley's idea of social surgery may be understood as anticipating many of the assumptions of the idea of a planned society, and genetic engineering. This full sense of social surgery does at least convey something of the sense of ostracism and exclusion involved when we speak of punishment. Here what would be stressed is the sense of loss or deprivation which punishment entails. The sense, in other words, of being cut off from social experience. Bradley denies that pain is a necessary ingredient in punishment, describing it as 'an accident of retribution', adding, rather disingenuously:

If a criminal defying the law is shot through the brain, are we, if there is no pain, to hold that there is no retribution? (*CE*, p. 164 n.).

Putting this example aside, it must surely be true that the deprivation involved in punishment alters an individual's awareness of himself and his surroundings.

As soon as we allow that the relationship between punishment and guilt is morally complex then the retributivist's case appears to be crucially weakened. If we allow such complexity then we must introduce external matters into the justification of punishment, so producing a chain of inconsistencies of the kind which led Bradley to introduce the idea of social surgery. Other philosophers have shared Bradley's view of the difficulties of retributivism at this particular point. McTaggart, for example, writes:

If we contented ourselves with using as a punishment whatever feeling of disgrace arose independently in the culprit's mind, the result would be that we should only affect those who were already conscious of their fault, and so required punishment least, while those who were impenitent, and so required it most, would escape altogether.[3]

McTaggart argued that the only alternative was to justify punishment by reference to its capacity to deter the criminal and prevent crime. But this alternative is, as Bradley recognizes, riddled with difficulties and inconsistencies, and so he is led to offer social surgery as a rational solution. The notion of social surgery is not a solution at all. It is a positivisitic, question-begging piece of sophistry. It depends on the pseudo-scientific premiss that it is possible to interfere rationally with the process of natural selection. The contrast this implies between reason and nature should, if Bradley is to be consistent in the application of his argument regarding contradictions, be superseded. This basic weakness is nowhere overcome, nor is there, indeed, any hint that Bradley is even aware of it. As a consequence, we are presented with a lot of talk regarding the amputation of the unfit, with no attempt to define terms, establish criteria of selection, etc. In a world governed by social surgery such an attempt at definition in terms which we could understand would be impossible. Virtue refers, not to something which men struggle for, but to something they are trained to want. Notions central to the principle of human autonomy would become redundant. For example, in the case of forgiveness, the necessary sense of moral failure would be absent; praise — nothing would ever be sufficiently difficult for a man to think of himself as having achieved it; punishment and mercy — men would never be in a position to deserve either; freedom — there would be nothing from which men could be described as being free, and, equally, nothing they would not be free to do, because their world would be empty of choice. To render virtue, praise, and punishment obsolete is to convert man into a machine. Social surgery does not eliminate relative disadvantage or amputate the unfit from the social organism. It destroys the idea of humanity altogether.

Bradley is led to such an untenable position because he considers that if justice is excluded then social surgery is the only alternative. But justice is excluded by virtue of his criticisms of retributivism. These were that as soon as the relation between punishment and guilt is made morally complex, as it would be by the presence or absence of repentance, then external considerations *must* be brought in which contradict the original internal requirement of guilt. This distinction could be elucidated in terms of the contrast between the moral and the political dimensions of punishment. Why should these dimensions be thought to contradict one another? Bradley seems merely to assume that they do. There are those who have seen the worlds of morality and politics as distinct, who have seen the gap between them as unbridgeable. For those who think they are worlds in opposition, political action is often construed as utilitarian, the dynamic being the calculation of consequence in which the possession of power is a necessary prerequisite. This often requires conciliation, negotiation, and compromise, and at this point, it is claimed, we observe the absolute distinction from morality. For from the moral perspective there can be no compromise, no making deals with virtue. It is this which constitutes the characteristic difficulty when moral considerations enter in. Bradley sometimes speaks in this way himself:

The state is forced to be unjust, and against this injustice the retributive view does not offer any protest (*CE*, p. 155 n.).

But why should we accept this assumption? Our interest is in its implication for the retributive view of punishment. Winch, for example, argues that for punishment to have a moral significance there must be an internal connection between punishment and crime. In other words, in its *moral* sense punishment *can* only be understood by connecting it with the nature of the crime. He contrasts this *internal* relation with the external one where punishment is contingently connected with the character of crime, where the punishment is connected not with the crime itself, but with the circumstances surrounding it, for example detection, arrest, and trial. It is not the nature of the crime which matters to the criminal but whether or not it is expedient for him to repeat it. Winch is arguing for a strong connection between punishment and repentance. But he recognizes, like Bradley, that such a view raises difficulties:

It may be said in objection to thus tying punishment to repentance that it makes punishment otiose ('a mere external addition'). Thus the argument would go, if the offender truly has repented when he comes to be punished, then there is nothing more for the punishment to achieve. On the other hand if the offender is not repentant, then whatever happens to him is not a punishment (in the 'ethical' sense of the word I have aimed to develop). In either case punishment can have no ethical sense.[4]

This is close to Bradley's criticism:

If you are to estimate morally, then, in proportion as the moral standard grows more inward, the genuine facts become inaccessible (*CE*, p. 154).

Why should this hold? If it does not then Bradley's criticism of retributivism is mistaken, and the sceptical deductions he draws from it, leading to the idea of social surgery, are false. There are two crucial points which the objection misses, the first of which is noted by Winch:

The form which repentance takes here cannot be understood apart from the need for punishment experienced by the penitent. It seems to me just to be a fact that some people do sometimes experience such a need, a fact which is made possible by the existence of the concept of punishment and the possibility of applying that concept in a certain way.[5]

It may be countered that this only shows that for *some* people punishment and repentance are connected in this way. But this objection may itself be refuted by following up Winch's remark regarding the existence of the concept of punishment. For its existence is surely social in character, implying a social dimension in the relation between the punishment and the wrongness of the act. In this sense, punishment is the expression of social condemnation. It is internally connected with moral indignation and disapprobation.

Bradley argues that 'common social morality is the basis of human life', but does not draw the conclusion that this includes, rather than excludes, the concept of punishment. If this is the case then reflection on the wrongness of the act for which the offender is being punished is at one with reflection on the moral condemnation which such punishment conveys. Punishment in the retributive sense cannot be separated from the cluster of moral concepts which alone inform a moral community, and so Bradley's criticisms fail. This sense of punishment, of being partially severed from the moral community, is referred to by some as being part of the pain which punishment involves.

It might be argued that if the person punished does not see the connection between punishment, social condemnation, and the nature of his wrongdoing then a logical gap appears which must be filled by non-retributive considerations. Now it is certainly true that there are cases where this occurs. Raskolnikov, for example, in Dostoevsky's *Crime and Punishment* does not see the murders he has committed as wrong, and so he cannot experience repentance. He says:

It was only when I fully realised the vileness of what I had done, that what was happening to me could really be a punishment for me.[6]

But what follows from this is not that non-retributive considerations need to be introduced, but that it is false to assume that repentance and punishment are connected in a simple or easy manner. Firstly, if punishment is thought of as a device for manipulating the punished in such a way as to produce a desired result then this is already to think of human beings as objects for training. To talk of a guarantee that punishment and repentance will always be tied is to conceive of punishment as a cure. And this is to adopt the pseudo-scientific view of punishment implied in the idea of social surgery. This is not only incompatible with any real understanding of moral character, it also renders the very idea of punishment unintelligible.

There is no reason, therefore, why retributivism should not allow for discontinuity between punishment and repentance, or that this should have an ethical sense. Secondly, it is a mistake to assume that this area can be excluded from the logical terrain of punishment. Indeed, some construe it as an essential requirement if it is to have a moral sense. Simone Weil remarks:

Men who are so estranged from the good that they seek to spread evil everywhere can only be reintegrated with the good by having harm inflicted on them. This must be done until the completely innocent part of their soul awakens with the surprised cry 'why am I being hurt'? [7]

Thus an element of contingency or asymmetry, a fracture between punishment and repentance, does have moral significance. Indeed, it is required if we are to speak of a criminal's coming to see the point of his punishment. More importantly, Simone Weil emphasizes that it is the innocent part of the criminal's soul which needs to be roused and illuminated. If punishment is a necessary condition of this it does not follow that we have moved away from guilt, but that the innocent part of the soul needs to be brought to bear on the criminal's understanding of the wrongness of his acts. Far from requiring the introduction of non-retributive considerations these features of punishment can be given ethical significance within the context of retributivism. If so then Bradley's criticisms of retributivism do not hold. This in turn means that his scepticism regarding the ideas of guilt and desert is also to that extent misplaced, with the consequence that the route which he feels impelled to take to the idea of social surgery is no longer necessary.

What conclusions can we draw by way of a prolegomenon to a future account of punishment? It seems clear that we need an understanding of the ways in which the experience of punishment is part of the criminal's understanding of what he has done. This involves placing the idea of punishment in the context of the moral community from which it draws its sense. It has too often been thought of as an isolated concept, separate from related concepts, moral condemnation, indignation, etc., which it serves to express. In this way retributivism may be construed so as to avoid the weaknesses

Bradley finds in it. Indeed, the idea of social surgery which Bradley considers the only possible elucidation of punishment is valuable as an indication of the kind of mechanistic view of the world which results if the criticisms of retributivism are allowed to get out of proportion, and deductions made from them which they cannot bear. The idea of crime as pollution, and of punishment as purification, is an ancient one.[8]

Philosophically, the best way to commemorate Bradley is both to assess his arguments and to seek to move on from them. I have argued that the weaknesses he detects in retributivism are not necessarily inherent, and I have defended a revised form of retributivism by examining further the moral significance of the relation between punishment and crime. Simone Weil emphasizes that it is the innocent part of the criminal's soul which needs to be touched before repentance for his wrongdoing can be achieved. But it does not follow, as Bradley thinks it does, that this necessarily weakens the connection between punishment and guilt. This would only appear to be the case if one thought of punishment in exclusively political or legal terms. Relations between these dimensions of punishment are complicated, but not, I would argue, for that reason devoid of ethical significance.

NOTES

1. Bradley's writings on punishment are mainly in *Ethical Studies*, 2nd edn., Oxford, 1927; and *Mr. Sidgwick's Hedonism*, 1877; and 'Some Remarks on Punishment', *International Journal of Ethics*, 4 April 1894, p. 269 ff., both reprinted in F. H. Bradley, *Collected Essays*, Oxford, 1969, pp. 71-128, and pp. 149-64.
2. 'Ethical Reward and Punishment', in Peter Winch, *Ethics and Action*, London, 1972, p. 211.
3. J. M. E. McTaggart, *Studies in Hegelian Cosmology*, Cambridge, 1901, p. 144.
4. Winch, op. cit., p. 219.
5. Winch, op. cit., p. 220.
6. As quoted in Winch, op. cit., p. 219.
7. Simone Weil, *Selected Essays*, 1934-43, Oxford, 1962, tr. Richard Rees, p. 31.
8. For a discussion of this idea see, for example, Douglas M. MacDowell, *The Law in Classical Athens*, London, 1879, p. 110. At the conclusion of his essay (*CE*, p. 163), Bradley quotes from Sophocles' *Ajax*, 'Tis not a skilful leech who mumbles charms o'er ills that need the knife.' I have attempted to show the ethical sense such ideas may have.

CHAPTER 6

Bradley as a Political Philosopher*

Peter Nicholson

I

When Bradley is included at all in the history of political
thought or political philosophy, he is usually depicted as an
apologist of 'conservatism'. This assessment, however, involves
several problems and misunderstandings. It also reduces
Bradley to a stylish exemplar of a political ideology, and
hinders his being taken seriously as a political philosopher.

I begin by outlining this well-established standard view of
Bradley as a 'conservative'.[1] Commentators on Bradley tend
to use the label 'conservative' very loosely, but clearly they
intend it derogatorily in order to indicate their views that he
sets the community's standards above the individual's, and
that he opposes all political reform or social improvement.
Hostile critics, concentrating on Essay V of *Ethical Studies*,
'My Station and Its Duties', have stressed his assertions that
the criterion of right and wrong is the good sense of the
man who has identified his will and judgment with the moral
spirit of the community; that to question society's morality
is to want to have no law but oneself, and to be self-conceited
and on the threshold of immorality; and that there is nothing
better than one's station in society and its duties (*ES*, pp.
196-202). Bradley is read as a complacent middle-class
champion of the status quo of Victorian England, with all its
privileges, injustices, inequalities, and miseries. Further, the
few political changes which he does suggest — and he is taken
to be advocating particular policies in his two articles on
politics — are seen as retrograde, involving greater injustice
and inhumanity.[2] That is the position commonly attributed
to Bradley; though one might feel that it should be termed

*I am grateful to W. H. Greenleaf, J. P. Horton, and J. Liddington for com-
ments on an earlier version.

not 'conservative' but 'reactionary', that is, as Bakunin once
defined the word, 'approval of a world where not reason and
the reasonable determination of the human will, but long
existence and immobility are the measure of the true and
the holy'.[3]

Whichever word one uses for it, how accurate is this
picture of Bradley's political thought as the partisan espousal
and defence of a particular political position? It must be
acknowledged immediately that very probably Bradley was
a Tory in politics. This is suggested both by the personal
political preferences which he occasionally expresses, and by
the accounts of those who knew him.[4] The former, however,
are very rare, and the latter tend to be anecdotal and un-
specific. Indeed it must be stressed how very little is known
of his views on issues of the day. We know that Bradley was
strongly Unionist in the Home Rule controversy of the
1890s, and that he had a rooted and passionate distrust of
Gladstone because he failed to support General Gordon in
the Sudan (Khartoum fell in January 1885).[5] We do not
know where he stood on such matters as the extension of
the franchise, votes for women, the eight-hour day, trade
unions, or progressive taxation; we cannot locate him in
relation to the various traditions of Tory and conservative
thought to be found in Victorian and Edwardian England;
nor can we even be certain that by the end of his life he
might not have looked favourably on the Labour Party
(which was joined by two of his staunchest philosophical
allies, Bosanquet and Haldane). All in all, though Bradley
probably was a Tory of some sort, there are not sufficient
grounds for concluding that he was the kind of reactionary
which the standard view makes him.

There is a more important point, however. Even if it could
be established in full and beyond dispute that Bradley's own
political convictions were a particular brand of conservatism,
of course it would not follow that his political *philosophy*
was conservative in the same sense. In fact, it is not; he
neither presents any kind of conservatism or conservative
policies as consequences of his philosophy, nor recommends
them in his philosophical writings. On the contrary, when
Bradley's discussions of politics are examined in full, he is
seen to hold that political policies cannot be deduced from

philosophy, that an adequate philosophical account of politics must accommodate differing political persuasions, and that political philosophy deals with political issues at a more fundamental level than that of party politics. These points will be considered in turn.

II

Bradley insists that philosophy's business is not to say what in particular is to be thought or done, but to reflect upon the facts of experience and theorize concerning what it finds.[6] Echoing Hegel, Bradley writes that 'all philosophy has to do is to "understand what is" ...' (*ES*, p. 193).[7] It is not philosophy's job to provide tests of reasoning, make scientific discoveries, teach religion, produce art, make the world moral, or run the state. The view that philosophy can say what it is right to do in morals or politics in particular cases, is a delusion which Bradley finds in utilitarians generally and in Sidgwick specifically. It confuses the reflective judgments of moral science with the immediate or intuitive judgments of the art of morals. In reflective judgment, a rule or principle is held before the mind, the particular case is brought under it, and a conclusion is drawn. This kind of deductive reasoning is appropriate in ethics and other branches of philosophy, but it is not what goes on in moral and political life. Ordinary people do not in fact make moral judgments, or acquire their moral standards, by consciously reasoning from principles and rules to a conclusion about what is right; rather, they see or feel that something fits the morality they have imbibed by precept and example and made their own. Should a new case arise, they automatically apply or extend the spirit of that morality, 'not by a reflective deduction, but by an intuitive subsumption which does not know that it is a subsumption' (*ES*, p. 196).[8]

Bradley believes that utilitarianism, with its principles set out as rules in a moral Nautical Almanack (Mill) or a systematic moral code (Sidgwick) mistakenly treats moral judgment as reflective instead of intuitive.[9] In addition, the delusion that ethics is practical erroneously assumes that there is always one right course of action, and that a moral code can prescribe it. Yet, no code can be complete; its clauses may conflict; and, moreover, duties clash. For all these reasons, sometimes the individual must decide for himself, with no guide but his own or another's intuitive judgment, and two individuals may legitimately make different decisions (*ES*, pp. 108 and 156–8).

Furthermore, utilitarianism's delusion that moral judgment is reflective is not only false in theory, it is also corrupt in practice. It has dangerous consequences because it is logically committed to turning moral science into casuistry, and that degenerates at once into finding a good reason for what one intended to do in any case (and ingenuity can bring every act, however bad, under some good rule). To introduce reflection upon principles into moral life confuses everything; it gives no real guidance, throws up insoluble dilemmas, and, destroying the ordinary person's instinctive understanding of morality, pushes him into making a merely private choice. That will not matter if he is a man of practical good sense, but 'what is to happen if men with no sense or hold on real life, but gifted with a logical faculty, begin systematically to deduce from this slippery principle' of ethics conclusions giving practical guidance? (*CE*, p. 116.)[10]

In sum, it becomes apparent that in Bradley's eyes utilitarianism is an even more deeply misconceived moral theory than had been argued in Essay III of *Ethical Studies*. He claimed there that utilitarianism misdefines 'good', fails to accord with the ordinary moral consciousness, and provides no indication how we know what is our duty, despite its claims to do precisely that. Now Bradley has contended that it operates with a mistaken conception of the logic of moral judgment. And that in turn can be seen to connect with another basic mistake which Bradley had dealt with earlier. For if moral philosophy is seen as a guide to practice, it is also expected to give a reason for acting in one way rather than another: from this, it is but a short step to asking 'why be moral?' But no answer, in moral terms, can be given to this question. Bradley is clear that 'why should I be moral?' is a senseless question, and that the only proper question is 'what should I do to be moral?' because it is a moral question (*ES*, pp. 58–64). So it is as part of avoiding a whole set of muddles in utilitarianism, that Bradley declares that moral and political philosophy, being reflective, cannot offer particular moral and political prescriptions because these are intuitive.

Whatever one's assessment of the merits of Bradley's opposition to utilitarianism and of his own position may be, it is clear that for him ethics, including political philosophy, is purely speculative. He is explicitly rejecting the utilitarian position that moral and political philosophy provide principles from which particular actions can be deduced. In Bradley's opinion philosophy cannot support particular ideologies or policies. Therefore, he could not consistently make conservatism a part of his political philosophy.

III

Of course, Bradley might be inconsistent, and do what he said could not be done. If, however, *Ethical Studies* did endorse any kind of conservatism, as has been alleged, it would have a fatal internal defect. For Bradley's avowed aim is to explain all the facts of morality, not to favour some at the expense of others, and not to explain away any of them. Hence to take account of moral stability and political conservatism, whilst ignoring moral progress and political unrest and reform, would produce a one-sided theory of the kind whose inadequacy he ruthlessly exposes in other moral philosophies. Therefore, if Bradley were promoting any political position, whether conservatism or revolutionary radicalism or whatsoever, he would not only be inconsistent with his claim that practical policies cannot be deduced from philosophical reflection, he would also fail to reach his goal of a comprehensive theory. My next task is to show that, when due attention is paid to the dialectical development of argument in *Ethical Studies*, it is clear that Bradley does not adopt one particular political position to the exclusion of others.

In much of *Ethical Studies* the pattern of argument is readily apparent. It is obvious, for instance, that Essay III presents hedonistic utilitarianism as unsatisfactory in various ways and requiring improvement. Essay IV does the same with a version of Kant's moral philosophy. But what the improvement is, and how it is effected, is not so obvious or widely agreed. Those who see Bradley as an exponent of reactionary conservatism treat Essay V as the culmination of the argument, and 'My Station and Its Duties' as his final moral theory. Others think that the development of Bradley's position continues in Essay VI and beyond, so that the moral theory he finally reaches is Essay VI's 'Ideal Morality' as supplemented by remarks in the remainder of the book. The superiority of the latter interpretation can be demonstrated by a brief rehearsal of the structure of Essays V and VI.

Essay V presents a theory of social organicism which emphasizes morality on its external side of the family, society, and the state, and claims that a man realizes himself by performing his function as a member of the community. The essay includes several sets of arguments. A crucial but little-noticed preliminary dialectic establishes that communities (families, societies, states) are real. Against the view that individuals alone are real, and against the view (unstated but implied) that communities alone are real, Bradley argues that both individuals and communities are real, and interdependent. So he asserts the sociality of individuals, but without saying that they are exclusively social, without denying their reality as individuals. In this essay, however, he concentrates on their sociality. The individual is, by birth and education, what he is, because of his community and his social relations. Consequently, his self-realization must take place in his community, and must be achieved by performing the duties to family, friends, colleagues, and government which are fixed by his station in that society. Next, the merits of this theory over that of Essay IV are argued, notably that it lays down specific duties for the individual instead of an empty injunction to do one's duty for duty's sake.

The inadequacies of 'My Station', however, are patent, for it cannot meet the conditions Bradley has already set in Essay II (for instance, no state can be an 'infinite whole', for even if all its citizens are fully 'members', it is always limited by other states). Bradley himself lists a series of objections to the theory of 'My Station' in the last few pages of the essay, in particular pointing out that the ideals of one's society may be defective in various ways and that there are other moral duties besides social duties. The conclusion of

Essay V is that although 'My Station' is the best theory considered so far, and in the main satisfactory, it is none the less one-sided and needs correction. Its basic defect is that, though it rightly stresses that individuals are social and must realize themselves in a community, it deals only with the external side of morality, and consequently cannot cope properly even with that. The necessary correction is supplied by 'Ideal Morality' in the next essay, where the internal side of morality, the individual's moral feeling and belief, is added, without losing sight of the external side. The ultimate moral standard is a personal ideal of perfection, and it includes non-social duties. The social morality of 'My Station' is the essential foundation for 'Ideal Morality', but it must be amended into a better version of itself, and supplemented by moral ideals of doing one's best in pursuit of the best in everything and everywhere and not just in one's social relations. Thereby the objections to 'My Station' are over-come: or rather, such of them are overcome as can be within the limits of morality and without going beyond it to religion. 'Ideal Morality' completes the dialectic of which 'My Station' was but one side.

So far as politics is concerned, Essay V can be seen to contain two opposite one-sided views; individualism, which gives the individual licence to accept or reject morality as he wishes, and organicism, which subordinates the individual to his society's morality. The former suggests radical change and instability, the latter suggests traditionalism and ossi-fication. Neither view is satisfactory, and both are corrected in 'Ideal Morality'. For this final theory, social morality remains as the basis, but is subject to change by individuals in the light of their personal ideals. Individuals have a duty to formulate the best ideals, and to identify and remedy any rottenness in their society. They are free agents, able to form their own characters and adopt moral ideas different from those imbibed from their society. 'Ideal Morality' recognizes that the content of moral rules must be supplied by individuals. At the same time it acknowledges that the formation and spread of personal moral ideals is itself a social process. For on the one hand, in adopting their own moral ideals, individ-uals necessarily are influenced by their membership of their society; and on the other hand any changes they initiate are subject to acceptance by the community. Thus Bradley has deliberately presented the conservatism or traditionalism of Essay V as a one-sided position integral to a one-sided theory, and therefore as something to be superseded. Moreover, the theory which supersedes it takes due account of the facts both of social and of individual standards, of morality's external side of social institutions and of its internal side of personal ideals. It makes room for both traditionalism and radicalism, requiring one to account for social stability and continuity, and the other for social change and reform. Bradley does not adopt any kind of conservatism in preference to radicalism: he contends that an adequate explanation of morals and politics must comprehend both.

IV

Then what about Bradley's two articles on politics, one of which has already been cited as evidence of his personal political opinions? In these articles Bradley adheres strictly to the position laid down in *Ethical Studies*. In his discussions of such practical matters as punishment and war, he carefully separates the reflective arguments of political philosophy from the intuitive judgments of political partisanship, and is explicit that it is not his job as a philosopher to suggest practical proposals for solving practical problems. Political philosophy's task is to identify problems, and to show that they must be taken seriously. Its aim is to examine critically ready-made solutions and party dogmas, to go back to first principles, and to substitute rational and consistent arguments for thoughtlessness, confusion, superstition, blindness, and prejudice.

At first glance, neither the issues that Bradley selects, nor the terms in which he discusses them seem to be quite what one expects from political philosophy. For example, he asks whether society has a right to pursue eugenic ethical surgery and to suppress its undesirable types, for instance to execute insane murderers or to refuse to rear at public expense unwanted children. These are not the grand and perennial themes of politics, but questions limited in scope and relevance, conditioned by and relative to particular historical circumstances. So too are the answers to them which Bradley canvasses. For instance, he frequently refers to 'the Christian party' as expressing one of the major alternatives, and to Darwinism as providing another. Indeed, he thinks Darwinism has raised the most important and urgent questions, by showing that constant selection and the extinction of the worse varieties, or at least their hindrance from reproduction, and the encouragement of the higher type, is essential to the welfare of the community. This is very dated. The whole argument for ethical surgery and social amputation — which, of course, Bradley is not advocating but is simply saying must be taken seriously — depends upon assumptions which would now be widely rejected. For it assumes that an individual is born a certain type, for example a dangerous criminal or a vile savage, and that his type is inherited by his child. Subsequent research has shown that such characteristics are not transmitted biologically but culturally, through upbringing, education, social conditions, and so on. Bradley himself came to see this later.[11] This different view of the facts, however, destroys the case for ethical surgery, and shifts attention to education and other forms of socialization.

Thus the level of argument in Bradley's political articles may seem to be low and subject to revision in the light of changing circumstances and factual knowledge. But this is a superficial impression. It applies only to what Bradley terms the 'means' to the moral end, and not to the moral end itself. That end is the welfare of the community in the first instance and, ultimately, the development of humanity; and what Bradley is at bottom concerned to discuss and have discussed are the fundamental problems of politics: the relation between individual and society, and the relation between one society and others. Within a state, the moral end is the good of the community, realized in its members. The community is morally supreme and has an absolute and unrestricted right to deal with its members as it sees fit. This is the principle which justifies punishment, conscription, taxation, and forcible appropriation of private property with or without compensation. The rights of individuals are conditional, and subordinate to the principle of general welfare. Between states, the moral end is the good of humanity, realized in states. The development of human nature is the absolute end which sets the limits both to national self-sacrifice and to national self-assertion. The welfare and even the existence of any particular state is subordinate to it. It can justify war and even aggression in certain cases. At both the national and international level, Bradley is vague about what 'welfare' means, beyond emphasizing that maximizing good is not the same as maximizing pleasure. Yet he does not need to be more specific, since however 'welfare' is defined, the problem of the relation between individual interests and general interests exists. It is agreed that from the moral point of view the general welfare does and must come first. Disputable practical questions, however, about how best to promote the general welfare, must be left to politics.

The philosophical aim behind Bradley's detailed consideration of specific political issues can perhaps be expressed best in the terminology of *The Presuppositions of Critical History* (1874). He argues there that the historian must use certain presuppositions (once he writes of an 'absolute presupposition'). For instance, he must make inferences, must work from his present experience, and must take for granted the uniformity of nature and its laws. Critical history is careful to rest on these necessary assumptions and on no others. In precisely the same way, Bradley's objective in *Ethical Studies* is to be critical and to spell out the presuppositions of morality: for instance, that a man is responsible for his acts, that virtue is intrinsically good, and that there must always be a gap between what men do and what they ought to do. Again, Bradley's aim in his political philosophy is to fasten upon the presuppositions of politics. He begins this task, though it is no more than a beginning, in *Ethical Studies* and the two political articles. Three presuppositions are prominent in these writings.

First, both the rights of individuals, and their duties, necessarily collide with those of other individuals; this is another way in which they must be conditional (*ES*, pp. 156–8, 196–7 n., and 224–8; *CE*, pp. 121–2 and 157). Second, as has been shown, Bradley notes the necessary moral superiority of the principle of the general welfare. This is presupposed, for example, by punishment. Hence part of his point in 'Some Remarks on Punishment' is that no justification of punishment, whether in retributive or any other terms, can work unless the moral primacy of society is already taken for granted, for otherwise society can have no right of punishment over its members. Third, a presupposition prior to those two and which it is the real function of Essay V of *Ethical Studies* to lay bare, is that politics presupposes a moral community. Politics presupposes morality, along with all its presuppositions.

A common pattern thus runs through Bradley's treatment of history, morality, and politics. When philosophy examines history it analyses the presuppositions of the historian; when it turns to morality, it builds a theory to comprehend all the facts and presuppositions of morality; and when philosophy comes to politics it investigates what the very existence of political communities presupposes, and searches for 'truths not to be refuted' (*CE*, p. 157). In his political discussions, therefore, it is not the particular and often limited issues which are important, but the principles and problems underlying them.

That Bradley does work at a fundamental level is demonstrated by the continuing relevance of those principles and problems. There are different controversies and doubts about exactly when and where individuals' welfare should give way to the general welfare, but there is the same recognition that the community must decide and that the general welfare comes first. Society still has limited resources, and has to make hard decisions in allocating them. Rights and duties continue to collide, and the state has to arbitrate between them to the disadvantage of some. Should public medical resources be deployed on treating serious illness affecting a minority, or on less serious illness affecting a majority? If an embryo can be tested for a crippling hereditary disease, should abortion be allowed, or should it be required? If a seriously defective baby is born, should its parents be left to decide whether it lives or dies? How much public money should be spent on overseas aid? Should the government spend heavily on nuclear weapons, or disarm unilaterally? Here are questions similar to Bradley's. They confront contemporary states (regardless of their particular political system) and are required to be decided for the general welfare. Philosophy, however, cannot decide between them, precisely because it operates at the level of presuppositions.

For no policies can be deduced from these presuppositions: whilst more than one policy can be rested upon them. For example, the principle of the primacy of the general welfare can justify retributive punishment in proportion to moral guilt; but equally it can justify overriding justice in favour of a measure of deterrence or mercy, or again it could justify social surgery (*CE*, pp. 152-62). Political philosophy can neither prescribe one of these policies, nor proscribe any.

V

I have argued that Bradley's writings on politics are philosophical, not political. None the less, it may appear that there is an inconsistency, because they do have a bearing on practical problems. What Bradley denies, however, is that political philosophy provides the kind of principles from which practical policies or decisions can be deduced in particular cases. This does not commit him to saying that philosophy has no other bearing on politics; nor does he in fact divorce philosophy from politics. Bradley's basic position is that political philosophy must take politics as it is, and construct a theory which covers all its presuppositions and facts. It can do nothing for those engaged in politics, if they pay it any attention at all, except remind them of the political realities they already know, and urge them to promote the best government of the community. The political philosopher can argue, for instance, that there should be a consistent principle of punishment, but he must leave to politics its choice and application. Utilitarians, however, go further: for example, in *On Liberty*, J. S. Mill does not simply assert the need for a principle to limit the interference of collective opinion with individual independence, but gives a principle based on his philosophy. This exceeds the scope of philosophy. Utilitarians debauch their intuitive understanding of politics. A false conception of philosophy deludes them, distorting their theory of politics and corrupting their practice. Yet this is the very point at which philosophy, as Bradley conceives it, bears most powerfully upon practice. For by criticizing and destroying the bad philosophy and false theory of utilitarians and 'thinking men', by freeing their minds, it can significantly alter their political practice. Philosophy corrects its own mistakes. It expels bad theory: it does not, however, offer any substitute which provides practical guidance. It is reflective judgment, and the most it can do is clear away obstacles to intuitive judgment.

Bradley never wrote extensively on politics. In the Preface to *Ethical Studies* he noted that his task demanded a greater acquaintance with the facts of the world than he possessed, and a clearer metaphysic than he had reached. Thereafter he seems to have been more concerned to develop and complete his metaphysics than to extend his knowledge of political and legal institutions. He wrote nothing else on politics besides the two articles discussed above, and they probably both belong to the period immediately after *Ethical Studies*.[12] Nevertheless, what Bradley does write about politics is sufficiently fundamental, and intermeshed with other parts of his philosophy, to support my claim that it is wrong to class him as any kind of conservative ideologist. His work as a political philosopher should be acknowledged.

NOTES

1. This paragraph is based on: H. Sturt, *Idola Theatri*, London, 1906, pp. 57–62 and 264–5; F. Thilly, *A History of Philosophy*, New York, 1914, 3rd edn. revised by Ledger Wood, 1957, p. 567; G. H. Sabine, 'The Social Origin of Absolute Idealism', *Journal of Philosophy*, vol. 12, 1915, pp. 174–5; G. Santayana, *Some Turns of Thought in Modern Philosophy*, Cambridge, 1933, pp. 56–7; G. H. Sabine, *A History of Political Theory*, 1937, 4th edn. revised by T. L. Thorson, Hindsdale, Ill., 1973, p. 666; L. S. Stebbing, *Ideals and Illusions*, London, 1941, pp. 61–2; Ralph G. Ross, *F. H. Bradley, Ethical Studies, Selected Essays*, New York, 1951, pp. x–xvi; D. Krook, *Three Traditions of Moral Thought*, Cambridge, 1958, p. 241; J. Bowle, *Politics and Opinion in the Nineteenth Century*, London, 1954, pp. 291–7; S. I. Benn and R. S. Peters, *Social Principles and the Democratic State*, London, 1959, p. 311; J. H. Randall, Jun., *Philosophy after Darwin. Chapters for 'The Career of Philosophy' Vol. III*, New York, 1957, ed. Beth Singer, pp. 112–14; A. Quinton, *The Politics of Imperfection. The Religious and Secular Traditions of Conservative Thought in England from Hooker to Oakeshott*, London, 1978, p. 72, and *Thoughts and Thinkers*, London, 1982, p. 194.

   Many of these writers commend the utilitarians for their active concern with reform; and link Bradley with Hegel, whom they also attack for complacement acceptance of bad social conditions and political oppression. Clearly, their interpretation of Hegel strongly influences their reading of Bradley. In my opinion that interpretation, too, is mistaken.

   The standard view of Bradley is not, of course, the only one. His conservatism is argued to be Burkean and progressive by A. B. Ulam, *The Philosophical Foundations of English Socialism*, Cambridge, Mass., 1951, discerned by F. P. Harris, *The Neo-Idealist Political Theory: its Continuity with the British Tradition*, New York, 1944, pp. 6-19. A few writers have taken what I agree is the correct view, and refrained from attaching any party political label to Bradley's philosophy: R. Wollheim, *F. H. Bradley*, Harmondsworth, 1959, 2nd edn., 1969; A. J. M. Milne, *The Social Philosophy of English Idealism*, London, 1962; and S. Candlish, 'Bradley on My Station and Its Duties', *Australasian Journal of Philosophy*, vol. 56, 1978, pp. 155-70. These three writers are also conspicuous for avoiding the mistake made by most of the exponents of the standard view, of isolating Essay V, 'My Station and Its Duties', from the rest of *Ethical Studies*, Oxford, 1927 (on this see section III below).

2. See 'Some Remarks on Punishment', *International Journal of Ethics*, vol. 4, 1893-4, pp. 269-84, and 'The Limits of Individual and National Self-Sacrifice', loc. cit., vol. 5, 1894-5, pp. 17-28. They are reprinted in *Collected Essays*, Oxford, 1969, and page references are to this edition.

3. 'The Reaction in Germany' (1842), in *Michael Bakunin: Selected Writings*, ed. A. Lehning, London, 1973, p. 51.

4. For some of Bradley's personal feelings on social matters, see the final paragraph of 'Some Remarks on Punishment', pp. 163-4. The most informative recollection of Bradley's political opinions is A. E. Taylor's obituary in *Mind*, vol. 34, 1925, pp. 1-12. Taylor knew Bradley well from 1891.

5. Taylor, loc. cit., pp. 5-6.

6. This paragraph is based on *Ethical Studies*, pp. 193-8; *Mr. Sidgwick's Hedonism*, 1877, sect. 8, reprinted in *Collected Essays*, pp. 104-16; and *The Principles of Logic*, 1883, 2nd edn. 1922, bk. II, part I, chap. IV, sects. 4 and 7-9, pp. 266-71.

7. This I take to be a translation of the statement *'Das was ist zu begreifen, is die Aufgabe der Philosophie'*, in the *Vorrede* to G. W. F. Hegel, *Grundlinien der Philosophie des Rechts*. T. M. Knox, *Hegel's Philosophy of Right*, Oxford, 1942, renders it: 'to comprehend what is, this is the task of philosophy' (p. 11). See too the opening of *The Presuppositions of Critical History*, 1874, in *Collected Essays*, p. 5.

8. Bradley is much influenced by Aristotle — witness his frequent quotations from and allusions to the *Nicomachean Ethics* — both on the nature of moral judgment and on the view that philosophy is 'theoretical'.

9. He refers to Mill's 'moral "Nautical Almanack"' in *Ethical Studies*, pp. 101-2, citing *Utilitarianism* (see *Collected Works of John Stuart Mill*, vol. X, p. 225).

10. Bradley makes clear he regards Sidgwick himself as one of the men of practical good sense (*CE*, p. 115).

11. 'Some Remarks on Punishment' and 'The Limits of Individual and National Self-Sacrifice' were published in April and October 1894. The latter was written in 1878 or 1879 (see opening footnote). The former may have been too. It was certainly written before 1891 (see its final footnote). Its views are sometimes identical and always consistent with those in the other article, in *Ethical Studies*, 1876, and in *Mr. Sidgwick's Hedonism*, 1877, for example pp. 121-3. Bradley's acceptance of Darwinism, therefore, probably belongs to the later 1870s. By 1924, when he was making notes for a second edition of *Ethical Studies*, he had greatly revised his view. In 1876 he said that 'civilisation is to some not inconsiderable extent hereditary' and that 'it is a very different thing, even apart from education, to be born of civilized and uncivilized ancestors'. A footnote in the second edition retracts this, stating that it is very doubtful whether civilized tendencies or the characteristics of any particular society are hereditary (p. 170 n.). This, of course, fits well with his original emphasis on the crucial role of socialization in moral development (Essays V and VII).

12. See note 11.

CHAPTER 7

Bradley's Theory of Judgment

Guy Stock

I wish to give an account of Bradley's theory of judgment which will show its connections with epistemological and metaphysical issues. My approach will, however, be piecemeal and at no point shall I attempt to state Bradley's theory. I shall simply build up a picture of it by drawing successive comparisons, positive and negative, with alternative theories of thinking and judgment.

In the first section I shall describe, by means of a comparison with Wittgenstein's *Tractatus*, how the role played by the notion of our *real world* in Bradley's theory of judgment differs from that played by the notion of *reality*. In the second section, I shall compare Bradley's anti-psychologism in logic with Frege's and attempt to locate in Frege's theory of judgment certain incoherencies which Bradley saw as implicit in the act/object schema of thinking to which Frege's theory conformed. In the final section, I shall consider Russell's and Bradley's theories as alternative ways of avoiding the difficulties in a Fregean theory and in doing so return to the theme of the nature of the distinction to be drawn between worlds, real and unreal, and reality.

I

A grasp of the difference between the notion of *a world* and the notion of *reality*, and consequently a grasp of the difference between the notion of our *real world* and the notion of *reality*, is essential to an understanding of Bradley's philosophy as a whole. It is essential to understanding what he means by *appearance* as opposed to reality. It is, however, a distinction that has its foundation in Bradley's logic. Moreover it is, I think, a distinction that in some way or other any theory which is to succeed in making sense of our capacity to think both what is true and what is false must allow for.

The notion of our real world can be seen to be exercised when, for example, a person takes, correctly or incorrectly, an object of some empirically discernible sort to exist somewhere in space and time as opposed to being a figment of somebody's imagination or merely fictional.[1] The notion of reality, on the other hand, operates on an entirely different level. In the context of Bradley's theory it is not an *idea* actually exercised by people in their acts of judgment. It is the notion that he points to when he suggests that the general form of judgment can be given by the formula: 'Reality is such that S is P.'[2] In other words it is the ultimate logical subject of all acts of judgment, true and false. The notion of reality therefore includes, but is essentially wider than, that of our real world, since it is not tied logically, in the way that the latter is, to the notion of *truth* or *fact*.

The motive for such a notion of reality has in itself nothing to do with Bradley's monism. In fact if one wants an analogue in terms of which to understand the role that the notion of reality plays within Bradley's theory then one can look to the radically pluralistic logic of Wittgenstein's *Tractatus*. Bradley's distinction between our real world and reality parallels that drawn in the *Tractatus* between (i) the world construed as all that is the case,[3] which is one out of an indefinite plurality of alternative possible worlds any one of which might have existed instead, and (ii) reality construed as the totality of simple objects or the substance common to all possible worlds.[4] It is the latter notion of reality which Wittgenstein uses when he says that to 'p' and to '—p', one of which must be true and one of which must be false, 'there corresponds one and the same reality'.[5] Any satisfactory theory of human thinking must be able to portray the false thought, in which a non-existent state of affairs is pictured, as 'reaching right out to reality'[6] or, to use Bradley's terminology, as having reality as its ultimate logical subject, just as surely as does the true thought. But if this is so, any satisfactory theory of human thinking must leave room for a distinction between the notion of reality and the notion of a world, since the latter notion is exercised in distinguishing our real world construed as all that is the case, from alternative possible worlds thinkable in thoughts false with respect to our real world.

Of course I do not want to exaggerate any similarity between Bradley and Wittgenstein. In most things they are totally opposed. Their positive accounts of thinking, for example, can be seen as lying at opposite ends of a spectrum. I do hope, however, that the comparison will at least have made a little clearer Bradley's notion of reality.

Also, I hope the reader will now be in a better position to understand the following statement of what I take to be the main 'controls' which Bradley would see as operating on his attempt to construct a theory of judgment.

First and foremost, like any acceptable theory, it must be internally consistent and be consistent with the existence of the facts which confront it — in this case the existence of human knowledge, error, and so on. Secondly it must be consistent with reality being 'individual, substantial and self-existent'[7] as opposed to being general, abstract, and adjectival, and thus with reality being essentially different in its nature from thought and truth. Thirdly it must be consistent with the actual *historic* existence in the real world of human acts of thought (true and false), acts of perception (veridical and non-veridical), acts of will (successful and unsuccessful), etc. — events without which the various bodies of human knowledge and belief, scientific and otherwise, to which we *now* have cognitive access, could not have come to exist.

With these controls in mind I would now like to compare Bradley's anti-psychologism in logic with Frege's and to locate what Bradley would undoubtedly take to be inadequacies in Frege's theory of judgment.

II

It is well known that both Bradley and Frege shared an anti-psychologistic stance in logic. I would like, however, to emphasize a radical difference between them in this respect.

Bradley argues that logic is properly concerned with ideas only in so far as ideas have a symbolic function.[8] But to say that logic is concerned with ideas, Bradley notes, is to run the risk of an ambiguity. It is, however, an ambiguity that can be readily illustrated and rendered harmless by reference to the distinction that can be drawn between a particular perceptible sign (say, a series of marks of a certain shape on a piece of paper) and the *meaning* that that particular possesses as an instance of a type in a given language. The word 'idea' can be used to mean either a *particular psychical occurrence* analogous to the physical occurrence involved in constructing a linguistic token with the intention of communicating something; or it can be used to mean something analogous to the *meaning* that such a token has as an instance of a type in a given language.

In the former sense of the term, all ideas, as Bradley says, 'are facts unique with definite qualities ... the same in all points with none other in the world' (*PL*, p. 4). In the latter sense of the term, different people can have the very same ideas: the very same perceptions, memory images, thoughts, intentions, and so on. And the same person can have the same ideas at different times in his life. Thus in the latter sense an idea is taken as a *universal* and, as Bradley says, 'can not as such exist ... can not be an event, with a place in the series of time or space ... can be a fact no more inside our heads than it can outside them' (*PL*, p. 7).

Bradley maintains that logic, for its special purposes, is properly only concerned with ideas taken as the universal, communicable contents of judgments considered in abstraction from their particular existence as psychological states of subjects. On the other hand, he emphasizes that from a broader philosophical standpoint this must be seen simply as an abstraction that is necessary for practical purposes within the special science of logic. It must under no circumstances be taken as entailing an ontology of eternal truths, meanings, or abstract universals (*PL*, p. 7 n.), existing or subsisting independently of people's psychological acts but capable of becoming at moments of time the objects of such acts. Bradley — and here again he is in agreement with Wittgenstein[9] — rejects the intelligibility of a schema which portrays the psychological acts of perception, thinking, judgment, and so on, as *derivatively* true or false depending on the truth-value of the object of the act. The psychological act or state itself must be portrayed as capable of being *underivatively* the bearer of truth or falsehood. Bradley sums up his view as follows:

truth in the end is not truth unless it is thought, and so is actually thought by this or that mind, and therefore is thought at some one time. But, for our logical purpose, we are compelled to abstract from this aspect ... We must in logic assume that truth, as truth, is itself out of time, and that, as truth, it does not and can not exist; though on the other side ... all truth must 'have' existence.[10]

Thus Bradley maintains that an abstraction that we must of necessity make in our thinking within the special science of logic can lead us into error at a deeper philosophical level. It can lead us into error if we take the distinction between the psychological existent and its communicable universal content to entail an ontology which requires a schema of thinking and judgment which, when thought out, proves internally inconsistent and unable to make sense of the existence of human knowledge, error, and so on.

This I think is precisely the form of the criticism that Bradley would have levelled against Frege's theory of judgment and I will now try to locate in more detail inadequacies that I am sure Bradley would have pointed to.

Frege's theory of judgment is expounded in terms of a three-realm metaphysics.[11] Frege's first realm is the external world of independently existing physical things cognitively accessible to people by sense perception at moments of time. His second realm consists of the inner psychical states and acts of people which hold or occur in time. To these psychical states and acts, Frege gives the name 'ideas'. But Frege argues that in addition a third realm must be recognized:

Anything belonging to this realm has it in common with ideas that it cannot be perceived by the senses, but has it in common with (external) things that it does not need an owner ... Thus for example the thought we have expressed in the Pythagorean theorem is timelessly true, true independently of whether anyone takes it to be true. It needs no owner.[12]

There is no particular significance in Frege's choice of an example from mathematics. Let us assume a person possesses a language containing existential and universal quantifiers, a stock of proper names whose referents are actually existing objects in Frege's first realm, a stock of well-defined empirical predicate expressions standing for concepts under which such objects can and do fall, and the usual logical connectives. Such a person will be able to construct a series of singular and general sentences, each of which will, on Frege's view, express a complete thought timelessly true or false. Moreover, the person will be able to understand the senses of the sentences he can construct, or in other words, he will be able to think at moments of time the thoughts they express, whether or not he knows the truth-values of those thoughts.

Hence Frege maintains in the context of his theory of judgment that we must distinguish from one another:

(i) The grasping of a thought, or in other words, the psychical, second-realm activity of thinking a thought. This is to be construed as corresponding to the act of understanding the sense of a sentence without knowing the truth-value of the thought that the sentence expresses.

(ii) The acknowledgement of the truth of a thought, or in other words, the psychical, second-realm act of judgment.[13] (We might note here that Frege elsewhere characterizes the act of judgment as the act of 'advancing from a thought to a truth-value'.)[14]

So for Frege, thinking is a psychical activity taking place in time. We can take it to be, in some sense, a constructive or synthetic activity corresponding in essence to the 'step by step' construction of sentences, the senses of which a person understands.[15] By possession of this synthetic capacity — a capacity which, incidentally, would correspond to what Bradley calls 'ideal construction' — an unlimited series of thoughts, true and false, will become cognitively accessible to a person. These thoughts themselves, however, will not be originated or be in any way affected by the synthetic activity of thinking.[16] The thoughts themselves, on Frege's view, must be taken to exist timelessly in a realm of non-actual *intelligibilia*. Their existence is as independent of the datable human acts of thinking as is the existence of physical objects independent of the perceptions by means of which people have knowledge of them.[17]

Now the problem with which I would like to confront Frege's theory concerns its ability to make sense of our capacity to have knowledge of particular objects existing in the world which are available to us by means of sense perception. To be fair to him, Frege does not purport to work out in any detail a theory of sense perception. He does, however, claim that 'visual sense impressions are certainly necessary for seeing things, but not sufficient. What must still be added is not anything sensible.'[18]

Frege has nothing more to say about the nature of this 'not anything sensible' but it would seem reasonable enough to give it a quasi-Kantian interpretation. We might therefore attempt to sketch out an account of sense perception that would, on the face of it, fit in with the above claim of Frege, in the following way. We could say that a sense perception is an inner or psychical state of a sentient being — an inner state of a kind that can be veridical or non-veridical. Thus the proper object of a sense perception when it is veridical can be said to be a *fact* concerning a particular existent object in the external world rather than simply the particular object itself. The reception of sense impressions from a particular object will be a necessary condition of a person perceiving any facts whatsoever concerning the object, but the merely passive reception of such impressions will not be sufficient for perception proper. The merely passive reception of a manifold of sense impressions from a particular object will constitute an *immediate* or non-discursive cognition of it. However, in order to perceive any facts concerning an immediately present particular the subject will need to exercise an active capacity for subsuming particulars under general concepts which have specific empirical contents.

It might well be argued at this point, in a Kantian fashion, that a person's ability to acquire concepts with specific empirical contents, in the first place, will require him to possess already a set of purely intellectual capacities of thought, in essence identical to those possessed in being able to use proper names, predicate expressions, quantifiers, logical connectives, and so on. In other words, it might be argued that the capacity to acquire empirical concepts as a result of the passive reception of sense impressions will presuppose possession of a set of active capacities of thought identical to those used in an absolutely pure form in making transitions within the predicate calculus. It seems to me that such purely intellectual capacities are plausible candidates for the 'not anything sensible' which Frege claims must be added to sense impressions if sense perception of specific objects immediately present to a person by means of his sense impressions is to occur.

But even if this kind of account of sense perception were itself internally consistent and did not have latent in it the absurdity of the thing-in-itself — as Bradley puts it, the absurdity of a reality 'which is unable to appear' (*AR*, pp. 113–14) — we can ask: is it really consistent with Frege's theory of judgment?

To get a clearer view of this question I would like to consider how an account of language might be combined with such a quasi-Kantian theory of sense perception. Since I shall return to this topic in the third section of this paper it will be convenient to work in terms of the model supplied by Russell in his logical atomism.[19]

When a person perceives a fact concerning a particular object immediately present by means of his sense impressions, the particular external object itself will be a *constituent* of the fact he perceives. Assuming the person to have mastery of a language, he will be able to construct a sentence, with a name of the external object as its grammatical subject, expressing a proposition which is true and which *is* the fact he perceives. The particular external object designated by the grammatical subject of the sentence will be the *logical* subject of the proposition and of the *judgment* that the person formulates and expresses by means of the sentence.

We can say, then, that on the quasi-Kantian account the theoretical role played by sense impressions is to enable particular objects in the external world to become at one and the same time constituents of perceived facts and the logical subjects of those genuinely singular propositions or judgments that constitute the ultimate foundations of any knowledge that human beings have of the external world.

We can now ask: is Frege's theory of judgment and his account of language with its distinction between the sense and reference of expressions consistent with sense impressions playing the above role in sense perception?

Let us now apply Frege's theory to the case of a person using a simple assertoric sentence with a singular term — what Frege would call a proper name — as its grammatical subject in order to express a current veridical sense perception. The person will understand the sense of the sentence he is uttering and in doing so will be thinking the thought. Since the thought is the content of a perception he will no doubt acknowledge the thought as true and thus will be performing an act of judgment. Given that the perception is veridical his act of judgment will be true in virtue of the thought which he is acknowledging *as* true being a truth. And if it is a truth it is therefore a *fact*. As Frege expresses it: 'What is a fact? A fact is a thought that is true ... The work of the scientist does not consist in the creation but in the discovery of true thoughts.'[20]

But what about the object in the external world? On Frege's account this will be the reference of the proper name which is the grammatical subject of the sentence used to express the perception. But the reference of the name could not conceivably be a constituent of the fact perceived — given that a fact simply is a true thought. A thought is the sense of a sentence, and only the sense of the proper name, not its reference, could possibly be an element in the sense of the sentence.

It follows that Frege could not consistently portray sense impressions as playing the theoretical role in sense perception that they are taken to play within the quasi-Kantian account. In fact it is difficult to think of a role for sense impressions within the Fregean schema. Perhaps a distinction similar to that once made by G. E. Moore could be drawn.[21] Moore regarded propositions as independently existing objects of psychical acts and took propositions themselves to be syntheses of concepts. Propositions were to be distinguished from concepts simply in terms of the complexity of the former. Thus true propositions of a certain kind were to be regarded as the proper objects of acts of sense perception and the simple concepts involved in them were correlated with sensations.

However, whether or not Frege were to adopt such a distinction, I do not see how he could avoid the consequence, embraced by Moore, that the objects of human sense perception are timelessly true *intelligibilia*. Frege's first realm thus collapses into his third. But this is surely absurd, since the idea of the third realm can only be given sense in contrast to the first and second realms. In terms of the controls which

Bradley saw as operating on any theory of judgment, clearly Frege's theory fails to be able to treat the reality which is the object of our thinking as 'individual, substantial and self-existent' and thus as essentially different in its nature from thought.

The explicit statement of Bradley's argument against any theory which like Frege's treats thinking and judgment as psychological relations holding simply between a subject and the *senses* of words and sentences (or what Bradley himself would call *ideas*) is made as follows:

(i) 'If judgment is the synthesis of two ideas, then truth consists in the junction of unreals' (*PL*, p. 46).

(ii) 'But reality is not a connection of adjectives . . . Its essence is to be substantial and individual' (*PL*, p. 46).

Hence:

(iii) 'Judgment . . . is not confined to ideas and can not by any means consist in their synthesis' (*PL*, p. 50).

Moore, Russell, and Wittgenstein[22] in their diverse ways, all were, or came to be, in agreement with Bradley that the particular existent psychological act or state itself must be capable of being portrayed as underivatively the bearer of truth and falsehood. To this end, Russell can be seen as making demands which entailed his rejection of Frege's distinction between sense and reference. It is to these demands and the contrasting accounts that Russell and Bradley give of human thinking, true and false, when its objects are particulars existing in the real or actual world, that I will now turn.

III

If the 'historic psychological act of sense perception' is to be portrayed as capable of being underivatively veridical, and thus as being underivately the bearer of truth to a person, Russell can be seen as making two demands. First, he argued that particular existent entities themselves must be capable of being immediately given in the experience or inner states of subjects. They must be capable of being given in a way which is independent of the subject's discursive faculty for thinking of the 'universal' properties and relations that different particulars can and do possess. Secondly, he argued that in language there must be names such that they are capable of being used in acts of judgment *merely* to designate particular existent objects and make those objects the logical subjects of simple predicates in judgments. Such judgments would imply nothing whatsoever other than what is explicitly asserted by the predicates used. Names capable of performing this function Russell called *genuine* or *logically proper names*. Judgments formulated by means of sentences having genuine names as their grammatical subjects would be singular or *atomic* judgments. The truth-value of such a judgment would be determined simply by the property or relation asserted in the judgment in fact holding. No other conditions obtaining or not obtaining in regard to anything else could possibly affect the truth-value of such a judgment. They would be *unconditional* truths.

Proper names of a kind that stand for particular objects as a result of having acquired, through past application, a meaning of a sort explicable by reference to facts, or alleged facts, about particular objects, cannot be genuine names. The truth-value of a judgment formulated by means of a sentence containing a name understood in the above way would depend not merely on what is asserted by means of the grammatical predicate. It would depend also on whether or not some object, taken by the person making the judgment to be the subject of certain truths, and understood by him to be the bearer of the name, actually existed. Russell maintained, therefore, that such judgments could not be genuinely singular even though grammatically singular sentences were used in their formulation. He concluded that they must in fact be *general* in logical form. So, as is well known, he argued that their logical form would be properly shown by formulating them in a conjunction of sentences involving the use of existential and universal quantifiers.

Given the picture of a knowing subject's relation to reality implicit in the Russellian account of generality, people *had* to be able to make genuinely singular judgments. It would be absurd, given the account of generality that Russell wished to give, to maintain that all judgments are really existential in form and therefore are really general in form. The sense that can be given to a general judgment, made within the sphere of our empirical knowledge, depends on the possibility of construing the quantifiers used in its formulation as ranging over the logical subjects of genuinely singular judgments which people at times actually make or which 'in principle' could be made at some place, at some time. The truth-values of the general judgments that people make in the empirical sphere can be uniquely determined, yes or no, only if such genuinely singular perceptual judgments are possible. Therefore Russell can be seen as concluding that a view like Frege's, according to which names of necessity have a sense and cannot simply designate, is incompatible with the view that the truth-values of general judgments that people can make in the empirical sphere are uniquely determined.

But to look at the structure of our empirical knowledge in the way that Russell does would be to look at it simply statically or simply *sub specie aeternitatis*. Russell, like Bradley, was aware that an epistemology must have, so to speak, its 'dynamics' as well as its 'statics'. Each knowing subject has a unique 'perspectival' viewpoint on the world of objects in space and time which are available for its knowledge by means of its waking sense perceptions. A human being will at each successive instant of his waking life be confronted by an indefinitely complex manifold of particular objects of various empirically discernible sorts about which he will be perceiving, with more or less explicit awareness, a manifold of facts. Assuming (as I am throughout) that the subject is a human being with a mastery of a language he will at moments of time be able to formulate the contents of particular perceptions in explicit acts of judgment.

Hence in the 'dynamics' of Russell's theory of knowledge the genuinely singular judgment returns to fulfil another role. The nameable particulars immediately present in sensation to a person, and about which he can at that moment of time perceive a manifold of particular facts, will constitute for him a 'source point' for the general judgments, true and false, which he can make about particulars more or less remote from him in space and time. Given a mastery of the ideas of spatio-temporal distance and direction (by an act that Russell calls 'logical construction', and Bradley would call 'ideal construction') a person will be able to think, at moments of time, of a strictly unlimited number of determinate positions in the spatio-temporal series containing the nameable particulars *here* and *now* present to him. And thus, given a mastery of a stock of empirical predicates, he will be able to construct, by the use of quantifiers, an indefinite series of general judgments (true and false) making claims as to the existence of objects of empirically discernible sorts at determinate positions in the spatio-temporal series containing the nameable particulars currently present to him. In this way all a person's thinking in any sphere of empirical knowledge will involve reference back to the particulars at the moment present to him in sense perception. Or, to put it the other way round, it will involve a constructive or synthetic act of thought on the part of the person, which will proceed from the nameable particulars, at each successive moment of time, present in his sense perceptions.

Now we can ask: how does Bradley's position compare with that of Russell on these issues?

Briefly it is as follows: In regard to what I have called the 'dynamics' of a theory of knowledge, Bradley's account coincides with Russell's. However in regard to its 'statics', Bradley's account is in the end totally at odds with Russell's. Bradley agrees that the empirical judgments, true and false, that we formulate by means of grammatically singular sentences are really existential in logical form. But he denies that names capable of *merely* designating particular objects are possible and therefore that so-called genuinely singular judgments of the kind demanded by a Russellian account of generality are possible. He therefore rejects the picture of human empirical knowledge according to which the truth-values of the general judgments we can construct are uniquely determined by a reality of facts capable of being formulated by sentences of the postulated sort. In *that* sense there cannot be in any sphere of human knowledge, empirical or otherwise, *absolute* or *unconditional* truths and falsehoods. Correspondingly, reality cannot be construed as a totality of *merely* sensible particulars related in the context of facts by purely intelligible 'abstract' universals.

To describe the details behind this argument would be

equivalent to giving a description of Bradley's theory of judgment. I cannot undertake to do this fully but I will attempt to indicate what seem to me to be the main features of Bradley's reasoning.

It is the absolutely basic premiss of Bradley's theory of judgment that a human being's fundamental point of cognitive contact with reality (that is, with the 'individual, substantial and self-existent') lies in his present, waking sense perceptions. As he puts it: 'We escape from ideas, and from mere universals, by a reference to the real which appears in perception' (*PL*, p. 69).

But of course to say this is not to say much. It is certainly not to say anything that Russell would disagree with. In fact Bradley's remark is to be construed, at least in part, as falling within the 'dynamics' of his theory of knowledge, and thus in part he is making a point very close to one made by Russell. Judgments about particulars present in a person's sensible environment and which we characteristically formulate by sentences employing egocentric demonstratives, Bradley calls 'analytic judgments of sense'. Thus when, for example, a person picks out a piece of white chalk from a box of coloured pieces and formulates the content of his current perception by means of the sentence 'This is white', he is making an analytic judgment of sense. 'Synthetic judgments of sense' are judgments about particulars of empirically discernible sorts not currently present in the person's sensible environment. Bradley argues, for fundamentally the same reasons as Russell, that a person's capacity to make judgments of the latter sort is dependent in a special way on his capacity to make judgments of the former sort. As he says:

Synthetic judgments are possible only by being connected with what is given at this very instant. The ideas of past and future events are projected from the base of present perception. It is only in that point that they encounter the reality of which they wish to be true (*PL*, p. 62).

However, Bradley maintains that this distinction between analytic judgments and synthetic judgments cannot be taken as marking an absolute distinction of logical form. The ideas of empirically discernible sorts of object that we employ in the formulation of analytic judgments and which constitute the ideal contents of our normal waking sense perceptions always imply an existence beyond the present momentary appearance. So also does our use of ordinary language proper names, even when those names are used in the formulation of judgments the logical subjects of which are present in perception, since their use implies the continuous existence of their bearers (*PL*, p. 61). It is not, Bradley argues, that we could not designate a unique momentary appearance present on a single occasion. He maintains, as is obviously the case, that we can if we choose give names to such things. But what is inconceivable is that we should be able *merely* to designate a momentary appearance and make it a logical subject of true or false predications. It is only possible to designate a momentary particular and make it a logical subject of judgment by thinking of it as having some empirically discernible character and as existing at an instant in a times series containing other instants from which its existence is excluded (*PL*, p. 61). Such judgments, therefore, of necessity involve the judging subject in an act of ideal construction, the intentional object of which is taken to exist and transcend the present moment.

Thus, although the ideal construction in terms of which a person can think of determinate times must be referred to reality as it appears in the ideal contents of his sense perceptions 'at the very instant', Bradley argues 'that the real, which appears in perception, does not appear in one single moment' (*PL*, p. 54). It is, accordingly, fundamental to Bradley's view, that reality is present in the ideal construction in terms of which, for example, we think (truly or falsely) of particulars remote in space and time just as much as it is present in the contents of our present sense perceptions. As he puts it: 'The contents of our perceptions, and the content of our ideal constructions, are both adjectives of the one reality' (*PL*, p. 75). And in holding this, of course, his theory differs from Russell's (*ETR*, p. 408): it marks, we might say, the difference between Russell's notion of a logical construction and Bradley's notion of an ideal construction.

Thus Bradley argues that even the most exiguous analytic judgments of sense, for example those formulable by means of grammatically singular sentences like 'This is white', must be taken to be existential in form. We can only make sense of the possibility of such judgments if we assume the judging subject to take, in the act of judgment, the designated particular to exist in a wider system or 'world' of particulars. And this world itself must be taken in the act of judgment to exist, or in other words, must be at that moment identified in this thought in terms of an ideal construction referred to reality *as* it is present in the contents of his current perceptions.

Therefore Bradley is adamant that neither 'this', nor any linguistic expression, could be capable of 'carrying over' a particular existent 'intact into judgement' (*ETR*, pp. 206-7) on the model of *mere* designation. Neither 'this' nor any word could 'mean what it stands for and stand for what it means' (*PL*, p. 168) — which *is* what was demanded by Russell of his genuine names.

Bradley does argue, however, that 'this' and egocentric demonstratives in general do have a necessary and distinctive role to play in language which is radically different from that played by the ordinary proper names we use. As he puts in an obscure but very important remark: 'The idea of "this," unlike most ideas, can not be used as a symbol in judgment' (*PL*, p. 67).

One way of beginning to understand what Bradley means by this remark, it seems to me, is to reflect on the fact that 'this' cannot play the same kind of role in the judgments that on occasions we formulate to ourselves as it does in the communication of judgments. On Bradley's view the primary linguistic function of 'this' is to draw the attention of other people (*PL*, p. 50) to some object in the immediate sensible environment which is already the focus of attention of the judging subject. Its use will, of course, normally also involve the use of adjectival expressions but 'this' itself does not describe the object. Nevertheless, Bradley maintains, 'this' like any word in a language must have a universal meaning graspable by different people. As I understand him, Bradley means by the *idea* of 'this' the ideas that a person must have in order to possess a full understanding of the meaning of 'this' in English — the ideas that would have to be exercised in explaining the meaning 'this' has. Bradley identifies two such ideas: namely, the idea of particularity or exclusion within a spatial or temporal series and the idea of immediate presence (*PL*, p. 67). However when 'this' is actually used on some occasion to formulate and communicate an analytic judgment of sense, say 'This is white', the above ideas cannot be taken to be used predicatively in the judgment. Of course one might attempt to analyse the content of the former judgment by some such sentence as 'The particular immediately present to me is white'. But then, as Bradley notes (*PL*, p. 69 n.), expressions like 'me' and 'present' must be construed as functioning in linguistic communication in a fundamentally similar way to 'this', and, moreover, it is difficult to see how their meanings in the judgment in question could be explained without the recurrence of 'this'.

Thus, on Bradley's account of the use of 'this' in the communication of judgments, 'this' might on a particular occasion of its use be said to *stand for* the particular object which is the logical subject of the person's judgment and which is the thing he wishes to draw attention to. Thus far it might be said to have a quasi-namelike function. However, so used it will not stand for that particular object in virtue of having acquired through its past use a general capacity to imply, when used by people in diverse spatio-temporal circumstances, distinguishing facts concerning that particular. But on Bradley's view this *is* how names, properly so called, do function. A person can on a given occasion use a proper name to stand for a particular object and make that object the logical subject of an explicit predication *only* because that name has come, through past use or by an act of definition, to be understood as implying the *existence*, in some sphere of knowledge or belief, of a particular object of a certain sort of which certain things are true. As Bradley puts it: 'The name of an individual must carry with it and imply certain attributes, or else its attachment to that individual becomes a psychological impossibility' (*PL*, p. 169, cf. pp. 80–1).

For Bradley, then, the judgments that people formulate at moments of time using proper names that have a currency in their language, are also to be regarded as existential in logical form even though the sentences used are grammatically singular and involve the person in making no explicit existential claim. Not unnaturally he treats judgments formed by sentences having definite descriptions as their grammatical subjects in a similar way. This he makes clear in a well-known passage, written long before 1905, in which he says:

'The King of Utopia died on Tuesday' may be safely contradicted. And
yet the denial must remain ambiguous. The ground may be that there is
no such place, or it never had a king, or he is still living, or, though he is
dead, yet he died on Monday (*PL*, pp. 124-5).

Therefore Bradley concludes that all judgments of the
kinds that we characteristically formulate by means of grammatically singular subject-predicate and relational sentences
are to be construed as being existential in logical form. As
he expresses it: 'All singular judgments have . . . been shown
to be existential' (*PL*, p. 81). And of existential judgments
themselves, Bradley says:

In existential judgment . . . the apparent is not the actual subject. Let
us take such a denial as 'Chimæras are non-existent.' 'Chimæras' is here
ostensibly the subject, but is really the predicate. It is the quality of
harbouring chimæras which is denied of the nature of things (*PL*,
p. 120).

Here, to return to the theme of the first section of this
paper, Bradley is to be understood as meaning by 'the nature
of things' the *real* world where that notion is to be distinguished from the notion of reality construed as the ultimate
logical subject of judgments, true and false. As Bradley notes
(*PL*, p. 71), 'It is one thing to seek the reality *in* that series
[of phenomena]; it is quite another thing to try to find it *as*
the series.'

At this point, it seems to me that we can use the idioms of
contemporary predicate logic to bring out the full force of
Bradley's reasoning. Quantifiers can be taken to be devices
for saying that *every* entity of a specifiable sort in a chosen
universe has a certain property or that *some* entities have.
The truth-value of a quantification, or act of judgment
formulated on some occasion by means of a sentence containing a quantifier, will therefore depend not merely on the
ideal content of the open sentence to which the quantifier
is attached but also on which universe the quantifier is
construed to relate to.

The notion of a universe as it is employed in the above
context is, I take it, precisely Bradley's notion of a world
where that notion is to be distinguished from the notion of
reality.[23] The entities of specific sorts within the chosen
world, and over which the quantifiers used in formulating
the quantification are taken to range, would be what Bradley

means by '*special* realities' or '*special* objects'.[24] However the chosen world relative to which the quantifiers are construed will *itself* of necessity be ideally specifiable and thus *itself* be a special reality. It will be something which, in the use of the quantifiers in that context, will *itself* be taken to be real or exist. But the same analysis could not be given of what is involved in taking a world *as a whole* to exist as is given of taking some entity to exist *within* that world. Unless, that is, through some advance in knowledge, it became possible to treat what had hitherto been regarded as a 'world' simply as an entity of a specifiable sort, existing, along with other entities of the same sort, within a wider world. In taking a specifiable world *as a whole* to exist, in formulating a given quantification, the ultimate logical subject of the judgment must remain unspecified.

The reality which must be taken to be the ultimate logical subject of our thinking on any occasion when we think either truly or falsely of anything can never be identified with any specifiable object of our thought no matter how widely or narrowly we cast the ideal net. But this of course is *not* to deny that reality is ultimately that of which we have knowledge when we succeed in thinking the truth with respect to any particular existing within a given world. But as Bradley points out, in a remark which I think is fundamental to all his thinking on truth, we must realize that 'the idea, which qualifies a finite sphere within the Whole, is [not] in the same sense true of the Whole' (*ETR*, p. 41 n.).

In other words, if we assume a quantification or judgment in which a predicate is asserted truly of a particular object of a specific sort existing within a certain world, that predicate could not be said to be true *of* that world. Nor could the ideal content of the judgment as such be said to be true *of* the world or, for that matter, true *of* anything. We may say that the content of the quantification was true *in* or *with respect to* a particular specifiable world: namely the world of entities over which the quantifiers employed in formulating the judgment were taken to range. But further, this notion of the ideal content of a judgment being either true or false with respect to a certain specifiable world is not the notion of a relation that could be taken to hold between the content of that judgment and reality *simpliciter*. The ideal content of a judgment which is true with respect to a certain world can become false if the quantifiers employed in its formulation are construed to relate to a different world. It is only with respect to a world the entities in which have already been specified by ideal contents which, under certain further conditions, would logically exclude or require yet further things, that we can give sense to the notion of a certain ideal content having to be either true or false. As Bradley expresses the matter:

'Caesar crossed the Rubicon', we say, 'or not'; but this 'either-or' is only true if you are confined to a single world of events. If there are various worlds, it may also be true that Caesar never saw the Rubicon nor indeed existed at all. And, with this, obviously our truth has ceased to be absolute (*ETR*, pp. 261–2).

Therefore Bradley concludes that all our singular judgments, even those that are true or false of particular objects actually existing in space and time, must be taken to be radically *conditional*. And it is important to see that Bradley's point here is not to be seen merely as a consequence of the 'dynamic' element in his theory of knowledge. It is not to be seen simply as a consequence of the 'egocentric predicament' of the knowing subject. Certainly Russell himself would agree that we cannot actually know explicitly the ultimate perceptible facts which determine the truth-values of *all* the existential and universal judgments that we can construct and understand the *senses* of. But Bradley is claiming much more than this. He is claiming that there could not be such ultimate perceptible facts and therefore the whole 'static' structure of our empirical knowledge implicit in the foundationalist account must be differently conceived. As Bradley puts it, using the metaphor of a chain for our empirical knowledge:

A last fact, a final link, is not merely a thing which we can not know, but a thing which could not possibly be real. Our chain by its nature can not have a support. Its essence excludes a fastening at the end. We do not merely fear that it hangs in the air, but we know it must do so. And when the end is unsupported, all the rest is unsupported. Hence our conditio*ned* truth is only conditio*nal*. It avowedly depends on what is not fact, and it is not categorically true.[25]

Hence Bradley's point here is to be taken as having an essentially logical foundation. It depends on a rejection of the possibility of a certain kind of name and therefore of a certain kind of judgment or proposition. It is most certainly not to be construed as sceptical in the sense of casting doubt on the existence of our empirical knowledge. It is an argument to the effect that we cannot construe the human knowledge that exists (for example in empirical science) to have a certain postulated logical structure and that, therefore, we must construe it differently.

Bradley emphasizes that the particular world with respect to which we wish to construe judgments like that concerning Caesar's crossing the Rubicon is our *real* world of objects and events in space and time. It is of course with respect to the world in which *these* our presently demonstratively locatable bodies exist, the only world within which we can *actually* think, either truly or falsely, about anything, the only world in which we can *actually* suffer, act, realize or fail to realize our desires and intentions, etc., that we are especially concerned to think the truth (cf. *ETR*, p. 468). Moreover Bradley emphasizes that we must of necessity in our actual thinking at any moment of time, in any sphere of knowledge or belief, work with a concept of truth which, so to speak, obeys the law of excluded middle (*ETR*, pp. 266-7). Once the ideal content of a judgment has been clearly defined, and the particular world with respect to which its truth is claimed has been clearly indicated, then we must take either it or its negation to be true. That, so to speak, is the way the human understanding works and we *must* adopt that principle in our thinking at any moment in any sphere.

But the world of particular objects of empirically discernible sorts which at any given waking moment we take to be actual and which we *then* distinguish in our thinking from particular things merely dreamt, imagined in literature or science, and perhaps once falsely believed to be actual, Bradley maintains cannot be marked off *as* actual by reference to any special features it has. For example the actual world is not to be distinguished by reference to the ideas of space and time. Those ideas are not to be construed as having any peculiar status. They are not, for example, to be taken as Kantian pure *intuitions*, which would enable space and time themselves to be portrayed as immediately known unique individuals. As Bradley puts it: 'We must get rid of the erroneous notion . . . that space and time are "principles of individuation," in the sense that a temporal or spatial exclusion will confer uniqueness on any content' (*PL*, p. 63).

Our ideas of space and time are *ideas* like any others and there is nothing in their contents that logically excludes the possibility of there being a multiplicity of spatially unrelated spaces and temporally unrelated times. Our ability to distinguish the particular spatio-temporal series with respect to which we wish to construe our empirical judgments must, Bradley argues, be taken to lie in our abilities to think of it as *the* one containing *these our* bodies and *these* other demonstratively locatable particulars of such-and-such empirically discernible sorts present now in the ideal contents of our current sense perceptions and logically connected thoughts. As he puts it: 'It is not by its quality as a temporal event or phenomenon of space, that the given is unique. It is unique, not because it has a certain character, but because it *is given*' (*PL*, p. 64).

Hence Bradley gives what David Lewis calls an 'indexical' account of actuality. And he would be in complete agreement with Lewis when the latter says: 'We picture the actual world — indefensibly — as the one solid, vivid, energetic world among innumerable ghostly, faded, wispy, "merely" possible worlds.'[26]

However, for Bradley (and now we are encroaching on the positive account of the Absolute that falls within his metaphysics), reality cannot be satisfactorily construed simply as a totality of thinkable worlds lying externally related to one another. We can think of such worlds, each with its own truth and falsity, and each with its own actual and non-actual, only by referring ideal contents of specific kinds to a reality which transcends them. On Bradley's view, to the individual, substantial, self-existent which is not merely *ideally* present at moments of time in the *contents* of our sense perceptions and thoughts which we take at moments of time to be true and false with respect to *this* and other worlds, but is also *immediately* present in the *existence* of our perceptions, thoughts, feelings, acts (bodily and otherwise), *qua* experiences — experiences to the nature of which our abstract bipolar thinking is patently inadequate.

NOTES

1. For example, *ETR*, chap. III, 'On Floating Ideas and the Imaginary', pp. 30-2; and chap. XVI, 'On My Real World', pp. 460-5.
2. *PL*, vol. II, Terminal Essay (TE), 'On Judgment', p. 630. In fact Bosanquet uses this formula much more frequently than Bradley does.
3. Wittgenstein, *Tractatus Logico-Philosophicus*, London, 1961, tr. D. F. Pears and B. F. McGuinness, 1-1.1.
4. *Tractatus*, 2.021 ff. and 5.5561; also *Notebooks 1914-16*, Oxford, 1961, p. 39, entry for 22.1.15.
5. *Tractatus*, 4.0621.
6. Ibid., 2.1511.
7. *PL*, vol. I, bk. I, chap. II, paras. 3-5, pp. 43-6; also para. 29, pp. 70-1.
8. The contents of this précis comes from *PL*, vol. I, bk. I, chap. I, paras. 1-9, pp. 1-10. I use the terms 'type' and 'token' which Bradley does not, but he clearly intends equivalent distinctions.
9. *Tractatus*, 5.541-2. For Wittgenstein a proposition is a perceptible sign in its projective relation to reality and therefore is *itself* a species of fact. And Wittgenstein held that the thought, *qua* psychological fact, must have constituents corresponding to the words in a propositional sign.
10. *PL*, vol. II, TE XI, 'On the Possible and the Actual', p. 704 n.; cf. also TE I, 'On Inference', pp. 612-13, and *ETR*, chap. XI, 'On Some Aspects of Truth', pp. 339-42, for some very Fregean sounding remarks about how we are constrained to think of truths.
11. G. Frege, *Logical Investigations*, Oxford, 1977, chap. I, 'Thoughts', esp. pp. 13-18 and 24-30.
12. Ibid., p. 17; cf. *ETR*, chap. XI, 'On Some Aspects of Truth', pp. 339-42.
13. *Logical Investigations*, chap. I, 'Thoughts', p. 7.
14. Frege, *Philosophical Writings of Gottlob Frege*, Oxford, 1952, tr. P. Geach and M. Black, 'On Sense and Reference', p. 65.
15. *Logical Investigations*, chap. III, 'Compound Thoughts', pp. 55-7. For an account of the 'step by step' construction of sentences see M. Dummett, *Frege*, London, 1973, chap. 2, pp. 9-24.
16. *Logical Investigations*, chap. III, 'Compound Thoughts', p. 61.
17. Ibid., chap. I, 'Thoughts', pp. 27-30. Frege does allow that thoughts 'must somehow be implicated with the temporal' and suggests that they can have 'inessential' properties which *do* depend on their becoming objects of the psychological acts of people at moments of time. In this way, Frege suggests, via psychological acts of thinking and willing, thoughts might be construed to be capable of becoming active at moments of time in the first realm of physical things.
18. Ibid., pp. 26-7.
19. It is at this point that one can see Russell's reason for demanding against Frege that names which designate particulars but which do not have 'predicable' meanings attached to them must be possible. Cf. Dummett, *Frege*, chap. 6, pp. 163-6, where Dummett obscures the real epistemological and metaphysical issues behind Russell's demand.
20. *Logical Investigations*, chap. I, 'Thoughts', p. 25.
21. 'On Judgment', *Mind*, 1899.
22. Cf. G. E. Moore, *Some Main Problems of Philosophy*, London, 1953, and B. Russell, *The Problems of Philosophy*, Oxford, 1912.

The account of Russell's philosophy that I give is a synopsis of his logical atomism in the period before he embraced a 'subjectless' neutral monist atomism. My sources would be mainly B. Russell, *Logic and Knowledge*, ed. R. C. Marsh, London, 1956, 'On the Nature of Acquaintance', 1914, pp. 127 ff., and 'The Philosophy of Logical Atomism', 1918, pp. 177 ff. I have not noted this synopsis of Russell since I do not intend it to be a scholarly historical account. I am happy simply to see it as a more or less coherent view of human knowledge and one which Bradley attacks.

23. Cf. for example, *ETR*, chap. III, 'On Floating Ideas and the Imaginary', pp. 30–42; also ibid., chap. XVI, 'On My Real World', pp. 460–9.
24. Cf., for example, *PL*, vol. II, TE II, 'On Judgment', pp. 623–30. But this distinction is used throughout the *PL*.
25. *PL*, bk. I, chap. II, para. 71, p. 100; cf. also TE II, 'On Judgment', p. 628; also *ETR*, chap. IX, 'On Appearance, Error, and Contradiction', pp. 258–9.
26. 'Anselm and Actuality', *Noûs*, vol. 4, 1970, p. 184. Cf. also, for a briefer treatment, D. Lewis, *Counterfactuals*, Oxford, 1973, chap. 4, pp. 85–6.

CHAPTER 8

Is Epistemology Incoherent?

Simon Blackburn

It must occur to many philosophers that themes prominent in recent epistemology and philosophy of language also dominate the writings of the British Idealists, the exponents of the so-called coherence theory of truth. One such theme is the interanimation of meanings, in the sense that a particular sentence expresses a belief only because of its relations to a great many other sentences expressing surrounding beliefs. Here is a passage from Joachim which strikes responsive chords:

No universal judgment of science, then, expresses in and by itself a determinate meaning. For every such judgment is really the abbreviated statement of a meaning which would require a whole system of knowledge for its adequate expression. It is this larger meaning, embodied more or less fully in such a system, which, so to say, *animates* the single judgments and gives them determinate significance.[1]

Elsewhere Joachim emphasizes the mistake committed by Descartes, and nowadays supposed to characterize 'foundationalist epistemology', of thinking of the system of belief in terms of the discrete links of a chain anchored at some determinate point in a confrontation with the world:

the ideal of knowledge for me is a system, not of *truths* but of *truth*. 'Coherence' cannot be attached to propositions from the outside: it is not a property which they can aquire by colligation, whilst retaining unaltered the truth they possessed in isolation.[2]

The whole system gains its authority from experience, and this introduces the other idealist theme: the judgmental character of observation. The idealists' particular enemy was the view that observation shows us facts directly in a way which enables us to understand what it is for judgment to correspond to such facts. When Bradley writes that 'merely given facts are the imaginary creatures of false theory', or that the given facts 'show already in their nature the work of truth-making' (*ETR*, p. 108), he is anticipating, in a Kantian vein, the doubts many philosophers feel about the myth of the given. And he emphasizes that even if at some point there existed a datum of sensation or feeling wholly unmodified by apperception, then firstly, we would not know of it, and secondly, it would need description and interpretation in order to become part of a system of science, and this reintroduces the work of judgment. When I open my eyes experiences flood in, but as far as the theory of knowledge or truth goes, they might just as well be regarded as beliefs. The senses are sufficiently impregnated with the 'work of truth-making' to be best regarded as just very fertile sources of belief. Of course, there are various different ways of developing this general theme, but for my purpose I want only to sketch its general character.[3]

Both themes point in the direction of a coherence theory of truth, if an adequate version proves statable. And both point towards some scepticism about traditional epistemology. This sums up in the charge that because of these conceptions of meaning and observation we can see that there can be no 'first philosophy': no 'God's eye view', or 'Archimedean point', from which the philosopher can survey our work of forming belief, and see whether we are delineating reality well or badly in that work. So when, for example, Rorty writes:

For the Quine–Sellars approach to epistemology, to say that truth and knowledge can only be judged by the standards of the inquirers of our own day is not to say that human knowledge is less noble or important, or more 'cut off from the world' than we had thought. It is merely to say that nothing counts as justification unless by reference to what we already accept, and that there is no way to get outside our beliefs and our language so as to find some test other than coherence.[4]

He does not intend merely to advert to the tautology that our best standards of enquiry are our best standards of enquiry. It is rather that because of the way in which our experiences and thoughts mutually infuse each other the philosopher's role is bound to be limited, and traditional epistemology falls outside the proper limits. I want to suggest, on the contrary, that when we appreciate how a coherence theory of truth has to be developed, we see how epistemology works as well.

I

The traditional charge against coherence theories of truth is that we can make up coherent stories ad lib, entirely without regard to the way the world is. By following our fancies, and paying attention only to consistency, we can generate comprehensive descriptions of possible but non-actual worlds. For any such description to be true of the actual world therefore requires more than its mere presence in such a set. A form of this objection is made by Russell.[5] Suppose we have a coherent and reasonably comprehensive description of some historical period — call the system S. Then we might maintain or increase coherence, and increase comprehensiveness, by adding the proposition that some late prelate died on the gallows $(S + E)$. But for all its membership of the system, E might be false. Bradley's ideal of comprehension and coherence gives us no reason to control admission to the system in anything like the sane accepted ways, and as a consequence not only admits falsehoods, but also allows increasingly divergent systems, each of which meets the ideal.

Bradley's response to this apparently devastating objection is interesting. Reminding us of the requirement that a system be made as comprehensive as possible, he says:

But imagine my world made on the principle of in such a case accepting mere fancy as fact. Would such a world be *more* comprehensive and coherent than the world as now arranged? Would it be coherent at all? ... The idea of system demands the inclusion of all possible material. Not only must you include everything to be gained from immediate experience and perception, but you must also be ready to act on the same principle with regard to fancy. (*ETR*, pp. 213–14).

He then points out that this requires the admission of contradictory fancies, and so is ruled out by the requirement of coherence.

At first sight this is an evasion. Russell's charge is that if S is comprehensive and coherent — I abbreviate this to CC — or approaches being so to some degree, then so is $S + E$, to a greater degree, in spite of the falsity of E. Bradley's retort is that a different set is not CC. This different set includes what I shall call an *entitling judgment*, telling how E got into the first set. So the set he is considering is $S + E + F$, where F tells us that E is the product of fancy. Bradley argues that this set is only CC if the principle on which E is allowed in is accepted, or in other words, if $S + E + F + G$ is CC, where G generalizes the principle implicit in adding E on the basis of F — i.e. endorses the admission of any old fancy. And this set is not CC, because the principle enjoins the admission of inconsistencies. But Russell wanted to consider only $S + E$. So Bradley missed his point.

Or perhaps Russell missed Bradley's. Let us call a system reflexive with respect to some set of judgments it contains, if it also contains a description of the title of those judgments to membership. Then Bradley clearly regards the aim that a body of belief be comprehensive as enjoining that so far as possible it be reflexive — in so far as a system contains elements without anything indicating their title to being there, it falls short on comprehensiveness. If this is the theory then Bradley is perfectly right to reply to Russell as he does, for whenever an addition to a system is proposed on some ground, the test may be run on the addition plus the principle implicit in accepting the ground. Of course, so far as the connection between membership of a CC system and truth goes, the victory may be only temporary. For the search should turn to an example where a judgment is proposed together with a title whose general acceptance does not yield incoherence, yet which is not true. Since we are poor creatures with limited capacities, we will expect there to be such. But before considering this, I want to press the present argument a little further.

In Bradley's view the fact that a judgment is the product of fancy cannot give the right pedigree to a candidate for admission to a system of belief. It can let in inconsistent pairs, destroying coherence. But quite what is the requirement? After all, the proper use of memory, perception, the testimony of others, induction, and calculation, can also let in inconsistent pairs, yet these are the very claims to title of most common-sense beliefs. It is easy to imagine epistemic situations where one proper use of these sources leads us to accept some judgment, and another leads us to reject it. Now when we recognize that we are in such a situation, we suspend judgment, because we operate the principle that we cannot add a belief to a system if we see that its title could equally be claimed by its negation. The aim of comprehensiveness assures us that this is an inferior situation, which could be improved until just one belief got the title. So now we should ask what control there is over the kinds of process which could count as improvement.

The problem is to arrive at some conception of why the proper — normal — use of perception, memory, and so on, should alone control the coherent and comprehensive systems of belief to which we should aspire. Bradley, like everyone else, believes that they should do so:

I do not believe in any knowledge which is independent of feeling and sensation . . . Our intelligence cannot construct the world of perceptions and feelings, and it depends on what is given — to so much I assent (*ETR*, p. 203).

The difficulty is that the assimilation of observation to judgment makes it seem as though our faculties are simply ready, cheap, and fertile sources of belief, by comparison with which even the richest imaginings give only the barest sketches of world. No imagination, however unbridled, can give us as rich a conception of merely possible worlds as we have of the actual one. But this does nothing to explain the negative authority of observation and other sober processes of enquiry. Why should not we augment them by other procedures when they fail to give us an answer? We can tailor imaginings for consistency when we have to. And if observation, memory, and so on, are sisters under the skin with invention, being merely productive sources of judgment, whence comes the authority which enables their deliverances, and no others, to enter into systems of belief?

The answer to this on behalf of the idealists must concentrate upon the notion of belief. For there is nothing at all odd about manufacturing a system of propositions of superior comprehension and coherence by a judicious use of invention. But the idealists were innocent of any Fregean doctrine desiring us to purge philosophy of psychology: they are talking of systems of judgment and belief, not of propositions in the abstract. This makes two differences. One is that whether we like it or not the senses control our beliefs in ways which are often unalterable. If we open our eyes we have little or no choice over what we see and what we believe; conversely, we cannot actually believe what we know ourselves to have just invented. Thus one problem with Russell's case is that you simply cannot add the proposition that the late prelate died on the gallows to your beliefs about the history of the time. You would need to go through some process of attaining conviction. I return to this point later.

The other point about systems of belief is that we require them to have a coherence which goes beyond mere consistency. This is what I shall call *extended* coherence, and it requires a certain harmony between an element of the system and its entitling judgment. Consider, for instance, these two propositions: p, and: p is the delivery of a process which, in the circumstances in which it was used, had a fifty-fifty chance of delivering $-p$. These are perfectly compatible, for normal values of p. They could both be members of a CC system of *propositions*. But they are not fitted to both being members of a CC system of *beliefs*. They could, indeed, both be held by some particular man. But there is a probabilistic chasm, between the confidence in the belief and the scepticism about its pedigree. Having high confidence in things which have a fifty-fifty pedigree is a bad disposition to give in to. Standard arguments show how a man with given desires — for example for money — would do badly if made to act out such a disposition — for example by betting. At least, the techniques show how he does badly if his disposition covers decidable issues.

Now the whole point of introducing fanciful beliefs as a challenge to a coherence theorist is that you can fancy what you like. The process is uncontrolled, in a way which means that it could just as well have issued in the opposite delivery. And of course this is just the point of contrast with observation and other sober practices of enquiry, which do not suffer from an even chance of delivering either a judgment or its negation, regardless of which is true on the occasion of use. At least, that is the natural thing to say. There may be a question of whether a coherence theory of truth can allow us to say it, and there is certainly a question of whether it is of much use to the coherence theorist when he has said it. But I want to turn aside from these questions temporarily, in order to draw in some epistemology.

Lack of extended coherence is an internal complaint in a system of beliefs. That is, checking on a particular commitment we might find that its title is not one which permits the degree of confidence with which it is held. Obviously there are local enquiries whose aim is precisely to find out whether this is so. Equally clearly, standard problems in epistemology seemed important precisely because they suggested some conception of a probability space, in which there are competing alternatives, and where our best entitlement only gives some cherished belief a poor chance of being true. So these suggestions can be seen as alerting us to a possible disharmony in our thoughts, noticeable to anyone walking round his boat, and not only to someone trying to hover in an unstable God's eye viewpoint above it. An opponent will retort that there is no reason to heed these suggestions: that our best science imposes its own implicit judgment of the competing probabilities, and that a philosopher has no right to suggest a different one. Our best science finds perfect coherence between our confidence in an external world, or many inductive predictions, or the belief in other minds, and the entitling judgments we can offer for such commitments. So if there is nowhere outside its system to stand, there is no way to challenge the system, even on the grounds of extended coherence. I want to suggest however that there is. We have to preserve coherence between our best science of best sciences, or in other words, our naturalized epistemology, and the endorsement of the probabilities implicit in those best sciences. And that is a coherence which can very easily slip. Preserving it is almost exactly like doing traditional epistemology. To illustrate the point I shall work through some of the more exuberant responses to worries about meaning and observation.

II

The problem which emerged in the last section was that of reconciling a broadly judgmental account of observation and memory, or other sober practices of enquiry, with some conception of their authority over what to allow into a CC system of beliefs. A purely conventionalist reaction to the problem simply reverses it: being an outcome of sober practices of enquiry is simply a title which *we* confer on judgments which as a community *we* accept. If this raises the problem of where the consensus arises in the first place, we enter into a historical enquiry, which will have nothing to point to but the linguistic and cultural arrangements which the community has inherited and under which it operates. The drift is that the approval of some peer group, or the arrangements of some linguistic or cultural circle, itself creates the fact that a particular opinion, or method of forming opinion, is correct. At any rate, this approval creates as many of such facts as we need, so that if the resulting conceptions of truth, rationality, and so forth, are rather meagre, that is the fault of philosophical traditions which have falsely promised us something richer. Until Professor Rorty's book it was hard to find a definite statement of this drift, although it could be sensed in various places, particularly, of course, in the later Wittgenstein. But Rorty is forthright in drawing the analogy with conventionalist accounts of such things as human rights, he cites:

the difference between moral philosophers who think that rights and responsibilities are a matter of what society bestows, and those who think that there is something inside a man which a society recognizes when it makes its bestowal.[6]

Now this purely conventionalist line must show how a belief together with this conception of its title may cohere together. The threat is that mention of conventional origins for an element in our epistemology is too close to mention of fanciful origins — in other words, that it imposes a conception of chances which cannot cohere with the certainty we attach to the element. Thus mention of conventions and arrangements of society to explain some feature is only reputable under strict conditions. We need a notion of alternative possible conventions or arrangements. We need a notion of why some convention is desired — in Lewis's terms, a notion of the co-ordination problem to which one system or another is the solution. And we need the explanatory claim that it is because of a reinforcing net of expectations about continued conformity that the fact to be explained exists and continues to exist — rather than, say, because of our brute natures or other external constraints. Now this kind of explanation, in itself a perfectly normal piece of human science, brings its own implications for chances, and these are not always welcome. Let me give an example of the threat.

Suppose we take a purely conventional attitude to Goodman's problem of projection. By this I mean accepting three things. We interpret 'entrenchment' in terms of the linguistic arrangements of the community. We suppose that those arrangements are simply the ones which happen to be favoured out of a space of alternative possible ones. So far as the needs, natures, or causal interactions of the community with the world go, these could equally have served: thus there is reason for a community to entrench some predicate, but not for it to embed 'green' rather than 'grue'. Finally we suppose that our commitment to one projection rather than to another inconsistent one is explained by which convention we have come to operate. The incoherence is then this: the mention of convention is relevant in so far as our natures, our causal interactions with emeralds, or knowledge of them, might perfectly well have left us forming a system which would in turn have led us to confidence that emeralds would be blue tomorrow. Convention takes up the slack between these things and whatever is necessary to form our actual system. But this is exactly on a par with admitting that our particular projection is the outcome of fancy — it is the outcome of something which does not vary with the colour of the emeralds tomorrow, something which, so far as that colour, or any causal connections with that colour, go, might equally well have gone one way or the other. Indeed the conventional status of a commitment is quite consistent with it being, in origin, the explicit outcome of a chance event. Whim, fancy, or the toss of a coin is just the sort of thing which chooses between equally attractive competing solutions to a problem of mutual co-ordination. The general point is that if our commitment is explained by convention, so that had the convention been different we would have had an inconsistent commitment, then unless there is a causal story showing how the way the convention was formed would be determined by which of the competing commitments is true, it will be incoherent to maintain the commitment. But if there *is* such a story, showing us why, for instance, in the world as we have it it would have been much more natural, or inevitable, for us to speak the one language, then the point of mentioning our arrangements and conventions is lost. Our predicting green rather than grue will be explained not by our linguistic arrangements, but by whatever story explains why we make *those* arrangements and not others.

If a chance event, or an event whose occurrence was chance so far as the truth of p goes, explains why one is committed to p as opposed to $-p$, then extended coherence fails. The incoherence is noticeable to anyone walking round his boat, for when a naturalized epistemologist invokes a conventional explanation of a practice, he imposes a definite chance of there having been other practices, and it is this chance which produces the incoherence. It is not imposed only by some *a priori* first philosophy, with an academic conception of probabilities, but by something presented as a straightforward piece of human psychology. Indeed, it should be clear that the naturalized epistemologist is particularly vulnerable to the point. For he forbids himself retreat to a peculiarly philosophical, external, and insulated position, from which reference to conventionality can be allowed, without destroying the certainties which we properly have when we are immersed in day-to-day living. He rightly disallows a distinction between an 'internal' judgment (the certainty that the emerald stays blue) and an 'external' theory of the probability that we should have arranged ourselves so as to find the contrary equally acceptable. The alleged distinction is anathema, precisely because it is the task of the philosopher to sketch a unified account of ourselves as capable of signalling the way the world is, and this requires a unified picture of the chance of our judgments as opposed to conflicting judgments being true. If convention enters at all, it enters as a piece of scientific explanation, carrying its own implications for the chance of correctness. So any coherence theorist should know that his job is not done if he reaches bedrock when he says that such-and-such a judgment emerges from *our* language, *our* arrangements, *our* games, institutions, conventions, and so on. To avoid extended incoherence, he needs also to find a view according to which our having formed those conventions, if it determines which judgment we accept, is itself a signal of the way the world is, and varies according to it.

I suspect that many philosophers find it tempting, at this point, to give up naturalized epistemology, and retreat to a kind of transcendental conventionalism. This means both taking comfort in reference to us, our ways and conventions, *and* disallowing consideration of the way we could have made alternatives, and of what chance there was of our doing so. Thus when a conventionalist response to Goodman's problem is attacked on the grounds that it is either naturally or even logically impossible to regard the manufactured predicates as genuinely free of reference to time or other divisions, a transcendental conventionalist replies that this is just what we would expect — given our conventions. Of course, he argues, we *say* that there are the differences people have laboured to point out, and these differences may show that we have no serious conception of what it would be for a community to count the artificial predicates as determining kinds, or as observational or primitive. But the transcendental conventionalist then tries to outflank the whole discussion: all this he urges is a matter of what *we* think, and what we think is the outcome of our immersion in our conventions. The transcendental conventionalist forswears the obligation that usually attends explanatory reference to convention — namely, that we discern a space of equally possible solutions to the co-ordination problem — because, he thinks, the conventions involved, since they somehow give the framework of our thought, also disable us from thinking about what other conventions would be. The position accepts, perhaps, Davidson's belief that in general we can make little sense of the notion of a rival way of doing things. But he insists still that it is we who confer authority upon our own way, via arrangements we have made and which determine our way of thought. Furthermore, if within that way of thought there are stable ways of assigning chances to belief, there is no potential incoherence introduced by seeing it as conventionally determined, because there is no genuine space of alternatives which we can identify, or to which we can assign probabilities, leading to the danger of extended incoherence.

Transcendental conventionalism has the usual attractions of theft. It is familiar in discussions of necessary truth, where, acknowledging that a rival way of counting or measuring or doing arithmetic is not really conceivable, or even that it is, so far as we can see, demonstrably inoperable, it adds the gloss that this is all so to *us now*, and the way we are now is supposedly a product of our linguistic arrangements. So the conventionalist stream flows past the rock of being unable to identify alternative conventions. But it does so only by losing its explanatory pretensions. If all approaches to conceiving of rival ways of thought (in the relevant respects) fail, there is no right to say that we have our way *because* of some arrangement or tradition or social set-up which could have been otherwise. For the explanation is only as good as the counterfactual, that if these things had been otherwise, the resulting way of thought would have had the opposing feature. But since it is admitted that we do not know what it could be for a way of thought to have the opposing feature, we can have no right to say this.

I commend the dilemma of taking reference to convention in a naturalized spirit, and facing the problem of keeping extended coherence, or taking it transcendentally and losing an explanatory value. It is, at least, a way of denying that we reach bedrock in reference to our ways. But how sharp is the first horn? Goodman's is a good example just because the rival ways of thought are supposed to be in actual conflict with ours, resulting in genuinely conflicting expectations. There would be nothing incoherent about seeing immersion in a convention as a fact which explains how we come to see a particular truth, if the alternative would have been just to miss it. Incoherence arises when the alternative would have been to believe the contrary, and when the matter determining the convention we operate shows no sign of varying according to which judgment is true. To illustrate the difference I can mention Quine's treatment of observation. When Quine writes 'a sentence is observational insofar as its truth value, on any occasion, would be agreed to by just about any member of the speech community witnessing the occasion',[7] what kind of authority is supposed to reside in the speech community, and how did that authority arise? If we imagine a different community, following different speech conventions, how are we to envisage their observation sentences comparing with ours? If they conflict, the threat of extended incoherence arises as before. If it is the *consentium gentium*, as Rorty takes Quine to imply, which determines that in saying some particular things we are reporting an observation, then unless we have some theory according to which that consent is a reliable sign of the fact reported, once again, we have incoherence. But having such a theory is just have a way of seeing our tendency to take a given report as a good sign that it is true, or in other words, of seeing ourselves as good signallers of the truth, which is just what classical epistemology wants to do.

The crucial distinction is between letting convention in our speech community explain how we come to make the various judgments we do, after using our senses, and letting it play a role in explaining why those judgments are the right ones to make. It cannot play the second role unless we can see our having made the convention as itself an indicator of the fact we are reporting, and this is usually no part of our general view of the world. The trouble, then, with the pure conventionalist response to the problem of the authority of observation is just that it tries to make our conventions play this second, incoherent, role. Now I do not know if Quine intended his account of observation to be taken in Rorty's way. Certainly he intended his definition to 'accord perfectly with the traditional role of the observation sentence as the court of appeal of scientific theories'.[8] But the traditional role was not just that of appeal to common consent regardless of the nature of that consent. In so far as common opinion entered into traditional epistemology, it was because it was common opinion amongst those who knew, or who used their faculties properly, or in other words, had more title than convention-following could give to being supposed to be reliable signallers of whatever they reported. And it seems to me that we can follow Quine's desire to study the relation between meagre input and torrential output in the believing observer, whilst respecting the need not to see that output as incoherently related to the truth of the belief. The question which now remains is how much difference the coherence theory of truth might make to our endeavours to preserve coherence in our conception of ourselves as responsive to observation.

III

If you form a belief about whether there is a cat in the

garden without putting yourself in the way of signs which vary according to whether there is a cat in the garden, you have as much chance of being wrong as being right. Sober practices of enquiry are precisely those which put you in the way of signs and signals which so vary. Responding to them is bettering your chance of being right, so it forms the essential coherence between the belief and its entitling judgment. Hence, a coherence theory of truth demands the proper respect for observation and such other practices as meet this desideratum: it insists on our being able to see the process leading to the belief as one which would vary with the truth of the belief — a process causally connected with the presence of the cat. Of course, it is we who have causal theories, including theories of our own responses to the way the world is. It is we who think that if there is a cat in the garden our experience will be one way, and if there is not it will be another way, and that the relevant difference is therefore a good sign of the presence of the cat. But since we do have such views, we should be satisfied with our respect for observation.

But at this point we face another version of Russell's objection, designed to show that extended coherence is not sufficient for truth, or that a gain in extended coherence may yet be a step away from truth. If we had bizarre views about confirmation, we could maintain extended coherence in a system with a good admixture of falsity. A fanciful process might come along with a fanciful story to the effect that the process is indeed a good sign of the way the world is. A good impostor will usually bring a fake pedigree. For instance, the idea might come into someone's head that he is spoken to by God, but at the same time it comes into his head that this is not itself a judgment that has just come into his head, but is itself the result of the fact that he is being spoken to by God. The problem will arise whenever we fall victim to mistaken interpretations of our experience, coupled with credible theories about why the interpretations are not mistaken. The objection is not that one could aim to bring this about, so that on a coherence view of truth we should expect bizarre techniques for forming belief. One cannot deliberately adopt a fanciful pedigree for a belief that has just come into one's head, for doing that demands convincing oneself that the pedigree is not what one knows it is. But a false belief and a false theory as to its reliability may both arise. So even if extended coherence is a necessary condition for truth, and even if it does something to rehabilitate traditional epistemological interests, or at any rate to unmask some of their successors, it cannot be sufficient.

Well, it cannot in the short term. A particular step, even with the right kind of title, may be an increase in comprehensiveness, yet a step away from the truth. But this, it seems to me, does not matter if we expect the step to be corrigible, as yet further increases are made. And this is generally so. Fake titles become exposed as our general theory of the way the world is improves. I don't think anyone has the right to assert that a falsehood might remain through all the potential improvements we can imagine in a system of belief. This touches on large issues which I do not want to go into here: it is at least not clear that it is a weakness in a coherence theory of truth that it is suspicious of a wholesale contrast between an opinion which would result from the best disposition of ourselves as signallers of how the world is, and an opinion which is true.

A different objection is that by giving the necessary causal role to facts, the coherence theory gives ground to some rival notion of correspondence. The causal processes which we embrace, in the effort to certify the extended coherence of a system of belief, must start with the fact that, say, the cat is in the garden, and end with our tendency to believe this about it. Only because of this does our tendency to believe vary in the right way with the fact. But if facts play this role, aren't they to be seen as extra-systematic, real beings of whatever ontological category, ready for correspondence? I do not think so. It is part of common sense to see that the fact that the cat is in the garden can cause all sorts of things — the fact that there are no birds in the garden, or the shadow on the parsley. If we dislike a style of description involving mention of facts as causal relata, we will substitute a preferred style. The essential is to keep a high probability for the conditionals: if I soberly believe that there is a cat in the garden, then there is; if I believe that there is not one, then there is not. I am a good instrument for registering cats.

I do not think that having these conditionals embedded in a system of knowledge gives ground to a correspondence theory, at least in any sense in which that could be a rival to a coherence view. It is, of course, notoriously hard to say just what is right about a correspondence theory of truth. But one appeal it might have is to direct our attention to just these belief-to-world conditionals: it stresses that there is a need to build a naturalized epistemology, a theory of our own best theorizing, respecting the need to give them a high probability. In that case, the coherence theory in my development is not so much a rival to a correspondence theory, but absorbs its virtues in passing. In the same way, perhaps more obviously, it absorbs the virtues of the so-called semantic conception of truth. At least, I cannot see that sympathy with the directions I have been exploring should make it harder to allow that '*p*' is true if and only if *p*, nor that the totality of such conditionals in a language should be capable of systematic recursive description. Such sympathy hardly leads one to deny that 'London' refers to London and so on.

Perhaps however there is more to observation than that because of it belief-to-world conditionals can be given a high probability. For in some areas we form opinion happily enough, and convince ourselves that we do so rightly, and go on to expand and improve comprehensive systems of such opinions, although nothing seems to correspond to observation. These areas are usually felt to be those about which a coherence theory of truth works best — mathematics, for example, or ethics. Whatever else we think about the processes of forming mathematical and ethical belief, we think that if we go through the processes correctly then when we end up believing, say that $2 + 2 = 4$ or that is is wrong to kick dogs gratuitously, we are likely to be right. I do not want my kind of coherence theory to flatten out the distinction between these beliefs and the rest. The best theory of the way we form such systems, and of why we may regard ourselves as doing so well, will have to cite their success in enabling us to cope with and live in the observed world. Otherwise they would be empty formalisms. Even within a coherence theory it seems to me that we can delimit different roles for different kinds of opinion, and our naturalized epistemology will lead us to see their entitling judgments in different ways. The main difference the coherence notion makes is that it enables us to give up resistance to saying that these kinds of opinion are genuinely capable of truth-values. The contrast with observed fact is just that coherence will not involve a belief in them. Our commitment to the entitling conditionals will not be part of a causal theory of ourselves.

I have deliberately talked of a drift or direction of thinking leading to sympathy with themes which are embodied in the coherence theory of truth. I have not actually given a definition of what that theory is. In not doing so I pander to the quietistic leanings of many philosophers who have thought about truth, to the effect that either the concept is redundant, or that our best understanding of it must always remain glowing in the totality of T-sentences of a language or that any attempted definition is somehow bound to fail. Perhaps the best thing to talk about is a coherence theory of belief, or of success in belief or the point of belief, or of epistemology. I do not much mind about this. If membership of the most comprehensive and coherent system of belief which the best use of our faculties could lead to is not truth, perhaps it is near enough. It is at any rate the best we are going to get, and it demands very high standards of inspection of our boat.[9]

NOTES

1. H. H. Joachim, *The Nature of Truth*, Oxford, 1906, p. 96.
2. Ibid., pp. 72–3.
3. A judgmental theory is developed, for example, by Richard Gregory, *The Intelligent Eye*, London, 1974, and Edward Craig, 'Sensory Experience and the Foundations of Knowledge', *Synthese*, 1976.
4. R. Rorty, *Philosophy and the Mirror of Nature*, Oxford, 1980, p. 178.
5. B. Russell, 'The Nature of Truth', *Mind*, vol. XV, 1906.
6. R. Rorty, *Philosophy and the Mirror of Nature*, Oxford, 1980, p. 177.
7. W. V. O. Quine, *The Roots of Reference*, Open Court, 1974, p. 39.
8. W. V. O. Quine, 'Epistemology Naturalized', in *Ontological Relativity and Other Essays*, Columbia, 1969, p. 87.
9. My thanks are due to Oxford University Press for permitting a degree of overlap between this paper and part of one chapter of my book *Spreading the Word: Groundings in the Philosophy of Language*, Oxford, 1984. In that chapter I try to address a problem raised by Rogers Albritton, that belief-

world conditionals will be too easy to defend on a full coherence theory, since that theory diminishes and perhaps distorts our view of what it is that we are good at signalling. The defence complicates things a little, and since it does not affect the main points I wanted to make on Bradley's behalf I thought it best to leave this paper as it stands.

CHAPTER 9

Bradley's Principle of
Sufficient Reason

James Allard

My title is suggested by a remark of Russell's. In one of the many places where Russell attacks Bradley, Russell comments that Bradley's view of relations depends on the view that all true judgments are necessarily true. In Russell's words, Bradley's 'opinion seems to rest upon some law of sufficient reason, some desire to show that every truth is "necessary"'.[1] I believe that Russell is correct here. Bradley does think that every true judgment is necessarily true. Russell's way of putting the point, however, is misleading. Bradley does not accept some abstract principle which compels him to adopt this; rather, his analysis of the logical form of judgments commits him to it. In this paper I will try to explain why Bradley adopts this view; that is, I will try to explain Bradley's 'principle of sufficient reason'.

The key to Bradley's view is the way in which judgments are necessary. If my reading of Bradley is correct, judgments are necessary in the way in which deductive arguments are necessary: the relationship between premisses and conclusion is logically necessary. Bradley arrives at this view by reducing judgments to abbreviated arguments and then analysing the judgments by analysing the arguments they abbreviate. As a result, when Bradley says that a judgment is true, 'true' is to be taken as referring to a property of the argument which the judgment abbreviates. The property of argument which Bradley picks here is soundness. Consequently, for Bradley a judgment is true if and only if the argument which the judgment abbreviates is sound. But an argument is sound only if it is valid; that is, if the material conditional formed by conjoining the premisses to form the antecedent and letting the conclusion be the consequent is necessarily true.

Consequently, on Bradley's analysis a judgment is true only if it is necessary in the way in which a valid argument is necessary. This analysis of judgments and the necessity which it imputes to them constitutes Bradley's principle of sufficient reason.

This, of course, only indicates Bradley's view in outline. To make it seem even remotely plausible, we need to examine in detail Bradley's analysis of judgments. And here Bradley's way of arriving at his conclusion is helpful. For out of his analysis of judgments it is possible to abstract the following argument which concisely summarizes his way of arriving at his conclusion.

(1) All judgments are hypothetical.
(2) All hypothetical judgments are abbreviated arguments.
∴ (3) All judgments are abbreviated arguments.

As it stands this argument looks valid, but hardly sound. We need to examine its premises in some detail in order to see the concerns which lie behind them.

Bradley's argument for (1) is not at all succinct. It sprawls through two hundred pages of *The Principles of Logic*. In these pages, Bradley tries to show two things. First, he tries to show that all categorical judgments (i.e. categorical grammatically) have the truth-conditions of hypotheticals. Second, he tries to show that disjunctive, negative, and modal judgments in all of their varieties are to be analysed as hypothetical, categorical, or a combination of the two. Taken together these two parts of the argument are meant to show that (1) is correct, that all judgments are hypothetical.

These parts are of unequal importance. The second part of the argument seems plausible by itself and Bradley spends less time with it. After all, disjunctive, modal, and negative judgments can be represented as functions of categorical judgments, so this part of Bradley's argument at least seems reasonable. The first part of the argument, however, seems to support an obviously false claim. Categorical judgments do not seem to be hypothetical. Thus, this part of the argument forms the linchpin. If Bradley can show that categorical judgments have the truth-conditions of hypothetical judgments, then he will be well on his way to establishing (1). Due to limitations of space, I will focus on this part of the argument for (1). I will assume that if it succeeds, then Bradley has demonstrated that (1) holds.

But even this part of the argument is exceedingly complex. There are many subvarieties of categorical judgments. Still, it is possible to follow Bradley in dividing categorical judgments into two main exclusive groups, universal categoricals and singular categoricals. By making his case with respect to judgments in these two groups Bradley can claim to have shown that all categorical judgments are hypothetical.

The case for universal categoricals is by far the easier case to make — so easy in fact that Bradley declines to make it. He merely points it out to his readers much in the same way as a contemporary philosopher might appeal to the intuitions of his readers. Still, several of the things that Bradley says call for comment. First, there is his use of the term 'judgment'. He defines this term by saying that 'judgment proper is the act which refers an ideal content . . . to a reality beyond the act' (*PL*, p. 10). 'Ideal' here is the adjectival form of idea, so the ideal content of a judgment is the idea or ideas which compose it. A judgment occurs when these ideas are attributed to an object (i.e. to a reality beyond the act). According to this definition, then, a judgment is the act of asserting something about an object.

There is one problem with this definition. Bradley treats judgments as truth bearers, as things which are true or false. It is not clear, however, how a mental act can either be true or false. We can avoid this problem by recognizing that judgment has process/product ambiguity. It can refer either to the mental act of judging or it can refer to the content of that act (i.e. what is specified in the sentence form 'S judged that p' by 'p'). It is in the latter sense that a judgment is true or false. Since Bradley's concern in this argument is with the truth-conditions of judgments, I will take 'judgment' hereafter to refer to the content of an act of judgment or, as we might now say, to a proposition.

This takes care of one problematic term, but two more remain, 'categorical' and 'universal categorical'. A categorical judgment, Bradley states, 'makes a real assertion in which some fact is affirmed or denied' (*PL*, p. 44). 'Real' here seems to mean unconditional. As the context of this particular quotation indicates, a categorical assertion is one in which a subject is said to be connected to a predicate or one in which this connection is denied. Their union or lack of it is the fact which a categorical judgment asserts. Since 'subject' and 'predicate' are not ideas, but things for which the ideas stand, a categorical judgment on this account is a subject-predicate judgment. That is, a categorical judgment has subject-predicate truth-conditions; it is true if and only if the individual denoted by the subject term has the feature denoted by the predicate term (or, in the case of a denial, if the thing denoted by the subject term lacks the feature denoted by the predicate term).

This leaves the term 'universal categorical'. As the name indicates, it is a subject-predicate judgment which is universal; that is, it asserts something about a class of objects. It has the form 'All *A*s are *B*s'. This, however, is not sufficient to define a universal categorical judgment. To use Bradley's language, the class in question cannot be 'a real collection of actual cases' (*PL*, p. 82). His point is that a universal categorical is not merely concerned with actual cases, but with possible cases as well. This is Bradley's way of saying that universal categoricals support counterfactuals. In other words, a universal categorical is a judgment of the form 'All *A*s are *B*s' which entails the judgment 'If this were an *A*, then it would be a *B*' (*PL*, pp. 82-3 and 355-7). If one accepts the claim that the difference between an accidental and a lawlike generalization is that the second, but not the first, supports counterfactuals, then Bradley is claiming that true universal categoricals are lawlike generalizations. Accidental generalizations, on the other hand, are reducible to finite conjunctions of singular judgments — hence they are singular judgments.

Bradley's way of using these terms perhaps indicates why he did not feel constrained to argue his claim that universal categoricals are conditionals. Treating universal categoricals as conditionals gives Bradley a simple account of why universal categoricals support counterfactuals. It is because a universal categorical, a judgment of the form 'All *A*s are *B*s', is about anything which might be an *A* and it asserts of such a thing that if it is an *A* it is also a *B*. Since this is what a counterfactual asserts of a thing which is not but which might be an *A*, it follows that some instantiations of universal categoricals are counterfactuals.

Aside from the ease of this way of explaining the relationship between lawlike generalizations and counterfactuals, there is an additional reason why Bradley may not have argued for this view. It is that it was already in his day on the way to becoming a dogma.[2] This, too, is a reason why Bradley did not defend this analysis at length. He merely states that universal categoricals are hypotheticals and passes on.

The second part of Bradley's case for (1) is considerably more difficult. Here Bradley has to show that singular categoricals are conditionals. Unlike universal categoricals, there seems to be no obvious reason to accept this analysis. It looks wrong. Nevertheless, Bradley does produce an intricate and interesting argument for this conclusion.

He does not, however, advance this argument for all singular categoricals. Rather, he advances it for the class of singular categoricals which seem to him to be the most obvious candidates for categorical status. He argues that even these judgments are conditional, and then extends his claim to cover all singular categoricals. His case thus rests on his claim that he has shown that a particular class of singular categoricals are in fact conditional.

This most obvious class is composed of what Bradley calls 'analytic judgments of sense'. The name is misleading, however, since 'analytic' is not used in a Kantian sense. Bradley calls a judgment analytic if it analyses something, so, as the name suggests, analytic judgments of sense are judgments which analyse what is sensed at the moment when the judgment is made. In his words they are 'judgments which make an assertion about what I now perceive, or feel, or about some portion of it' (*PL*, p. 49). Bradley does not specify exact criteria for identifying such judgments (in fact he denies that there is an exact distinction to be drawn (*PL*, p. 108, n. 7), but he does provide numerous examples. 'This tree is green', and 'I have a toothache', both count as analytic judgments of sense. They are contrasted with synthetic judgments of sense, which are about sense, but not just as it is experienced by the judger at the moment of judgment. Thus judgments like 'This road leads to Rome' (when the judger is in Paris) are synthetic judgments of sense since they are about what is sensed, but as synthesized from different experiences rather than as given at the moment the judgment is made. Bradley's argument that singular categorical judgments are conditional thus rests on his analysis of analytic judgments of sense. He claims that they are not categorical and, consequently, that no other singular judgments are either.

Two considerations back this claim. The first is Bradley's attempt to show that singular categoricals cannot be treated as subject-predicate judgments; the second is his alternative analysis, that they are conditionals. Since the only support Bradley gives for his own analysis is that the first analysis is wrong, the heart of his argument is his critique of the subject-predicate analysis. For convenience in reference, I will call this critique Bradley's abstraction argument.

If I have interpreted Bradley correctly, the aim of the abstraction argument is reasonably clear. Unfortunately, the way in which Bradley initially states this aim makes it seem unduly paradoxical. He introduces it by saying that so-called singular categorical judgments are all false (*PL*, p. 93). However, a few pages later he qualifies this claim to bring out its force. He states that such judgments are false *if* taken as categorical. In his words:

Now I am not urging that the analytic judgment is in *no* sense true. I am saying that, if you take it as asserting the existence of its content as given fact, your procedure is unwarranted (*PL*, 97).

I take this to state the real point of the argument: that so-called singular categoricals are false *if* they are construed as categorical. The abstraction argument is thus a *reductio* on the claim that so-called singular categorical judgments are really categorical (i.e. really have subject-predicate form).

In a schematic form the argument is this.

(4) If a judgment is true, then it corresponds with a fact.[3]
(5) Singular categoricals abstract from fact (*PL*, p. 94).
(6) Judgments which abstract from fact do not correspond with any fact (*PL*, p. 94).
∴ (7) Singular categoricals are false (*PL*, pp. 93–9).

Although the purport of the various premisses is as yet unclear, the argument does look valid (barring unsuspected ambiguities in key terms).

It also looks unsound. While (4) and (5) seem plausible, at least from a traditional point of view, (6) does not. There is no obvious reason why judgments which abstract from fact should fail to correspond with fact. However, a closer examination reveals that Bradley is using 'correspond' in an unusual way and that given this usage, (6) is less problematic than it seems. It is rather premiss (4) which is the controversial premiss. Premiss (4) contains two crucial terms, 'correspondence' and 'fact'.

The first crucial term, 'correspondence', is my term, not Bradley's. I have introduced it because the argument clearly turns on some view about the nature of truth for which Bradley provides no label. Thus, he makes claims like:

There are more ways than one of saying the thing that is not true. It is not always necessary to go beyond the facts. It is often more than enough to come short of them (*PL*, 93-4).

The point here seems to be that judgments are false unless they state the facts exactly, neither adding to them nor subtracting from them. This concern is also present earlier in *The Principles of Logic*[4] and in other places in Bradley's work (*ETR*, p. 225). What emerges from these passages is the view that judgments are true if and only if they bear a certain relation to fact. Following tradition I have called this relationship correspondence.

As the passage I have quoted above indicates, Bradley does not clearly specify what the relation I have called correspondence comes to. This much, however, is clear. A judgment is true if and only if it stands in a one-to-one relationship with the facts, so that each element in the judgment represents some elements in the fact and conversely. This is what I take Bradley to indicate when he says that false judgments come short of the facts or go beyond them.

The third crucial term in (4), 'fact', is what makes (4) so controversial. For Bradley uses 'fact' as a name for the given. In his words:

The fact, which is given us, is the total complex of qualities and relations which appear to sense (*PL*, p. 94).

As subsequent remarks make clear, Bradley does not really think that the given is relational. Although he sometimes describes it in these terms, he is usually careful to qualify such descriptions (see, for example, *ETR*, pp. 176-7). In his view, the given is not a set of discrete elements, but rather what he calls immediate experience. Instead of being atomistic, as empiricists would have it, the given is 'a continuous mass of perception and feeling' (*PL*, p. 95). It is 'a sort of confusion' or 'a nebula' in which the various aspects are blended into a whole (*AR*, p. 419). This nebula is what Bradley calls fact.

These accounts of the crucial terms in (4) indicate why (4) is *the* controversial premiss in the argument. For (4) says that a judgment is true if and only if it stands in a one-to-one correspondence with the given. Since virtually no judgments stand in such a correspondence with any likely candidate for the given, it would appear that (4) would require that most if not all judgments be false. Because it seems so paradoxical to assert this, it is difficult to see why Bradley accepted it. Yet his reasons for accepting it are what make the abstraction argument interesting rather than merely bizarre.

In *The Principles of Logic* Bradley does not question the correspondence theory of truth. He seems to regard correspondence with fact as the only viable account of the nature of truth, although he accepts coherence as the criterion of truth. Consequently, his defence of (4) is a defence of his interpretation of correspondence. It is a best explanation defence. Bradley claims that the only other account of correspondence, the empiricist account, has serious problems which his account avoids.

As Bradley understands it, the empiricist account depends on the claim that distinctions in thought indicate differences in reality. This, of course, is one way to put Hume's claim that things which are distinguishable in thought are really different.[5] What makes this claim important in this context is the fact that the correspondence theory of truth requires that judgments correspond with reality. For if things which are distinguishable are really different, there is no reason at all to require that correspondence hold between a judgment and the entire given. It is sufficient for the truth of a judgment for the judgment to correspond to something distinguishable in experience. And this is what empiricists do require. On their account judgments are true if they correspond with distinguishable things.

None of this satisfies Bradley. He rejects the empiricist claim that things which are distinguishable in thought are really different and with it the claim that a true judgment need only correspond to distinguishable things. His way of doing this, however, is roundabout. He attacks the empiricist view of the given which the claim about distinguishability presupposes. This undermines the empiricist view of correspondence. His criticism is an attempt to show that empiricists have failed to support their view of correspondence adequately.

In order for Bradley's strategy to succeed, he needs to criticize the portion of the empiricist view which supports the claims he wishes to controvert. This portion is the insistence that the given is atomistic. According to this view, the given is composed of simple sensory qualities which exist independently of other sensory qualities. No claim about one sensory quality entails anything about another sensory quality. Since these qualities, or sensory atoms, do not depend on other qualities for their characteristics, and since they are simple, our ability to distinguish two sensory qualities shows that they are different. In this way the empiricist view of the given supports the claims about distinguishability and hence correspondence. Bradley thus needs to attack the assertion that the given is atomistic. In doing so he uses two arguments. First, he claims that an atomistic account of the given is factually false, while, second, he claims that it leads to paradox.

As far as the first criticism goes, Bradley is content to assert that reflection on experience shows that the empiricist account of the given is wrong. As I have already mentioned, Bradley's view of the given leads him to the view that the given is not like a set of atoms. To use his metaphor, the given is a nebula (which as far as I can tell only means that it is not atomistic). In so far as one can speak of such a nebula having parts (and Bradley does so with apologies, *CE*, pp. 631-2), these parts are mutually dependent. They have the features which they have in virtue of their connection with other parts. It is thus factually false that the given is atomistic.

This criticism explains Bradley's position, but hardly justifies it. It is not at all clear that the nature of the given is a factual matter, nor that we can know it through simple reflection. Even Bradley admits this (*ETR*, pp. 159-201).

Furthermore, Bradley's account of the given depends on a claim which empiricists would almost certainly reject, the claim that aspects of the given are mutually dependent. Empiricists would reject this for two reasons. First, they would claim that dependence is a relation and that relations are not given, but are rather the product of mental activity.[6] Second, they would claim that if relations were given, they would be simple impressions like other things which are given and so they would have independent existence. In other words, the empiricist reply to Bradley would be that his criticism in turn presupposes an incorrect account of relations. This focuses the issue on the nature of relations and it is this issue which Bradley's second criticism addresses.

The second criticism is that empiricists cannot explain the role of relations in the given. The official empiricist doctrine, of course, is that no relations are given. But as Bradley points out, if this is so, then it is difficult to understand how what is given comes to be related. Even if one accepts the view that the given is composed of sensory qualities like reds, yellows, and oblongs, it also seems to be the case that some of these qualities are given at the same time. But if this is so, then they are co-present and co-presence is a relation. So empiricists do need to give an account of the relations between sensory atoms. This, Bradley claims, they cannot do.

His criticism is in the form of a dilemma. Empiricists have the choice of treating relations as independently existing impressions (i.e. relations which do not actually relate anything) or as given impressions which actually do relate terms. The trouble is that neither of these alternatives is acceptable. The first leads to an infinite regress, while the second requires giving up the claim that the given is atomistic.

Bradley's more important argument concerns the first alternative. If relations are atomistic (i.e. independent of their terms), then empiricists need to explain how they come to be related to their terms. But it is hard to see how empiricists could do this. If they say that a relation relates relations and terms then the difficulty simply recurs. They now need to give an account of how the relation which relates the original relation and its terms does this. Since this new relation is, like other relations, an independently given item, the result is an infinite regress. This account of relations is non-explanatory.

The second alternative is that empiricists can avoid this unpleasant consequence by giving up the claim that relations are independently existing. On this account the regress is avoided by saying that some of the items in experience are not atoms but molecules. They are composed of related terms. But while this avoids the difficulty, it also requires empiricists to abandon the claim that relations are added to experience by thought.

Either way, empiricists have failed to support the claim that everything which is mentally distinguishable is really different. If relations do not exist except when relating terms, then the terms and the relations can be mentally distinguished without being really different (i.e. independently existing). But if this is so, then the truth of a judgment is not guaranteed by correspondence with distinguishable items in experience. As Bradley points out, these items may not be capable of independent existence, so corresponding with them will not constitute corresponding with fact. If terms are given but relations are not, then it is a mystery how things ever come to be related. Bradley concludes that empiricists have failed to provide an account of the given which supports their view of correspondence.

This completes Bradley's case for (4). He has not argued that the empiricist view is incorrect, but rather that it is at best incomplete. His view seems to be that it is clear that a judgment which corresponds with the given corresponds with fact. It is not clear, due to the incompleteness of the empiricist case, that a judgment which corresponds to an abstracted portion of the given corresponds to fact. Consequently, (4) is preferable to its only serious competitor.

Given this view of (4) it is easy to see why Bradley accepts (5) and (6). (5) says that singular categoricals abstract from fact. This is obviously true in the sense that judgments about specific things are selective. They do not purport to describe completely the given, but rather to describe specific elements in the given. That is, they are abstractive. Premiss (6) likewise seems obviously true. Abstractive judgments, judgments which purport to be about selected aspects of the given, fail to correspond in any element-by-element way with the entire given. But if 'correspondence' means standing in such a relationship, then (6) is obviously true. Consequently (7) follows, and Bradley has given his reasons for thinking that all subject-predicate judgments are false.

As it stands this is a paradoxical conclusion, made more so by Bradley's manner of presentation. The paradox vanishes, however, if this is seen as a *reductio* on the attempt to treat so-called singular categoricals as subject-predicate judgments. Bradley's point is that if such judgments, judgments like 'The tree is green', are treated as subject-predicate judgments, then they are false. Since this consequence is absurd, we should adopt a different account of the logical form of so-called singular categoricals.

Bradley, in fact, claims that so-called singular categoricals are conditionals. In his view · such judgments implicitly suppose that certain conditions obtain, and, on the strength of such an assumption, assert that something else is the case. The implicit assumptions thus form the antecedent of the conditional, while what is explicitly asserted forms the consequent. Take, for example, a judgment like 'This tree is green'. On Bradley's analysis this judgment is about what is immediately given to the judger. The judger asserts that, given present conditions, this tree is green. By analysing such judgments as conditional, Bradley is able to claim that they are about the whole of the given (*PL*, pp. 97–8).

This analysis also has another consequence. It makes so-called singular categoricals, universal judgments. In the above case, the judgment about the green tree fits any situation in which the given has the same form that it had when the judgment is made. Thus the judgment turns out to be universal; it is not about any particular situation or thing, but is rather (as we would now say) a universally quantified conditional (*PL*, p. 104).

This concludes Bradley's case for (1). He has argued that both universal and singular categoricals have the truth-conditions of conditionals. If we grant the plausibility of treating disjunctive judgments, disjunctions of categorical judgments, and negative judgments as elaborations of categorical judgments, then Bradley has shown that all judgments (at least of normal form) are hypothetical. With this his case for (1) is complete.

The remaining premiss is (2). Like (1), (2) represents Bradley's solution to a particular problem, the problem of assigning truth-conditions to hypothetical or conditional judgments. Some conditions, for example material conditionals, pose no problems here, but others, like counterfactual conditionals, pose serious problems. Since Bradley treats both singular and universal categoricals as conditionals which support counterfactuals, he clearly must deal with the problems posed by counterfactual conditionals. Indeed, this is the kind of conditional which he takes as a model for analysis.

There are basically two ways to provide truth-conditions for counterfactuals. One approach is to take them at face value and say that they not only seem to be about unactualized possibilities, but that they are about unactualized possibilities. This approach leads to truth-conditions stated in terms of possible worlds. The other approach is to treat counterfactuals as dealing with the actual world. This requires analysing counterfactuals so that they are not (as they seem to be) statements about possibilities. The most successful analysis along these lines is the metalinguistic analysis. According to this analysis, counterfactuals are either condensed arguments or backed by arguments. They are claims about what is deducible from a body of statements, hence the appellation 'metalinguistic'.[7]

Since Bradley views modalities themselves as properties of judgments, he adopts the second, or metalinguistic, analysis (*PL*, pp. 197–201). For him conditional judgments are abbreviated arguments. They are true if the argument they abbreviate is sound, and false otherwise. This, of course, means that there is in principle no difference between judgments and arguments. The difference is merely a matter of emphasis. When we are concerned with logical consequence we treat judgments as abbreviated arguments, while a concern with the way in which they represent reality will lead us to talk of truth and falsity. Bradley talks both ways according to the issues under consideration.

Bradley begins his analysis by asking the question, 'What do hypothetical judgments assert?' According to his definition of 'judgment', every judgment must make some assertion or refer some content to reality. It is on the basis of this reference that a judgment is true or false, for Bradley holds a correspondence theory of truth (*PL*, pp. 41–2). Consequently, if what the judgment asserts corresponds to reality, then the judgment is true, while if it fails to correspond, then it is false. It follows from this that an answer to Bradley's question will state what a hypothetical judgment asserts, and by doing so, will also state what reality must be like if the judgment is true. Answering Bradley's question thus requires giving truth-conditions for hypothetical judgments.

There is a difficulty here, because it is hard to see what reality must be like if a hypothetical judgment is to be true. Obviously, its truth depends on neither the truth of the antecedent nor of the consequent. This is why Bradley says that neither is asserted. What is asserted is the connection between the antecedent and consequent, but this does not seem to correspond with any fact (*PL*, p. 86). The relationship between antecedent and consequent seems to be more than a factual relationship. It has a logical component.

Bradley's solution to this problem is unsatisfactory, as he became aware (*PL*, pp. 111–12, n. 41), but it does allow us to state his view of the truth-conditions of hypothetical judgments. According to Bradley's view, a hypothetical judgment asserts that reality has a certain disposition and that this disposition is such that if the antecedent of the judgment is taken as true, then because of this disposition, the consequent will also be true.

An example will make this clearer. Speaking of the judgment, 'If you had not destroyed the barometer, it would now forewarn us', Bradley says:

In this judgment we assert the existence in reality of such circumstances, and such a general law of nature, as would, *if we suppose* some conditions present, produce a certain result (*PL*, p. 87).

In other words, a hypothetical judgment asserts that there are certain circumstances and certain laws of nature which, in the presence of an additional condition (i.e. what the judger supposes) result in a further circumstance. The supposal here is the antecedent, while the result òf further circumstance is the consequent. The disposition which is asserted of reality is represented by the scientific law, and the conditions present are the conditions under which the law is operative. A hypothetical judgment thus asserts that reality is characterized by a scientific law which, in the presence of the antecedent and the circumstances under which the law operates, will result in the truth of the consequent.

What this analysis tells us is that a hypothetical judgment asserts that there is a connection between its antecedent and its consequent. It does not, however, tell us anything about the nature of this connection. It merely tells us that if in the appropriate circumstances we suppose the antecedent, then the consequent will result. Bradley attempts to explicate this connection by commenting on the nature of supposing, or, as he puts it, supposal. 'A supposal is', he says,

an ideal experiment. It is the application of a content to the real, with a view to see what the consequence is, and with a tacit reservation that no actual judgment has taken place. The supposed is treated as if it were real, in order to see how the real behaves when qualified thus in a certain manner (*PL*, p. 86).

Although this description is metaphorical, Bradley's meaning emerges from it rather clearly. His point is that hypothetical judgments report the results of thought-experiments. 'Ideal' is an adjectival form of 'idea', so an ideal experiment is an experiment conducted solely with ideas, that is, a thought-experiment. To conduct such an experiment, 'one applies a content to the real', that is, one treats the antecedent of the judgment as true. This is done with the proviso that the antecedent is not actually being asserted, it is only an assumption. This is what Bradley means by saying that it is done with 'a tacit reservation that no actual judgment has taken place'. One then observes the real to 'see' how it 'behaves'. Obviously, we do not literally see what happens, but we can come to a conclusion about what would happen. This conclusion is stated in the consequent. A hypothetical judgment thus encapsulates a thought-experiment.

This quotation tells us nothing about the way we come to a conclusion in an ideal experiment; that task is reserved for the long account of inference which forms the bulk of *The Principles of Logic*. It is clear, however, that Bradley sees this operation as logical rather than as psychological. In his view one of the distinguishing marks of an inference is being an ideal experiment (*PL*, p. 431). As an ideal experiment, a hypothetical judgment is thus an inference or an argument.

We can now summarize Bradley's view of the truth-conditions for hypothetical judgments. A hypothetical judgment is true if the argument it abbreviates is sound.

To determine soundness, one treats the antecedent as a true premiss. To the antecedent one adds premisses stating the relevant scientific laws and premisses describing the circumstances under which the antecedent is assumed to be true. If the consequent of the hypothetical is a logical consequence of this set of premisses, then the hypothetical is true. If it is not a logical consequence, then the hypothetical is false.

This view raises a number of interesting issues, but I will not pursue them here. My concern here is to note that this account of the truth-conditions of hypothetical judgments requires that hypothetical judgments be treated as condensed arguments. This is exactly what premiss (2) states. Hence, this account of the truth-conditions of hypothetical judgments is Bradley's argument for (2).

We can now see why Bradley thinks that all judgments are necessary. It is because, (3), they are condensed arguments. This follows from (1), that all judgments are conditional, and (2), that conditionals are condensed arguments. Since all judgments are condensed arguments, they are necessarily either valid or invalid. Premisses (1) and (2) thus constitute Bradley's principle of sufficient reason. In themselves they are straightforward (whatever one may think of the arguments backing them) and together they require that judgments be necessary.

Understood in this way, 'Bradley's principle of sufficient reason' is more interesting than Russell's criticism suggests. In suggesting that there is some (no doubt obscure) principle which Bradley accepts, Russell was giving Bradley less than his due. He was reinforcing the stereotype of Bradley as a Hegelian idealist who accepts paradoxical views, a Bradley who, as a matter of fact, is found only in the pages of his critics. The real Bradley is far removed from such a position. The real Bradley based his arguments on detailed logical analysis.

NOTES

1. 'Some Explanations in Reply to Mr. Bradley', *Mind*, NS, vol. XIX, 1910, p. 374.
2. See Robert Adamson, *A Short History of Logic*, Edinburgh, 1911, p. 250. This chapter of Adamson's book originally appeared in *Mind*, 1884, as a critical notice of *The Principles of Logic*.
3. Bradley never states this premiss in these words. It is, however, implicit throughout the argument of Chapter II. For example, during the course of

the abstraction argument, Bradley states, 'To make it [i.e. the judgment] both categorical and true, you must get the condition inside the judgment. You must take up the given as it really appears, without omission, unaltered, and unmutilated' (*PL*, p. 98). The second sentence here seems to require that true judgments correspond with fact.

4. *PL*, pp. 41-51. I have discussed the argument in these pages at length in 'Bradley's Argument against Correspondence', *Idealistic Studies*, vol. X, no. 3, Sept. 1980.

5. David Hume, *A Treatise of Human Nature*, Oxford, 1888, p. 18.

6. See, for example, John Locke, *An Essay Concerning Human Understanding*, bk. II, chap. XXV.

7. For a comparison of these approaches, see David Lewis, *Counterfactuals*, Oxford, 1973, pp. 65-77.

CHAPTER 10

Holism and Truth

David Holdcroft

My concern is primarily with Bradley's theory of truth, and the main question I wish to raise is whether it is a consequence of his holism. I shall first outline Bradley's theory of truth, and then say something about holism. I shall conclude by discussing some of the ways in which Bradley's general position is holistic, and their connection with his theory of truth.

The order of discussion that I have adopted follows that of *Appearance and Reality* though I have sometimes drawn on *Essays on Truth and Reality* for clarification or amplification.

I

(i) Reality

Bradley repeatedly says that a theory of truth goes hand in hand with one of reality.

It is impossible, in my opinion, to deal with truth apart from an examination of the nature of reality. Not merely has every one (though perhaps only at the back of his mind) a view as to reality which is sure to affect his result. The very questions as to truth with which a man begins, involve in the end an answer to certain questions about the nature of things (*ETR*, p. 310).

Appearance and Reality reflects these remarks. To begin with there is an account of the nature of reality, which then leads into a discussion of the nature of truth.

Bradley's fundamental thesis about the nature of ultimate reality is that:

Ultimate reality is such that it does not contradict itself; here is an absolute criterion. And it is proved absolute by the fact that, either in endeavouring to deny it, or even in attempting to doubt it, we tacitly assume its validity (*AR*, p. 120).

Three points call for comment. This is a theory of ultimate reality; but Bradley does not claim that we ordinarily experience this reality, or that we can understand what it is like in detail:

What is impossible is to construct absolute life in its detail, to have the specific experience in which it consists. But to gain an idea of its main features — an idea true so far as it goes, though abstract and incomplete — is a different endeavour. And it is a task, so far as I see, in which we may succeed (*AR*, p. 140).

This can be put by saying that if the *general* features of ultimate reality are accessible to thought, its detailed nature is not. Secondly, the criterion is in a certain sense absolute, which means for Bradley that it is not intellectually corrigible. Thirdly, the principle of contradiction is not for Bradley just a formal principle; the thesis that ultimate reality is not contradictory does not mean simply what can be put in the formal mode by saying that any description of ultimate reality must be consistent, but means in the material mode, roughly speaking, that reality is a harmonious and intelligible whole in which there are no 'bare' conjunctions.

Bradley goes on to develop his fundamental criterion:

. . . all appearance must belong to reality. For what appears is, and whatever is cannot fall outside the real . . . The character of the real is to possess everything phenomenal in a harmonious form (*AR*, p. 123).

Moreover, Bradley argues, ultimate reality forms one system, and is experience — in a special sense of 'experience' admitting of no distinction between subject and object.[1] So the development of the initial criterion can be summarized thus:

. . . the Absolute is one system, and . . . its contents are nothing but sentient experience. It will hence be a single and all-inclusive experience, which embraces every partial diversity in concord (*AR*, p. 129).

(ii) Truth

At first sight this account of reality seems rather naturally to suggest absence of contradiction, which in Bradley's terminology amounts to coherence, as the criterion of truth. Indeed, it might be argued that the metaphysics provides a justification for such a criterion.[2] But on reflection it appears that if only the most general features of ultimate reality are accessible to thought, then the project of developing a theory of truth hand in hand with one of reality is less straight-forward than it seemed to be at first sight. For if the detailed nature of ultimate reality is inaccessible to thought, what truths could we formulate about it? So that if by 'truth' is meant 'absolute' or 'unconditional' truth, then it is perhaps not surprising that Bradley concludes that, apart from a small number of unconditional truths about the most general features of reality, there are not, and could not be, any *absolute* truths. A conclusion which, at first sight anyway, seems to leave him without any theory of truth at all.

Briefly, the way in which Bradley comes to the conclusion that, with the exception of truths about the most general features of reality, there are not any absolute truths, is as follows: 'In judgment an idea is predicated of a reality' (*AR*, p. 144). The predicate is not a mental image, but 'a mere feature of content' and as such ideal:

The predicate is a content which has been made loose from its own immediate existence and is used in divorce from that first unity (*AR*, p. 144).

So that whereas in reality everything has two aspects that are inseparable, 'a "what" and a "that"', an existence and a content' which are 'distinguishable only and are not divisible' (*AR*, p. 143), the judgment presents the content, the 'what', as separate from the existence of the subject, the 'that', and so divides what in reality is only distinguishable.

But the fact that it involves a vicious abstraction is not the only defect of judgment. For the subject possesses an aspect that the predicate, because it is ideal, lacks, namely existence. Because this is so:

Judgement is essentially the re-union of two sides, 'what' and 'that', provisionally estranged. But it is the alienation of these aspects in which thought's ideality consists (*AR*, p. 145).

Bradley's point is, I think, that thought divides what in fact is not divided, the 'that' from the 'what'. As a result they have discrepant characters which prevent them from being reunited, for one, the subject, exists, whilst the other, the predicate, is *merely* ideal.

It is at this point, after these thoroughly discouraging pre-liminaries, that Bradley introduces the notion of truth: 'Truth is the object of thinking, and the aim of truth is to qualify existence ideally' (ibid.). But, Bradley maintains, truth can never attain its goal which is 'the predication of such content as, when predicated, is harmonious, and removes inconsistency and with it unrest' (ibid.). This is so since 'because the given reality is never consistent, thought is compelled to take the road of indefinite expansion' (ibid.). So absolute truth is unobtainable.

This highly condensed argument is perhaps the most important of Bradley's arguments designed to show that absolute truth is unobtainable. Certainly, if by a 'given reality' he means one of which we have an experience that we can describe in detail, then it is not difficult to see why in his terms a judgment will inevitably fail in its goal of consistently describing that reality. For suppose the given reality R is a, then our judgment will be of the form 'Ra'. But this will not be a consistent description of R, since no explanation of why a, which after all is different from R, inheres in R has been given.[3] We can try to remedy this defect by stating the conditions x under which R is a, so that our judgment now becomes $R(x)a$. But it is clear that the remedy calls for a similar cure, since a statement of the conditions will involve a new predicate b, and so on.

In this context it is worth mentioning that if sometimes the argument to the conclusion that judgment is incompletable develops out of the contention that predication is inconsistent, it *sometimes* develops out of the contention that judgment, because ideal, is incurably general. As we have seen, Bradley argues that there are important differences between a predicate and the reality of which it is predicated. One such difference has already been noted; the fact that the subject exists whilst the predicate is ideal. But there are at least two other important differences. Firstly, the reality of which a judgment is asserted to hold has an unlimited degree of detail, whereas the content of a judgment does not. Secondly, the reality of which a judgment is asserted to hold 'claims the character of a single self-subsistent being' (*AR*, p. 156) — though at the same time it has the 'discrepant' character of immediacy — while the content of a judgment does not. This seems to boil down to saying that whereas reality is particular, the content of a judgment is general and selective. We can try to remove these differences between reality and judgments by specifying the conditions in which the predicate holds of reality, but this is a cure which once embarked on simply calls for another cure of the same type, and so on.

Undoubtedly, at the root of this argument is a belief on Bradley's part that a judgment must relate to reality in virtue of its own explicit content alone, so that an attempt to relate a judgment uniquely to one part of reality by the use of demonstratives is beside the point.

> Your judgement means what ideally it contains; and contrariwise, what you have not explicitly expressed and included in it is not reckoned. And, if so, no possible appeal to designation in the end is permitted. 'This', 'my', 'now' and the rest will mean once for all exactly what they internally include and so express. Your meaning has always on demand to be made explicit and stated intelligibly within the judgement (*ETR*, pp. 234–5).

However arrived at, the argument that judgment is necessarily incomplete has many variations, as we shall see; but there is a particularly clear statement of it in 'Coherence and Contradiction'.

> The assertion of any object *a* is R*a*. Here, if R is not different from *a*, you have really no assertion. But, if R is different, you either deny this difference and so have a false assertion, or else you qualify R (that is a higher *R*) both by *a* and this difference. Hence you have now asserted a manifold. But, as soon as you assert of *R* a manifold ... there arises at once a question as to the 'how'. You cannot fall back on mere sense ... Hence you have to seek ideal conditions, and this search has to go on indefinitely (*ETR*, p. 229 n.).

The argument that judgments are incompletable seems to develop out of the arguments mentioned earlier, each of which can be seen as raising a difficulty with the supposition that absolute truth is obtainable — with the exception, of course, of truths about the most general features of reality. These arguments are, firstly, that from the ideality of judgment to the conclusion that judgments necessarily introduce a division at a point at which there is none in reality. Closely connected with this conclusion is the argument that predication itself is inconsistent; and closely connected with the contention that judgment is ideal is the argument that judgment is incurably general. And, as we have seen, the argument that judgment is incompletable can be developed from either of these last two arguments. So schematically the overall structure of Bradley's argument is as follows.

Judgment is ideal

Predication is inconsistent   Judgment is incurably general

Judgment is necessarily incompletable

What this brings out is the central importance of the argument
that judgment is ideal in Bradley's thought.

It must be added that not only does Bradley think that —
with the exception of judgments about the most general
features of reality — judgments are incompletable, but that
he adds, for good measure, that if thought were to obtain
its object, truth, it would thereby commit suicide.

> In every judgement the genuine subject is reality, which goes beyond
> the predicate and of which the predicate is an adjective. And I would
> urge first that, in desiring to transcend this distinction, thought is
> aiming at suicide (*AR*, p. 148).

It is not difficult to see why. To attain truth, thought would
have to cease to be ideal, and thus cease to be thought.

No doubt it is possible to argue that I have misrepresented
Bradley in various respects: but it seems incontrovertible that
his conclusion is that absolute truth is unobtainable except
when our subject-matter is the most *general* feature of reality.[4]
In that case, however, it seems that we can hardly take
coherence as the criterion of truth, since there seems to be
nothing for it to be a criterion of. And if it is a criterion it is
a very odd one, yielding the result that, with the exception
of a very restricted set of cases, the property that it is a
criterion of is always absent.

So perhaps the proper conclusion is that Bradley's metaphysics leads to scepticism, and not to the conclusion that
coherence is the criterion of truth.

(iii) Degrees of Truth

Bradley himself acknowledges that this conclusion might be
drawn:

> While admitting that thought cannot satisfy us as to reality's falling
> wholly within its limits, we may be told that, so long as we think, we
> must ignore this admission. And the question is, therefore, whether
> philosophy does not end in sheer scepticism — in the necessity, that is,
> of asserting what it is no less induced to deny (*AR*, p. 154).

After a recapitulation of the arguments already considered, those designed to show that truth is unobtainable, he restates the problem: To attain its object, truth, thought would have to commit suicide. So is there not something incoherent in the project of trying to discover truth? To this he replies:

Thought desires for its content the character which makes reality. These features, if realized, would destroy mere thought; and hence they are an Other beyond thought. But thought, nevertheless, can desire them, because its content has them already in an incomplete form. And in desire for the completion of what one has there is no contradiction. Here is the solution of our difficulty (*AR*, p. 159).

This seems to say that the content of each judgment has something in common with reality, and since it has something in common with it there is nothing inconsistent in trying to approximate more and more closely to it. If this is so, then Bradley is in effect saying that the solution to the problem of the fundamental and unbridgeable discrepancy between the nature of ultimate reality and the nature of thought is the doctrine that truth and reality have degrees;[5] and if this is not what he is saying, it is very unclear what solution he proposes. Certainly, if there are degrees of truth and reality, then, though at the end of the day thought and reality must remain discrepant, the project of describing reality would not be completely pointless, since we can hope to approximate more and more closely to absolute truth.

Setting aside judgments about the general features of ultimate reality, Bradley's theory of the degrees of truth consists of the following apparently logically independent theses.

(a) Truth has degrees.
(b) No judgment is completely true, or completely false.
(c) Every judgment is both partially true and partially false.

(a) Criteria of a judgment's degree of truth

In *Appearance and Reality* Bradley says first what the criterion of a judgment's degree of truth is, and then what the criterion of truth is. This order of exposition is slightly curious since the former would seem to depend logically on the latter. Certainly, in the absence of a criterion of truth, it is difficult to see how there can be a criterion of the degrees of truth, for without a criterion of truth we have no explanation of the term 'truth' in the phrase 'degree of truth'.

Bradley introduces his criterion of a judgment's degree of truth in the following words:

> Our judgements hold good, in short, just so far as they agree with, and do not diverge from, the real standard. We may put it otherwise by saying that truths are true, according as it would take less or more to convert them into reality (*AR*, p. 321).

This is a criterion he repeats many times (see *AR*, pp. 323, 327, 440, and 475). It seems to be intimately connected with his thesis that the judgment '*Ra*' is really of the form '*R(x)a*' *in which the function of the bracketed element* '*(x)*' *is to* spell out the conditions in which *R* is *a*. Clearly this spelling out could be more or less explicit, and Bradley's idea seems to be that the more explicit it is the fewer conditions we would need to add to make the judgment into one that is absolutely true.

But, as Bradley sees, we have no right to call this a test of a judgment's degree of *truth* unless we have a criterion of truth. There is, however, such a criterion which, he maintains, is at bottom the same as the criterion of ultimate reality:

> Perfection of truth and of reality has in the end the same character. It consists in positive, self-subsisting individuality ... Truth must exhibit the mark of internal harmony, or, again, the mark of expansion and all-inclusiveness. And these two characteristics are diverse aspects of a single principle (*AR*, p. 321).

In other words, the test of truth is consistency together with comprehensiveness — what in *Essays on Truth and Reality*, he came to call 'coherence'. Moreover, the fact that this is the criterion of truth explains, Bradley thinks, why his criterion of a judgment's degree of truth really is a criterion of degrees of *truth*.

> Hence to be more or less true, and to be more or less real, is to be separated by an interval, smaller or greater, from all-inclusiveness or self-consistency. Of two given appearances the one more wide, or more harmonious, is more real (*AR*, pp. 322–3).

There are, I think, many problems with Bradley's proposal. But before discussing them, it seems sensible to sketch the rest of his theory to get as clear a perspective as possible. It is important to note that if one thing the doctrine of the degrees of truth is meant to explain is how, given the unbridgeable discrepancy between the nature of thought and that of ultimate reality, the pursuit of truth can be rational, then the doctrine has other roles to play. One question for Bradley's metaphysics is why, if ultimate reality, is as it is, it should appear to be so different; and the doctrine of the degrees of truth and reality is meant to suggest an answer to that problem (cf. *ETR*, p. 273, *AR*, p. 482). And Bradley is also rightly concerned to protest against idea that truth is the province of science alone.

And we shall find that our account still holds good when we pass on to consider higher appearances of the universe. It would be a poor world which consisted merely of phenomenal events, and of the laws that somehow reign above them (*AR*, p. 328; see also *AR*, p. 334).

But if science, morality, religion, etc., all, to some degree, embody the truth, ought we not to ask to what degree they are true, and what contribution each makes to the overall truth? Certainly Bradley thought we should:

And this standard, in principle at least, is applicable to every kind of subject-matter. For everything, directly or indirectly, and with a greater or less preservation of its internal unity, has a relative space in Reality (*AR*, p. 333; see also *AR*, p. 330).

(b) No judgment is completely true or completely false

Given the doctrine of the incompletability of judgment, the thesis that no judgment is completely true is a direct corollary of Bradley's criterion. The thesis that no judgment is completely false is, on the other hand, more problematical. Bradley's claim is that a false judgment can become closer to the truth by supplementation which spells out the conditions on which it rests.

Error is truth when it is supplemented. And its positive isolation also is reducible, and exists as a mere element within the whole. Error is, but is not barely what it takes itself to be (*AR*, p. 173).

Uneasily one feels that supplementation would in many cases leave one with a different judgment from the one that one started with. But the crucial point is that Bradley's metaphysics seems to require a theory of this sort. For if error were not ultimately eradicable, then ultimate reality could not be an all-inclusive and harmonious system.

(c) Every judgment is both partially true and partially false

To my knowledge Bradley nowhere discusses the criterion of

degrees of falsity. But I suspect that he simply took it for granted that this is a judgment's distance from the truth, so that the further away it is the more false it is, and of course less true. In that case (c) is simply a corollary of his criterion and of (b).

(iv) Some Criticisms

Assuming for the moment that Bradley's criterion of (absolute) truth is acceptable, there seems an obvious difficulty with his criterion of a judgment's degree of truth. Since no judgment is completable, we can give no sense to the claim that fewer conditions are needed to complete one judgment than are needed to complete another. However many additions we made to either judgment it is incomplete.

Interestingly, Bradley sometimes formulates his criterion differently, though without any clear recognition that the formulation is different. One such formulation is stated thus: '... the amount of either wideness or consistency gives the degree of reality and also of truth' (*AR*, p. 332). This formulation is, in some respects, an improvement on the previous one since we can at least tell whether a judgment or theory *T* accounts for *more* of the phenomena than another *T′*. But though the fact that it does might be a reason for preferring *T* to *T′* — though without a theory of inductive support it is perhaps not clear that it is — does this new formulation give a degree of *truth*? Since Bradley has to say that we cannot have a completely inclusive theory, so that there is no such thing as *the* uniquely true theory, we cannot say how much would have to be added to any given theory to make it completely inclusive. So though *T*, relative to what we know, is more comprehensive than *T′*, is that a reason for saying that *T* is closer to the truth than *T′*? Might it not turn out that a recalcitrant experience can only be accommodated by a more massive revision in *T* than is necessary in the case of *T′*, so that *T′* has more staying power? Schiller put the point well:

We cannot assume that the road to truth runs in a straight line, that we are approaching truth at every step . . . One might as well assume that the right route up a mountain must always be the one that goes straight for the summit, whereas it may only lead to the foot of an unclimbable cliff, and the true *route* may lead a long way round up a lateral *arête*. This simple consideration really disposes of the assumption that we can declare one theory truer than another, in the sense of coming nearer to absolute truth, without having previously reached the latter; and the history of the sciences fully confirms this inference by furnishing many examples of theories which have long seemed all but completely true and then have had to be discarded, while others which looked quite unpromising have in the end proved far more valuable.[6]

There is perhaps yet a third formulation of the criterion of degrees of truth. The essential idea here is that the nearer to the truth a judgment is the less transformation it will have to undergo to become part of, as it were, *the* true theory. Whilst this idea is intuitively appealing, the difficulty seems to be the same as with the first suggestion. Since the true theory simply is not in principle formulable, what sense can be given to the idea of the transformation necessary to become embedded in it?

It is not clear then that either test gives a degree of *truth*, even assuming that Bradley's criterion is unproblematic. But this assumption is questionable. The problem is that in *Appearance and Reality* he says that 'Truth must exhibit the mark of internal harmony, or, again the mark of expansion and all-inclusiveness, (*AR*, p. 321), which is, I think, meant as a criterion. But on his own showing, no judgment can be either consistent or all-inclusive, so the test picks out nothing whatsoever, unless it picks out those true judgments about the most general features of reality which are said to be absolutely true.

There are, Bradley argues, a number of reasons why, on his criterion, such judgments are absolutely true. Firstly, the denial of these judgments is absolutely impossible, in the sense that the denial of them is self-contradictory: 'It is, indeed, an attempt to deny which, in the very act, unwittingly affirms' (*AR*, p. 476). Moreover, such judgments are all embracing, so rest on no conditions, and hence do not call for completion of the kind that other judgments call for. So the judgments in question are consistent and absolutely comprehensive: 'There are certain truths about the Absolute, which, for the present at least, we can regard as unconditional' (*AR*, p. 480).

It is none the less evident that even if there are judgments whose denial is absolutely impossible, they must suffer from some defects — indeed all the defects that thought, because it is ideal and involves predication, is heir to. This Bradley concedes.

Now in any truth about Reality the word 'about' is too significant. There remains always something outside, and other than, the predicate . . . In brief, the difference between subject and predicate, a difference essential to truth, is not accounted for (*AR*, p. 482).

The conclusion he comes to is 'that, in the end, no possible truth is quite true' (ibid.). Nevertheless there is a distinction to be made between truths that are *intellectually* corrigible, and those that are not, and this distinction replaces that between conditional and absolute truth. But even if the distinguishing feature of truths about the most general features of reality is that they are not intellectually corrigible, they are nevertheless corrigible in the sense that these truths give only a one-sided picture of reality; inevitably so, because thought is but one aspect of reality:

And . . . this self-completion of thought, by inclusion of the aspects opposed to mere thinking, would be what we mean by reality, and by reality we can mean no more than this (*AR*, Appendix, p. 493; see also *ETR*, p. 272).

At the end of the day it is not easy to say whether Bradley thought that there are (absolute) truths that satisfy the test of consistency and all-inclusiveness. But it seems to me that if coherence has a serious claim to be the test of truth, it must be in principle possible for something to pass that test. Moreover, Bradley's account of the criterion of a judgment's degree of truth cannot properly be so called by him unless he is able to give some account of truth itself. As it is, even if coherence is a criterion of truth, Bradley's theory seems to have an unusual feature in that it proposes a criterion of truth, but nowhere says what truth is.

Unquestionably, whatever Bradley thought, the difficulties with treating coherence as a criterion of truth which judgments about the most general features of ultimate reality measure up to, are, on his own showing, formidable. For if such judgments do pass the test, then in spite of the fact that they are ideal, general, and involve predication, and in spite of the contention that multiple predication is inconsistent,[7] then the contention that ultimate reality is one in many and is experience would be consistent. But can Bradley really maintain that? Discussing this case, he says:

Even the judgements that Reality is one in many and is experience, would be untenable, if we meant by these judgements to deny that Reality is in any sense more. But no such denial should be the intention of our judgement. What we really exclude here as senseless is the idea of any 'other' falling outside of our predicate, and able to be set over against it in idea as being itself also an attribute of the Real (*ETR*, pp. 323-4).

But though we cannot say it, reality is in some sense more. And even in the case of this judgment, the predicate falls short of its subject.

It is then perhaps difficult to defend the view that Bradley's solution to the problem of the discrepant nature of reality and thought is successful. But I want now to argue that the kind of problem that Bradley saw arises very naturally on certain quite plausible assumptions, and that this makes it both an interesting and difficult problem.

II

(i) Duhem and Quine

No doubt a holist would deny the existence of atomic propositions and facts, if the notion of an atomic proposition is that of a proposition that is unanalysable (i.e. simple), and whose truth or falsity is independent of that of other unanalysable propositions. But the denial of atomism is obviously compatible with weaker and stronger versions of holism. For instance, Duhem's claim that the physicist can never submit an isolated hypothesis to the test of experience, but only a whole set of hypotheses, can be construed as a rejection of atomism for physical hypotheses, since the confirmation of any particular hypothesis obviously goes hand in hand with that of others if he is right. Even more clearly, Quine's statement that 'our statements about the external world face the tribunal of sense experience not individually but only as a corporate body',[8] is a rejection of atomism. But Quine's thesis represents a stronger version of holism than does Duhem's, since it is meant to apply to any statement whatsoever, and to imply the interconnectedness of all sentences of a theory. It is not clear to me what argument, over and above

Duhem's argument about confirmation, Quine has for his stronger thesis, but it does seem to be unquestionably stronger.

(ii) Implications for Truth

A strong version of holism such as Quine's seems to imply that different and incompatible theories are consistent with whatever observations we have, or will have; so that our actual experience now and in the future is inadequate to determine the truth of our theories. Presumably, Quine would accept this, since he accepts the stronger thesis that different and incompatible theories are compatible with all possible observations, a thesis which he suggests follows from the thesis that our statements face the tribunal of sense experience as a corporate body.[9] Moreover, if we combine Quine's thesis that our sentences form an interconnected fabric, with the possibility that reports of future experience may not be consistent with existing theory, then whatever our convictions about a given theory, for all we know we may be forced to revise that theory.

So the combination of holism together with an empiricism that makes experience the ultimate arbiter seems to lead to the following conclusions: however convinced we are of the truth of a given theory we may be forced to revise it, and this process of revision once embarked on may be interminable, since the new theory may itself need revision, and so on. Moreover, if this process could terminate, we still would not have the true theory, since different and incompatible theories are compatible with all possible experience.

What account of truth is possible on this account? A correspondence theory of the sort worked out by the Logical Atomists would seem to be ruled out, since it requires an ontology of atomic facts and propositions. But what can be said positively?

In *Word and Object*, Quine sketches an answer:

What reality is like is the business of scientists, in the broadest sense, painstakingly to surmise . . . The question of how we know what there is is simply part of the question . . . of the evidence for truth about the world. The last arbiter is so-called scientific method, however amorphous.[10]

He goes on to say that:

At any rate scientific method, whatever its details, produces theory whose connection with all possible surface irritation consists solely in scientific method itself, unsupported by ulterior controls. This is the sense in which it is the last arbiter of truth.[11]

This, however, does not mean that Quine endorses Peirce's idea that truth can be defined as 'the ideal theory which is approached as a limit when the (supposed) canons of scientific method are used unceasingly on continuing experience'.[12] For the notion of limit is undefined for theories; and anyway, incompatible theories are consistent with all possible experience.

At this point it is hard not to see sceptical conclusions looming: but Quine thinks that they can be avoided.

It is rather when we turn back into the midst of an actually present theory, at least hypothetically accepted, that we can and do speak sensibly of this and that sentence as true. Where it makes sense to apply 'true' is to a sentence couched in the terms of a given theory and seen from within the theory complete with its posited reality.[13]

What saves this conclusion from the charge of relativism is, Quine argues, simply the fact that we take our notion of scientific enquiry seriously, so that we change our beliefs 'here and there for the better', and in so doing modify our conception of the posited reality.

I don't see why Quine should not say that from the point of view of our scheme at a particular time we may speak as if some things are true not merely relatively; it is only when we see that our scheme may have to change that we are prevented from doing this.

(iii) Implications for Ontology

Quine's holism is presumably epistemological. One interesting question is whether it has any ontological implications. This is a difficult question. It is not clear to me that the holism *per se*, strictly speaking, even rules out an ontology of independent particulars and atomic facts; though it would make this ontological posit epistemologically idle, thus ruling out a correspondence theory of truth. And even if it does rule out an ontology of atomic facts, it surely does not rule out one of the facts; at most it requires them to be interconnected. It is true that Quine himself has changed from positing an ontology of individuals, sets of individuals, sets of sets, etc., to postulating a field theory. This, however, is not due to a change in his conception of holism, but to developments in science; there are good reasons for preferring field theory.[14]

So I conclude that epistemological holism itself does not entail a unique ontology.

III

(i) Bradley and Holism

Bradley does I think subscribe to a version of epistemological holism that is very similar to Quine's. The obvious point to seek a parallel with Quine's views is in the argument that judgment is necessarily incompletable. It is true that in *Appearance and Reality*, the argument rests initially on logical considerations. Because its subject exists whilst its predicate is merely ideal, a judgment is not consistent. The remedy is to specify the conditions in which the predicate holds. The function of this condition is clearly to give an explanation, so at this point considerations to do with explanatory adequacy are introduced. Unfortunately, Bradley argues, a question in turn arises of the way in which the predicate involved in the condition relates to reality necessitating the introduction of a new condition, and so on. This seems to amount to the conclusion that a proper grasp of any judgment involves a wider system of judgments. And if it is protested that this is hardly a demonstration of the interconnectedness of all judgments, Bradley certainly writes at times as though this is what it in effect is.[15]

Now it would be very difficult to argue that any substantial conclusions follow from his version of epistemological holism on its own, any more than they do from Quine's. It is only when the holism is combined with a thoroughgoing empiricism that is fallibilist and non-foundational, and makes experience the ultimate arbiter,[16] that the theory of truth presents a series of difficult problems. For the thoroughgoing empiricism rules out the possibility of an appeal to a reality that is in principle non-observable, so we cannot say that our judgments could be true even though we cannot know whether they are or not; whilst epistemological holism rules out a correspondence theory of truth. Moreover, if no judgment/theory is completable because it inevitably rests on conditions which it cannot explain, then it is difficult to see what room we have for the notion of *the* uniquely true theory. So it is not difficult to see how, at this point, someone might conclude, as Bradley did, that unless we can make sense of the idea that judgments/theories can approximate to the truth, though they can never attain it, the inevitable conclusion is scepticism.

Schematically, the argument of the last paragraph can be set out thus:

Judgment is necessarily incompletable   Empiricism + fallibilism
                    ↓   ↓
No correspondence theory   Experience is the ultimate arbiter

No uniquely true theory

No doubt the thesis that experience is the ultimate arbiter, so that no aspect of reality is in principle unobservable, is not ontologically neutral; so it cannot be argued that no ontological assumptions are involved in the argument. However, if I am right, the account that Bradley gives of ultimate reality is not assumed by the argument, so it would be wrong to say that his problem over truth arises simply from his view of the Absolute, though it is true that his metaphysics are one source of the problem. But is this really so?

(ii) Bradley and Ultimate Reality

I argued that Quine's holism *per se* has fewer ontological implications than might be thought at first sight; although the way in which he combines epistemological holism with a thoroughgoing empiricism seems to raise a number of problems for the theory of truth, it does not tell us either how those problems can be solved, or what ontology to adopt. Analogous remarks apply, I think, to Bradley.

As I said, if his account of ultimate reality is correct, then the theory of truth has a series of additional complications to deal with, but it seems to me that there is a problem over truth for Bradley whether or not his account of the Absolute is correct. This is so because all the material necessary to mount an argument that there is no uniquely true theory is present without the theory of the Absolute. The question whether this substantial ontological thesis is correct is a separate question that cannot be settled by noting that Bradley is an epistemological holist, an empiricist, and a fallibilist; just as the question whether Quine's commitment to an ontology of individuals and sets of individuals is correct, cannot be settled in the same way.

In conclusion I should say that in drawing this parallel between Quine and Bradley I do not wish to suggest that they have a great deal in common, for there are deep differences,[17] but rather to see just what is Bradley's problem over truth, and to suggest that since it arises out of a number of quite plausible assumptions it is no small problem.

NOTES

1. *AR*, pp. 128–9: 'I mean that to be real is to be indissolubly one thing with sentience. It is to be something which comes as a feature and aspect within whole of feeling, something which, except as an integral element of such sentience, has no meaning at all.'
2. See S. Haack, *Philosophy of Logics*, Cambridge, 1978, p. 91.
3. Predication is treated as part of 'Appearance' in the first part of *Appearance and Reality*, and so condemned as contradictory.
4. And even this conclusion is not unproblematic: see sect. (1), para. iv, of this essay.
5. See *AR*, p. 431: 'The Absolute is each appearance, and is all, but it is not any one as such. And it is not all equally, but one appearance is more real than another. In short the doctrine of degrees in reality and truth is the fundamental answer to our problem.'
6. F. C. S. Schiller, *Logic for Use*, London, 1929.
7. By 'multiple predication' I mean predicating *a* and *b* of the same subject without differentiating separate aspects of the subject to wihich *a* and *b* respectively belong. This is prohibited by Bradley's version of the principle of non-contradiction. See *AR*, p. 501.
8. W. V. O. Quine, *From a Logical Point of View*, New York, 1961, p. 41.
9. In 'On Empirically Equivalent Systems of the World', *Erkenntnis*, vol. 9, 1975, p. 313, Quine writes: 'This holism thesis lends credence to the underdetermination theses. If in the face of adverse observations we are free always to choose among various adequate modifications of our theory, then presumably all possible observations are insufficient to determine theory uniquely.'
10. W. V. O. Quine, *Word and Object*, Cambridge, Mass., 1960, pp. 22–3.
11. Op. cit., p. 23.
12. Ibid.
13. Op. cit., p. 24.
14. W. V. O. Quine, 'Whither Physical Objects?', in *Essays in Honour of Imre Lakatos*, ed. R. S. Cohen *et al.*, Dordrecht, 1976, p. 498.

15. See *AR*, p. 409. This too is Wollheim's view. See his *Bradley*, Harmondsworth, p. 94, where expounding Bradley's doctrine he writes: 'From which it follows that it is impossible to talk of one fact without talking of all facts: for the only correct way of talking of one fact is to assert it in the apodosis of a conditional judgment whose protases contains the assertion of all other facts.'
16. See 'On Truth and Coherence', *ETR*, p. 202.
17. Bradley, for instance, would not have agreed with Quine's dictum that scientific method is the highest court of appeal. For a discussion of a different parallel between Bradley and Quine see M. Cresswell, 'Can Epistemology be Naturalised?', in *Essays on the Philosophy of W. V. O. Quine*, eds. W. Shahan and C. Swoyer, Hassocks, p. 109.

CHAPTER 11

Bradley on Relations*

Brand Blanshard

Empiricists pay scant attention to relations and as a rule give inadequate accounts of them. Rationalists pay them more heed, but differ widely in their accounts of them. The reason in both cases is that it is so hard to find the right place for them among the objects of our knowledge. On the one hand, they are not objects of sense. We hear tones, for example, but not the relations between them; when we hear two notes of a melody, we do not hear the relation of before and after between them; even when we hear two notes in a chord, we do not hear the relation of higher and lower, for that is inaudible; it is not in the realm of sound at all. Are such relations, then, grasped by the intellect? That does not seem right either. Hearing two notes as successive or perceiving two trees as one to the right of the other seems hardly an intellectual operation. Kant thought the best we could do with relations of time and space was to make them neither data of sense nor concepts of the intellect, but 'forms of pure perception', falling somewhere between the objects of sensation and thought.

Relations seem more challenging as one comes to realize how many kinds of them there are. Every number, for example, is related to every other, and when you include all their multiples, roots, fractions, squares, and cubes, you have an infinity of infinities of relations in this field alone. Every pain and pleasure has a degree of intensity, and these are all interrelated. I am the same person I was yesterday, yet also different, and whatever changes shows at every minute these relations of identity and difference. One painting is more beautiful than another, one act more moral than another, one speech more eloquent than another, one history more

*The final section of this paper, defending a non-Bradleian type of internal relation, has been omitted with the author's permission.

comprehensive than another, and these relations seem inexhaustible, even in kind. My mind at this moment contains desires, sensations, ideas, and emotions; all of them are interrelated. The sheet I am writing on is white, smooth, and oblong, and these qualities have relations of inherence in a subject — coexistence, mutual exclusiveness, and utility to an end. The judgments I express in consecutive sentences are either consistent with each other or inconsistent, but are related in either case. I am related to other persons as brother, husband, cousin, neighbour, fellow citizen. I am related by perception to a thousand books, papers, pens, pictures, and implements that are round me in the room. I am tired as the result of a walk this afternoon and am related by innumerable other strands of causation to the past. All this is only a beginning. We are spiders living in a vast web of relations. It is no wonder that philosophers have doubted and debated how to deal with these elusive filaments.

On this point, Bradley seems to have been confident. He has a theory that applies to all relations alike, and we shall begin with a brief sketch of the places he assigned them in the world. He gave them three different places; for they appeared, though in different senses, at three levels of experience. First is the level of immediacy. This is the earliest form of consciousness in the history of either the individual man or the race, and it consists of what James called a 'buzzing, blooming confusion'. The child confronting the world in his first days has, or rather is, a field of consciousness. We may be sure that he has pleasures and pains, hears sounds, sees colours, and feels pressures and even fears. But as yet he picks none of these things out of the continuum, and takes none of them for what they are. There are no spoons or bottles, dog or cat, father or mother, recognized as such, in his world. What exactly that world is like we do not know and shall never know, for if by an impossible feat we should put ourselves back into it with our mature minds, that act itself would destroy its character. No doubt beneath its surface, numberless qualities are being felt; and these qualities are related to each other not only by difference, but by many more specific relations. But neither the qualities nor their connections have been singled out for notice, still less for the process of naming, which will do so much to aid in the process of fixing and holding them later on.

Very well, immediacy is the bottom level, the primitive swamp, from which knowledge emerges. What does such emergence mean? It means making explicit the things, qualities, and relations present only implicitly in the primitive continuum. How is this done? In general by the forcing of ideas to the surface through tensions within the continuum. The child reaches for what has given him the taste of sugar and is brought up short by the taste of salt; next time he hesitates. The want for the sweet taste is still there, but so is the memory, however vague, of the salt, and the collision tends to force the thought of both into explicitness. The child notes the difference, and soon begins to note also the conditions under which each quality appears. Further, groups of qualities tend to cluster together, and to move together across his field of vision; these he comes to recognize as things — the red ball, the kitten, the pleasant bottle. Recognition is incipient perception; it is the grasp of what is given in the light of a character brought over from the past. And with the coming of perception we are fairly launched into the world of common sense, the world of things and qualities in relation. It is a realm in which there are no loose qualities, but all are grouped into attributes of this thing or that; in fact it is the world we live in for the rest of our days, the familiar, orderly, lawful, stable, dependable world of common sense.

If immediate experience is the first level in Bradley's account of the mind, this plateau of things in relation is the second. It is not merely the plane on which we live; it is the plane to which the great succession of common-sense philosophers have devoted their attention, such people as Hobbes and Locke and Hume and Mill. Because they deal with the things and persons and qualities we know, they seem peculiarly close, congenial, and intelligible to us. Bradley differed from them profoundly and in the most uncompromising way. In the opening three chapters of *Appearance* he brings his most withering rhetorical artillery to bear in the attempt to blast this familiar scene to pieces. Though we live in a world of things in relation, he dismisses their relations as self-contradictory, and so destroys that world as a whole. At the end of Chapter III, after twenty-three short pages,

Bradley writes: 'The reader who has followed and has grasped the principle of this chapter, will have little need to spend his time upon those which succeed it. He will have seen that our experience, where relational, is not true; and he will have condemned, almost without a hearing, the great mass of phenomena' (*AR*, p. 29).

One might think that this conclusion would give a good reason for stopping there. But over four hundred pages are still to come. The fact that common sense is riddled with contradictions does not mean for Bradley that there is nothing real at all. For, peeping through the interstices of the web of relations in which we live is a realm of reality in which the contradictions are transcended and everything is melted and blended into an intelligible whole. Bradley struggles with stubborn patience to show how the facts of separate persons and things, of error and evil, of qualities and relations, must after all be elements in one seamless experience. He thus belongs to that tribe of mystical monists to whom empiricism and change and even the plurality of things are unsubstantial phantoms among which it is foolish for reflective minds to rest. He is of the tribe of Parmenides and Plotinus, of Spinoza and Hegel. The mysticism appears in the contention that, in the third and highest stratum of development, the realm of things and relations, of human discourse and discursive thinking, will as such have disappeared. It is not that they will be destroyed altogether, for the Absolute consists of its appearances. It is rather that appearances change their appearance when seen in a wider context, and, seen in their absolute context, may be thoroughly transformed. In such an experience the realm of things and relations resolves itself into a single undivided immediacy, an immediacy which contains all the salvageable remnants of ordinary experience, but blended into a whole as immediate as that from which the long ascent began.

These are the three planes of Bradley's ascent to the Absolute. Of the first of them and the mind's movement to the second we shall say nothing, partly because the battle waged by James, Ward, and Bradley with the associationists over the way experience begins has now been won, partly because in the first chapter of *The Nature of Thought*[1] I have said what I have to say about the emergence of judgment from immediacy. In this paper I shall consider two points only: Bradley's attack on the common sense world of qualities and relations; and his attempt to show that they can be absorbed into the higher immediacy of the Absolute. Both are brilliant dialectical forays, but they do not now seem as decisive as when I first read them, sixty years ago.

I

1. Bradley's main argument against the reality of relations is stated in Chapter III of *Appearance and Reality*. It is in substance this. Suppose that A and B are connected by the relation R. Now R is not an adjective of either term, taken singly, nor of both together. It is a distinct entity which lies in some sense between them. 'The links are united by a link, and this bond of union is a link which also has two ends; and these require each a fresh link to connect them with the old . . . If you take the connexion as a solid thing, you have got to show, and you cannot show, how the other solids are joined to it' (*AR*, p. 28). How are A at one end and B at the other related to the entity that comes between them? If it takes a relation R to provide the bond between A and B, it will take another relation R^1 to provide the bond between A and R, and another still, R^2, to provide the relation between A and R^1. And this leads straight to an infinite regress. The same can of course be said about R's relation to the term at the other end, B. This demands a like set of intermediaries, and also a set that has no end. Now if both A and B are connected with R by chains that have no end, then they are not connected at all. Their relation depends on the completion of two infinite series, which is in both cases impossible. Thus to say that they are intelligibly related is a self-contradiction.

Is this argument valid? I think not. Bradley has been misled by a metaphor. He is thinking of a relation as if it were another term, as if A-R-B were three beads on a string, and then the relation of R to A or B will present the same problem as that of A to B. But R is not the same sort of being as its terms. It is neither a thing nor a quality. It is a relation, and the business of a relation is to relate. When I say that one box is *in* another, I am not saying something cryptic and unintelligible — unless indeed I make *in* a third box outside the inner one and inside the outer one; and then I must go on to produce an explosiion of boxes that would be shattering. Bradley seems determined to find mystery where there is none; and if he can pull a metaphysical rabbit from his hat in the form of the little word 'in', it is surely because, like magicians of a cruder kind, he has put it there. There is nothing unintelligible in saying that five is a larger number than three, that a league is longer than a mile, that Titian was an older man at death than Keats. If such statements are not intelligible, then nothing is. Of Bradley's argument here, Broad has remarked: 'Charity bids us avert our eyes from the pitiable spectacle of a great philosopher using an argument which would disgrace a child or a savage.'[2] We must accept the point, if not the rhetoric.

2. After arguing, convincingly enough, that there can be no qualities without relations and no relations without qualities, Bradley argues that even with relations, qualities cannot be joined. Of any that seem to be joined, he says:

> there is hence a diversity which falls inside each quality. Each has a double character, as both supporting and as being made by the relation. It may be taken as at once condition and result, and the question is as to how it can combine this variety. For it must combine the diversity, and yet it fails to do so. *A* is both made, and is not made, what it is by relation; and these different aspects are not each the other, nor again is either *A*. If we call its diverse aspects *a* and *α*, then *A* is partly each of these. As *a* it is the difference on which distinction is based, while as *α* it is the distinctness that results from connexion . . . *A*'s unity disappears, and its contents are dissipated in an endless process of distinction (*AR*, p. 26).

I have failed to see the force of this argument because I fail to see the difference between *a* and *α*. Let us suppose the relation between *A* and *B* is that of *larger than*; *A* is larger than *B*. That means that *A* must possess something on which the difference is based, in this case its margin of size, which is *a*. Let us agree that, noticing the difference, we see that it is the margin of size that makes the two distinct. The reference to this element is the result of our distinguishing the two sizes, and it is called *α*. But surely these two elements are the same. What differentiates the things compared is the margin of size possessed by A; what we note as the result of distinguishing is precisely the same. If it were not, our process of distinction would be worthless, since it would have missed the real difference. Bradley's attempt to find in A two differing parts, one the basis of difference, the other the result of distinction, is thus itself a distinction without a difference. The two parts, a and α, are fictions. And even if they existed, the argument would still fail. For its point is to show that the chasm between the two is unbridgeable. This is supposed to be shown by argument (1), which we have just found to be untenable.

So far as I can see, these are the only arguments for the unreality of relations given in the vital Chapter III. Most of this chapter is devoted to a proof, which is hardly necessary, that relations are impossible without qualities, and qualities without relations. And yet, as we have seen, Bradley can say at the end of the chapter: 'The reader who has followed and has grasped the principle of this chapter, will have little need to spend his time upon those which succeed it'. It is curious that with two shots of what we can only call a dialectical popgun he should really have supposed that he had dispatched the whole world of man and things, qualities and relations. However, in fairness it must be added that he did not rely on these exclusively. There are arguments that he adduced elsewhere which should be considered along with these.

3. In dealing with the unity of the lump of sugar, Bradley denies that there is any characterless 'it' to which the qualities belong. He then suggests that in asserting about the sugar we are perhaps predicating one quality of another, or of the rest as a whole. To use his own emphatic words:

One quality, A, is in relation with another quality, B. But what are we to understand here by *is*? We do not mean that 'in relation with B' is A, and yet we assert that A *is* 'in relation with B' . . . No, we should reply, the relation is not identical with the thing. It is only a sort of attribute which inheres or belongs. The word to use, when we are pressed, should not be *is* but only *has*. But this reply comes to very little. The whole question is evidently as to the meaning of *has*; and, apart from metaphors not taken seriously, there appears really to be no answer. And we seem unable to clear ourselves from the old dilemma. If you predicate what is different, you ascribe to the subject what it is *not*; and if you predicate what is *not* different, you say nothing at all (*AR*, p. 17).

The trouble with this neat dilemma is that you can readily seize it by its first horn. Bradley is assuming that the 'is' here used must be the 'is' of identity, and he sets aside the 'is' of predication as 'not taken seriously'. But this would rule out the greater part of our judgments. Of course we do make judgments of identity. If I say, 'Cicero was Tully' or 'salt is sodium chloride', I mean to identify two apparently different things. According to Professor Wollheim, Bradley wanted to reduce all judgments of the subject-predicate form to statements of identity.[3] If he did, he was clearly wrong. When, looking at the sugar, I say, 'That cube is white', I am doing nothing so absurd as identifying a shape with a colour. I am using *'is'* in a different sense, the sense of predication. In this kind of relation of subject to predicate Bradley finds an impenetrable mystery, which he calls 'marriage without a *modus vivendi*'. He finds it utterly unintelligible how a cubical shape could be white or the surface of an apple smooth, or sugar sweet. And we must grant to him that such assertions are absurd if they assert identity. A shape is not a colour or smoothness, nor is sugar identical with sweetness. But surely we are saying nothing so absurd. We are saying that white *belongs* to the cube, that the surface of the apple *possesses* smoothness, that sweetness may be *attributed* to the sugar. Bradley dismisses all these relations as illegitimate and unintelligible. But are they? Certainly most men, even after reflection, would not consider 'sugar is white' a leap into intellectual darkness. No doubt it is possible to raise questions about such statements. *Why* does the lump look white, the surface feel smooth, the taste seem sweet? These are definite questions that have definite causal answers, and to one who, like myself, holds causal necessity to involve logical necessity, they are questions which, if yet unanswered, are at least in theory answerable. There is nothing contradictory in them. Bradley's dilemma, therefore, has a broken first horn. You cannot say that if subject and predicate are different, then the judgment must be thrown out as meaningless. Even if it needs analysis, it remains a meaningful statement.

4. These seem slender grounds on which to base the abolition of the worlds of science and common sense. It has been

suggested by C. D. Broad, however, that these are not the sort of considerations that really moved Bradley.[4] The true consideration is rather that terms and relations alike are abstractions from an underlying unity, and one has no right to assume that these elements, when dissected out from this unity, remain what they were within it. 'Everywhere in the end a relation appears as a necessary but a self-contradictory translation of a non-relational or super-relational unity' (*ETR*, p. 309, n. 1). It is not merely the primeval swamp of vague feeling from which our terms and relations have been dredged up; it is also the present field of consciousness, the mass of our present immediate experience. The terms and relations used in judgment are torn by abstraction from this unity, and what reason have we to suppose that the naked abstractions that we drag out of it are unaffected by their violent removal? The pens and papers, tables and chairs before us are made of the experience offered us, but they are not *as such* there in the continuum; they are the bare bones extracted from it by our own disruptive and stripping intellect. And the distortion will never be made right again, never made an intelligible whole, until all these disjointed bits and pieces are brought together again into unity.

Broad is probably right in thinking that considerations of this kind had much to do with Bradley's curt dismissal of the common sense world. Are they convincing? To a certain extent they are. The sharply discriminated things and qualities of daily life are constructed out of the material of experience; there is no other quarry to draw them from; and the abstracting and construction are done by our own intelligence. The things around us are not part of the permanent 'furniture of the world', since they are the creatures of our own minds and of forebears like ourselves. They are evanescent fabrications, like the palaces of Prospero, and will no doubt disappear with their creators.

Are they therefore to be called unreal? I confess that I do not see why they are less real than the continuum out of which they emerged. Of course so far as the fabric of qualities and relations is found incoherent, they must, as Bradley held, be appearances only. But it takes more than the firecrackers of Part I of *Appearance* to blow them away. If we are to call them unreal, must we not carry the argument on to the very continuum from which they are quarried? That continuum is composed of experience, and Bradley lays it down as self-evident, to be sure, that experience is the ultimate stuff of the world. Whatever is, is experience. But this is dogmatic and disputable. Indeed to most contemporary science and philosophy it is false. Unless astronomy, for example, is to be thrown aside as an illusion, there was a universe long before sentience emerged from it, a universe that will persist long after consciousness has had its day. For Bradley to build the universe itself out of one of its own transient products was arbitrary and question-begging.

Many, including myself, who were carried away by the confident dialectic of Part I of *Appearance* did not quite realize what they were accepting. To show that something was contradictory was to show that it was unreal, and if it was unreal, then it could not as such exist or occur at all. Was this credible? Bradley, as he sat at his desk penning those chapters, never moved his pen, never in fact wrote them at all, for time, motion, and change are all self-contradictory. If asked, he would say that he sat in his chair, but of course he did not, for all spatial relations are likewise masses of inconsistency. His room, his books on the wall, the window, the Christ Church meadows, the Isis in the distance, these too were of course illusions. A quadrangle or two away lay the Merton library, where the big leather folios are bound to the shelves by chains so that light-fingered young monks should not make off with them, and where the ghost of Duns Scotus is alleged to linger. Only no monks ever worked there; there could have been no Duns Scotus; for that matter there never was an England; there was no Conqueror, no Shakespeare; history is a mirage. Strictly speaking, no other persons have ever lived, for they would have been related to each other by likenesses and differences all of which were illusory. Indeed Bradley himself was an illusion. His thoughts were events in time, which therefore could not have happened; they were related to each other at least by sequence and association, which, as relations, were unreal. The very reasoning by which Bradley proved the world of common sense to be unreal must therefore itself have been unreal.

Strangely enough, the force of this line of reflection was

never fully realized until G. E. Moore used it in his 'Defence of Common Sense'. The argument was simply that when the whole world of unquestioned conviction about time and space, change and movement, self and others was weighed in the balance against the metaphysical argument designed to show them unreal, common sense enormously outweighed its rival in the balance. It was far more likely that there was something amiss in the abstract argument than that the world in which men had lived securely for millenniums was one vast illusion. One would think that this argument would carry weight with Bradley, since coherence with experience was his test of truth. But he preferred to trust some rather wiredrawn considerations of logic.

II

With the conclusion of the first part of the *Appearance*, the world of common sense lay in ruins, and one might have thought the case for scepticism complete. But the very weapon with which Bradley had laid about him so destructively in the first part of his book he used in the second as his main tool of construction. That weapon and tool was the law of contradiction. What violated it had no standing and was condemned as illusion. But illusion is not just nothing at all. Something that may, as such, fail the test of contradiction. may by rearrangement be made into something consistent and restored to a degree of reality. The judgment that the Greeks defeated the Persians at Marathon in 390 BC is an error and untrue. But it is not unadulterated illusion. It can be rendered consistent with itself and with what we know of history merely by substituting a four for a three. Bradley takes under review again the structure of time and space, of things, of causality, of selves, of judgment and truth, which he had dealt with so hardly, and concludes that there is much in the realm of appearance that can be salvaged. True, it can be saved only by being shown to be coherent, and he has already proved to his satisfaction that it cannot be coherent as a plurality of related things or qualities. If unity and coherence were to be achieved, relations must be left behind. How could this be done? Bradley thought he had his cue in the immediacy he had already shown to lie below the level of explicit qualities and relations. This immediacy embraced implicitly the qualities and relations that emerged from it; why should there not be an immediacy above them into which they were all absorbed again, but now in unbroken unity? Finite things and events would dissolve into attributes which flowed into each other by necessity; the world would be a unity in which there were no accidents and no separable parts to contemplate; indeed, since there could be no separations, contemplative thought itself would have merged with its objects and as such disappeared. Thus the end of the road for human enlargement lay in a mystical state in which selves and things were alike transcended in a kind of nirvana.

The many ingenious considerations by which Bradley attempted to find coherence again in his bombed-out world we cannot here examine. The question we must ask is whether he has shown in principle that during the journey or at the journey's end the philosopher can dispense with relations. I do not see how the answer can be anything but No.

1. Consider first Bradley's Excalibur of destruction and construction, the law of contradiction. Is it not evident that, whether used destructively or constructively, its use depends on relations at every point? To show that between two alleged facts there is a contradiction is to admit a twoness and a difference that were already there; the finding of a contradiction only introduces a further difference where the existing difference sufficed to prove unreality. More significantly, since contradiction is itself a relation, and relations are unreal, contradiction itself must be unreal, and the law of contradiction which spells it out must be untrue. And how can you introduce as a test of truth or reality that which is itself untrue and unreal? By his own theory of relations, Bradley is using one illusion to dispel another.

The same holds of Bradley's use of consistency and coherence in the work of construction. Two judgments, to be true, must be consistent; but consistency is a relation and therefore an unreality; so the judgments are not really related after all. Coherence, as he conceived it, goes further. It involves both consistency among all facts and internecessitation among them. This system includes a perhaps infinite number of facts and relations, and the whole vast structure is vitiated by plurality and relatedness. It may be replied that at the end of the road neither plurality nor relations remain; they have been lost through transfiguration in a higher state. But then the aim of thought is not at truth after all. Its end is not the comprehensive understanding which we have been so often assured was its goal. Indeed truth itself has become an illusion.

2. This is worth seeing in another way. Bradley tells us that truth embraces two things, a content of thought on the one hand and on the other an object of which it is true. In the brilliant second chapter of the *Logic* he argues — successfully, I think — that that of which the judgment is true is neither its grammatical nor its logical subject, but a 'reality beyond the act' of which the content of subject and predicate is jointly asserted. Is the aim of thought to know or understand this reality while remaining distinct from it, or actually to identify itself with the real? In *The Nature of Thought* I argued that the relation of thought to object was a relation of potential to actual, that for thought to reach its referent would be to develop itself into identity with its object. And I still think that thought is a teleological activity in the sense that its ultimate controlling end is the full understanding of reality.

But understanding is one thing and identification is another. I no longer believe that the aim of thought, in particular or in general, is to lose its identity in its object. When I think of 'Dragons of the prime,/That tare each other in their slime', I am not trying to become these creatures, nor when I think of Gibraltar is my thought trying to convert itself into rock. Bradley too at times seems to espouse this denial. 'No idea in the end can, strictly as such, reach reality; for, as an idea, it never includes the required totality of conditions. Reality is concrete, while the truest truth must still be more or less abstract' (*AR*, p. 351). Yet he also says that as thought nears reality at the end of the process, it refuses to stay 'abstract'; it rushes across the bridge that divided it from its object and embraces and coalesces with it. 'There is a subject and a predicate, and there is the internal necessity, on each side, of identity with the other side. But, since in this consummation the division as such is transcended, neither the predicate nor the subject is able to survive. They are each preserved, but transmuted' (*AR*, p. 352). In achieving the Absolute, thought and truth 'commit suicide'. If one may compare small things with great, my own reflection has followed the opposite course. I do not know what it would mean for thought to become Gibraltar, even the transmuted Gibraltar that is 'somehow' contained in the Absolute. And in declaring this suicide, Bradley is deserting what he has long been presenting with eloquent persuasiveness as the philosopher's aim, the achievement of complete understanding, the grasp of an all-comprehensive and necessary system of *truth*. Now you cannot at once maintain that this is the ultimate end of thought and also that this same end is the suicide of thought, truth, and system all together.

3. It may be replied that discursive or relational thought is necessary as a ladder, but that it may be thrown down once we have scaled it to the top. That was Wittgenstein's method in his baffling *Tractatus*; a meaningful result had been attained by a series of steps which in the light of the result were meaningless. This will not do. Once more you cannot have it both ways; you cannot say both that the rungs are rotten and that they are not. If you ask us to accept your conclusion because it has been reached on a series of solid rungs, you cannot also expect us to accept it once you dismiss them as worm-eaten. If they are sound, you cannot expect us to jettison as worthless what has carried you safely through. Now Bradley does obviously believe in the discursive reasoning that he has used throughout the *Logic* and *Appearance*; he is impatient and even scornful of those who would question it. To those of us who have followed with admiration the illuminating reasoning of these two books, it is not good enough to be told at the end that, in view of an ineffable vision, all this subtle analysis and cogent argumentation is to be brushed aside like a spider's web. When mysticism and logic come in conflict, logic commonly wins.

My own choice is to preserve the ladder and forfeit the empyrean to which it is supposed to lead. It is not that I should reject an Absolute or question Bradley's main account of the philosophic enterprise. That enterprise is to start anywhere or with anything and keep pressing the question, Why? The question can be answered only in terms of a necessitating context. One explains X by A, B, and C, given which X has to be what is it. But can one stop with A, B, C? No; the question must be renewed with each of them, and thus the circle of determinants grows larger. Can one fix its circumference anywhere? Certainly not with present knowledge; the circle started by the pebble dropped in the ocean, or by the flower in the crannied wall, moves out beyond the horizon. As one follows it further, one becomes convinced, with Bradley and Spinoza, that the same would be true wherever one dropped the stone, indeed that every point on every circle is a point of intersection between many lines of connection, causal and necessary, and that the world is a vast network of such explanatory lines. There is no reason to think that any thing or any event falls outside this network, or that the disappearance of pebble or flower would not be registered in the remotest star. It is this infinite web-work of connections, visible throughout to the eye of intelligence, even if for the most part unseen, that constitutes for me the Absolute. There is no need to travel the long road only in the end to be drawn with every other recognizable thing into an all-devouring bog.

4. There is another point to consider about Bradley's merging of all relations into a fog or bog. We are told that though nothing would be discernible, everything would be there. Nothing, of course, falls outside the Absolute, for that would leave it partial and incomplete. The obverse side of this is that everything that exists, everything that in any sense *is* finds inclusion there. But this is contradiction again. For we are expressly told that phenomena, as phenomena, do not find inclusion there. The bookshelves that fill the wall opposite me contain thousands of distinguishable existents and thousands of distinguishable relations. Are these members of the Absolute? Not for Bradley, for as they stand they are shot through with inconsistencies; and in the Absolute they are represented by surrogates which are their real selves and from which all vestiges of the illusory have vanished. That means that the books, the colours, the letters that I see have

vanished also. But if so, then these things are *not* in the Absolute; they are *as such* excluded. Indeed the Absolute has been eviscerated of the phenomenal world as a whole. Thus Bradley faces a dilemma. Either he admits phenomena as such into the Absolute or not. If he does, he is admitting what, by his own insistence, is unreal and illusory, and thus has an Absolute no longer. If he does not admit them, his Absolute is not all-comprehensive and dies by privation. The things and relations of common life may be illusions, but illusions exist; they are not mere nothings. A place must be found for them in the Absolute, and it cannot be done.

NOTES

1. *The Nature of Thought*, London, 1955.
2. C. D. Broad, *Examination of McTaggart's Philosophy*, I, London, 1933, p. 85.
3. R. Wollheim, F. H. Bradley, Harmondsworth, 1959, p. 75.
4. Broad, op. cit., pp. 86–98.

CHAPTER 12

F. H. Bradley's Metaphysics of Feeling and its Place in the History of Philosophy*

James Bradley

I want to present a simple and strictly historical thesis: that neither Bradley's position in the history of philosophy, nor any important aspect of his metaphysics, can properly be understood without reference to the theory of immediate experience.

More often than not Bradley calls immediate experience 'feeling'. And I shall follow him in this. For while he has been variously cast as Hegelian, as a rationalist, as a platonist, as essentially a British Empiricist, as a critic of empiricism, and as a mere aberration in an otherwise unspoiled philosophical culture, the term 'feeling' usefully conveys what is in fact the central thrust of his metaphysics. He attempts, that is, to secure and guarantee the monism of the German post-Kantians, yet not through Schellingian intuition or Hegelian dialectic, but by means of a transformed account of the native Lockean theory of sensation — an account which would establish his own work as the legitimate issue both of British Empiricism and German Idealism.

Unlike others, then, I will not be interpreting Bradley's philosophy in terms of logical form, as paradox, metaphor, or analogy; nor psychoanalytically, as a symptom of infantile or linguistic neurosis. My claim is that if Bradley is to be understood, he must be understood in terms of the substantive content of his thought and of the theoretical problematic in which it was developed.

*This paper owes much to the teaching and inspiration of Professor D. M. MacKinnon and Mr. Gerd Buchdahl.

I

The central factor in Bradley's problematic is, I believe, that the thinkers of his generation perceived the radical intellectual and social changes which took place in their time as a series of dislocations or disunities — above all, in terms of a dichotomy between nature and spirit. On the one hand, the new scientific discoveries were being philosophically elaborated in mechanistic, epistemologically dualist, and agnostic terms,[1] while on the other hand, the available alternatives lacked cogency — as the critique of Matthew Arnold mounted by both Green and Bradley indicates. Arnold himself had in fact perceived that a 'time of criticism' was needed, during which 'the ideas of Europe' could penetrate the national culture; but, as Edward Caird insisted, the real 'age of criticism' could be inaugurated only by philosophers who had actually studied those ideas.[2]

Now the German post-Kantians had directly addressed the nature–spirit problem. In this regard, as against the reductive, mechanistic materialism of the French Enlightenment, their achievement is the qualitative differentiation of nature and society. They did not, however, abandon the Enlightenment ideal of a fundamental unity of both, and in line with this ideal they set out to resolve what they saw as Kant's dualism between consciousness and things-in-themselves. Thus, for the early Schelling, nature and spirit are the equivalent expressions of an identical subject-object which is their eternally present, pre-given source and origin, and which as such is at any time accessible by means of an esoteric intellectual intuition. In contrast, Hegel, in the *Phenomenology of Spirit*, develops a historical dialectic which manifests the exoteric realization of reason in the social order. Consequently, the identical subject-object is not for Hegel a given but a product; only now, in the epoch consequent upon the French Revolution, can it be retrospectively recognized to have been *an sich* from the start.

As is evident everywhere in their work, it is the reconciling identical subject-object of the post-Kantians which constitutes the connection between the British Idealists and their German predecessors. Yet this connection, properly understood, does not turn them into 'Anglo-Hegelians'. For all abandon the dialectic of history as the road to monism.

Briefly, the difficulty was that even nature had a history now. The vast dimensions of cosmological and evolutionary time were perceived as eroding the significance of human development, and, from the early 1870s onwards, the new astrophysics lent increasing support to the view that the universe was moving towards a final state of quiescence.[3] In consequence, the qualitative differentiation of nature and society no longer needed to be made; the problem was their reconciliation. And in this situation it was hardly likely that socio-historical experience would be seen as offering an adequate ground or basis for the identical subject-object. Even Caird's evolutionary Absolute was first of all established and defended as the necessary outcome of the German tradition, while Green's monism was arrived at by way of a critique of empiricism and Kantianism, and Bosanquet's derived from a logical criterion of coherence or wholeness. In order, however, to understand Bradley's account of the identical subject-object as grounded on the theory of feeling — i.e. his *ratio cognoscendi*, the guaranteeing foundation of his thought (and my sole concern in this paper) — it is necessary to specify more closely the problematic in which it was developed.

II

T. H. Green is of course a crucial influence. To overcome that 'heavy burden on the human spirit'[4] which he sees as a consequence of the empiricist antithesis between spirit and nature, Green criticizes Locke and Hume in terms of a disjunction: either the real is nothing more than a flow of discrete sensations, in which case knowledge of relations, as the work of the mind, cannot be knowledge of reality; or the order of sensations is determined by relations, and the real is thus in the last resort the work of the mind.

Green's disjunction owes a great deal to his immediate native predecessors, especially James Mill. His interpretation of British philosophy — Hume as sceptic rather than naturalist — is a retrospective account of the consequences of Mill's view of the world as the structureless abode of pure, particular feelings. And his theory of Eternal Reason is exactly the converse of that view: if feeling is structureless, mind alone must constitute the ordering structure of the world.

Now Bradley endorses Green's critique of the dualism of mind and matter inherent in empiricism and Kantianism (cf. *ETR*, p. 199). But he rejects Green's version of the identical subject-object as Eternal Reason. Green indeed asserts that the Eternal Reason may be indifferently viewed as feeling or thought.[5] Yet because he assumes with the empiricists that sensations or feelings are structureless, discrete particulars, he either treats them as an unintelligible surd, and thus loses his unity, or he asserts that the order of experience can only be the product of relating Reason, and thus, in order to preserve the unity, abolishes the feeling. Against Green's dualism, Bradley will interpret feeling, not as a series of discrete sensations which requires a structuring mind, but as a continuous whole of content constituting a non-relational unity of subject and object. And against Green's rationalism, Bradley will uphold the Reidian 'instinct' of his well-known epigram on metaphysics (*AR*, p. x; cf. *PL*, p. 591, *ETR*, p. 228) — he will try with this theory of feeling to preserve the distinction between thought and existence.

In discussing the origins of his theory of feeling, Bradley himself refers to the psychology of Aristotle and of Hegel as his sources (*PL*, p. 515). And this, though usually ignored, is of some significance. First — hardly surprising in the Oxford of his day[6] — he mentions Aristotle, not Plato. And the reference is to Aristotle's denial of psychological atomism; his view of sense-content as a kind of continuum which persists through and in change and is the ever-present basis of every stage of experience. Secondly, Bradley cites Hegel's *Philosophy of Mind* (para. 399 ff.), where Aristotle's view is presented in terms of immediate feeling and goes hand in hand with a genetic or developmental theory of the individual and the race: feeling as the first stage of mental evolution. Bradley starts, then, neither with Hegel's *Phenomenology*, nor with his *Logic*, but with his psychology (cf. also *AR*, p. 508 n., *ETR*, p. 153). And supported by Wundt's theory of 'total feeling', psychology always remains an integral element in the presentation and defence of Bradley's own account of feeling.[7]

But what of course transforms the psychological theory of feeling into the core and basis of Bradley's thought are the specific metaphysical functions which that theory has to perform. And here he owes a great deal to his nineteenth-century predecessors in the empiricist tradition – particularly J. S. Mill.

For Mill set out to replace Hamilton's doctrine of the relativity of mind and matter, Ego and Non-Ego, as the basic data of consciousness, with his own neutral stuff of discrete feelings. Of course, Mill himself admits that the continuity of feeling is as real as the sequence, but confesses that this is unaccountable, a 'final inexplicability'.[8] What conclusions Green drew from this we know. But to Bradley, reading Green and Mill together, a different conclusion could be drawn. After Mill's confession, the ground is ready for feeling to be defined, with Hegel, as a continuous whole; and, with that, it is only a short step from Mill's position to feeling taken, in Mill's manner, as both psychologically and logically primary – a creature at once mental and metaphysical. Bradley's all-too-evident ambiguity here is a result of grafting Mill's sensationalism on to the original unity of the post-Kantians.[9] And it is these two sources which account for the subjective language in which he will always elaborate his monism, even though feeling is in fact held to be neither subjective nor objective in nature (*AR*, p. 128, *ETR*, p. 159). Yet, so understood, Bradley's feeling will at least allow him to avoid the difficulties presented both by Green's rationalism and Hegel's dialectic in establishing the ultimate unity of nature and spirit.

III

The use to which Bradley puts feeling conceived as a given non-relational unity can be simply stated: from *The Principles of Logic* onwards his main doctrines have that theory as their premiss (cf. *AR*, p. 494). Of course, Bradley is regarded as an intellectualist, at least to the extent that while it is admitted he maintains a supra-rational conception of Reality, the doctrines which entail that conception are held to rest on purely logical or internal analyses of our concepts. His account of relations, for instance, is universally presented as if it were modelled on Hegel's critique of the Understanding. But it is then difficult to know why he refuses to follow Hegel's dialectical logic into the realm of Reason. And this refusal only becomes intelligible when it is recognized that Bradley's own critique of thought is prosecuted from the start on a thoroughly sensationalist, if anti-atomistic, basis.

Such a view does not, however, carry the unlikely implication that every one of his arguments is premissed on the theory of feeling. When, for example, in Chapter II of *Appearance and Reality* he is considering the Spencer–Huxley account of relations as independent, term-like entities which are given as separate impressions or feelings alongside the terms they relate, Bradley can hardly reply merely by invoking his own alternative theory of feeling. Instead, he convicts his opponents of incoherence, i.e. of offering an account of relations which fails to explain their relatedness. And this done, he can then go on to argue (*AR*, chap. III, para. 1) that relations are the work of the mind, i.e. that the objects of cognition are constituted in and by our cognitive activity itself.

Now it is here that we meet the idealist dimension of Bradley's thought — the most significant register of his debt to Hegel and of his kinship with Green and Bosanquet. For all agree that there is no such thing as the direct apprehension of particulars, whether ideas, sense-data, physical objects, or anything else. And this position renders especially significant the otherwise unexceptionable point that all our ideas or concepts are essentially contrastive in nature, i.e. that they cannot be introduced on their own but are necessarily bound up with one another. For, once granted that there are no directly apprehended particulars, this essential character of ideas also becomes the essential character of ideally constituted objects. Because all the property-terms by which we can characterize determinate objects are essentially contrasted with others, and because we have no knowledge of objects otherwise, then the characterization of an object as possessing a quality is at the same time its characterization negatively as not possessing others. The red object is thus essentially not-blue; its contradictory is its contrary and all its relations are internal or essential to it. In short, its identity is an identity-in-difference.

So far Bradley and the idealist concur. But the ground on which he advocates these doctrines is markedly different from theirs. Bosanquet, for instance, following Hegel, regards what is given as no more than the indeterminate 'this' of present perception. And he maintains that, as such, it is completely assimilated in the process of cognition; the sensible particular is nothing outside the mediating system of universal concepts. Now Bradley agrees that sensation or feeling — as non-relational — fulfils none of the conditions of knowledge of objects *qua* known — hence the areas of accord already mentioned. Nevertheless, he maintains that the specific 'this' comes always as continuous with or embedded in a non-relational whole of feeling (cf. *PL*, pp. 51-6, 94-8, and 659; *ETR*, pp. 174-6). And it is on account of its holistic character that Bradley denies that feeling is reducible to ideas or relations. Explicitly insisting that if there were no given whole the relational form would be unquestionable (cf. *ETR*, p. 190; *CE*, p. 674), he argues that in fact our knowledge of objects both depends upon, and is condemned as incoherent by, feeling so understood. In consequence, Reality cannot be identified with the system of thought.

This is all clearly evident in Bradley's account of relations in Chapter II, paragraphs 2 and 3, of *Appearance and Reality*. Usually of course, his position there is held to rest on a logical or internal incoherence in the concept of terms and relations as such. But that is Hegel's view,[10] not Bradley's. Bradley's argument, rather, is that while on the one side a term is known only as it is differentiated in virtue of its relations, on the other side it is given as an element in the whole of feeling — and so 'cannot wholly be made by', but 'must come to', its relational differentiation (*AR*, p. 25; cf. pp. 159 and 501, and *ETR*, p. 193). As such, a term has a 'double nature' (*AR*, p. 26) as both 'given' and 'made'. And while no hard-and-fast line can be drawn between these two aspects, neither can they be reconciled in any higher synthesis of dialectical logic. For in the nature of the case, the term *qua* given cannot be assimilated to or identified with its relational differentiation, i.e. it cannot be rendered intelligible (para. 2). And on account again of the sensible nature of a term (para. 3) — the argument here does not work equally from both sides like Hegel's, but depends on the term *qua* given —

relations cannot 'bear a relation' (*AR*, p. 27) to their terms in the proper sense, i.e. relations do not, as they claim, constitute the natures of their terms.[11] Thus the relational form is condemned to incoherence in any attempt to explain fully the nature of the connections we find in the world.

It is of course often suggested that in Chapter III of *Appearance and Reality* Bradley is either assuming or implying the ridiculous view that relations do not relate, i.e. that they are not relations. But in fact his point is that while relations indeed approximate to, or 'inadequately express' (*AR*, p. 125), actual connections, these connections are not relational in nature. So relations *do* relate for Bradley, but not because they themselves have any relating power. Rather, relations relate only in virtue of the non-relational unity given in feeling. Far from constituting the connections we find in the world, it is upon the given unity that the relational form depends (cf. *AR*, pp. 125 and 512; *ETR*, pp. 200, 231 n., and 239; *PL*, pp. 695-6).

Bradley's account of relations is, then, premised upon the theory of feeling (whatever may be thought of that). Yet I cannot adequately defend such an interpretation of all his main doctrines here. It would require too much space, for instance, to show how, far from upholding the rationalist view that, as an absolute necessity of thought, the law of non-contradiction is also an apprehension of logical necessity in the being of things, Bradley's definition of consistency in fact rests on the given unity of feeling (cf. *AR*, pp. 123-6, 461-2, 504, and 508; *ETR*, pp. 312-14). Or, again, that when in Chapter XIV of *Appearance and Reality* he defines reality as experience, 'the very ground on which [he] stand[s] ' is, as he says, that experience is given as 'a whole' (*AR*, p. 128). But even though assertion is no substitute for argument, I hope I have at least said enough to suggest that, once recognized as premised upon the theory of feeling, Bradley's doctrines are quite distinct from those with which they are normally identified.

Such a view must not however be taken to imply that the theory of feeling itself remains fixed and unchanging from *The Principles of Logic* to *Essays on Truth and Reality*, despite the difficulties all too obviously attached to it. Admittedly, Bradley's thought is usually regarded as having been presented in its completest form in *Appearance and Reality*, *Essays on Truth and Reality* being treated as a collection of supplementary essays. But this is far from being the case; the theory of feeling in fact undergoes radical development in the course of Bradley's career. And so it had to.

In *The Principles of Logic* the whole of feeling is little more than an anti-atomistic device — Mill with the continuity put in, so to speak. As such, it is described as a 'congeries of related phenomena' (*PL*, p. 8 n.), which is said both to contain relations (*PL*, p. 94) and to be non-relational in nature (*PL*, p. 96). Yet its main purpose is already clear: to secure the conditional nature of judgments as abstractions from 'the presented whole' (*PL*, p. 97) and so guarantee the distinction of thought and existence against a 'cheap and easy Monism' (*PL*, p. 591). In line with this intention, feeling had more or less become an unreservedly non-relational whole by the time of *Appearance and Reality*. Yet nowhere in that work does Bradley make any attempt to secure or defend it as such. In fact he is guilty there of treating the theory of feeling as self-evident and unquestionable, no doubt encouraged by the confluence of varied sources which, as we have seen, impelled him towards it. And it is precisely this confluence of sources which in *Appearance and Reality* leads Bradley to present feeling in so confused a fashion — as merely subjective and psychological in nature, as a genetically prior 'stage' of development and, more properly, as a logically prior ground. But even though he never quite gives up Hegel's genetic theory, nevertheless Bradley's mentalist tendencies in *Appearance and Reality* are more a matter of his debts to Hegel's psychology and Mill's sensationalism reinforcing each other than of any significant element in the theory of feeling itself. For by the time of *Essays on Truth and Reality*, Bradley had developed an account of feeling which is not only purged of the earlier obfuscations, but also shifts the post-Kantian concern with the demonstration of the identical subject-object on to a wholly new basis. And here his greatest debt is to his critics.

IV

Not surprisingly, the theory of feeling had to face serious challenge from philosophical psychologists like Ward and James.[12] They concur with Bradley in rejecting an atomistic, in favour of a continuum, theory of sensation. But they maintain in different ways that the presentational continuum is relational in nature. Such a view Bradley cannot of course accept: the given non-relational unity is the premiss of his metaphysics. And this makes the question of non-relationality doubly difficult for him. For Bradley is claiming, not (as is usually thought) that there is, impossibly, an 'experience' of unity without an experiencing subject, but that the non-relational unity of subject and object is given and manifest as such *within* the subject-object relation of knowledge. And he attempts to secure this crucial claim in his well-known but none too well understood essay 'On Our Knowledge of Immediate Experience' (*ETR*, chap. VI).

Bradley's starting-point here is a remark made in criticism of him by G. F. Stout. And this, though usually ignored, is of some importance in specifying his exact intentions. Stout says: 'Immediate experience is in no sense *knowledge of itself*. It does not *characterise itself* either as being mere feeling or as being this or that sort of feeling' (my italics).[13]

Now Bradley of course agrees that there is no such thing as immediate knowledge. But he puts Stout's statement in the form of a question: 'How can immediate experience *make an object of itself . . . know about itself?*' (*ETR*, p. x, my italics; cf. pp. 160 and 181). And here he is not asking how, impossibly, feeling can 'know itself' in the sense of become self-conscious, or be anything more than immediate and unknowable, outside of the subject-object relation of knowledge. Rather, the problem at issue is the epistemic status of feeling. In asking how feeling can have 'knowledge of itself', Bradley is referring to and taking up *Stout*'s definition of that phrase and turning his critic's assertion into a question: Does the given non-relational unity of feeling 'characterize itself' as such at the cognitive level?

Now as non-objective and non-relational, feeling cannot be a presentation in any usual sense (cf. *PL*, pp. 109, n. 19, and 517 n. 8; *CE*, p. 377 n.), nor can it properly be said to stand

in any relation to the objective world (*ETR*, p. 177).[14]
Consequently Bradley argues in Chapter VI of *Essays on
Truth and Reality* that the unity of feeling manifests itself
at the level of subject and object by means of the role it
plays in the cognitive determination of both terms. And it
is by means of that role that the given unity characterizes
itself as such, i.e. as the non-objective 'condition' and 'background' of the subject-object world, which is 'verified by
its working' (*ETR*, pp. 182 and 188) in the processes of
objectification.

Bradley is thus presenting in this chapter what, since
Dewey, we would call a 'functional' account of the role of
feeling. And he arrives at that account by means of an
analysis of what, since Dewey, we would call individual
problematic situations. The situations that Bradley analyses
are indeed almost trivial in what the Deweyites would call
their 'normality' and 'concreteness'. But while there is no
space to examine them here, their import is clear enough:
in Chapter VI of *Essays on Truth and Reality*, Bradley's
treatment of feeling has moved from the confused anti-
atomism of *The Principles of Logic*, through the mentalism
and dogmatism of *Appearance and Reality*, to a theory
which is grounded in the nature of our investigative experience
and which finds there the basis and justification for metaphysical philosophy. Bradley has anchored the identical
subject-object of the post-Kantians, not in intuition, or
dialectic, or 'reason', but in what his opponents too confi-
dently call the 'empirical' world.

Chapter VI cannot, then, be regarded as such a watershed
in Bradley's thought as his Deweyite commentators naturally
claim, using it as a lever with which to include him in the
already over-populated pantheon of proto-pragmatists.[15]
But nevertheless, as their enthusiasm for the essay suggests,
it has a significance in modern philosophy which British
commentary has notably failed to appreciate. This can, I
think, best be shown through a brief comparison with
Deweyite pragmatism.

An enlightened Deweyite steeped in Dewey's *Logic: The
Theory of Inquiry* (New York, 1938; henceforth *LTI*), and
unusually well-informed about Bradley, would be readily
prepared to admit that his colleagues, even Dewey himself,

have made mistakes in interpreting Bradley's development. After all, he could equally well point out that Bradley systematically misunderstood Dewey's concept of 'practice'. But scoring exegetical points would not be to his purpose. Rather, he would want to acknowledge both the historical importance of, and pragmatist debt to, Bradley's transformation of the empiricist doctrine of sensation: his shift from atomistic particulars to the whole of feeling or 'total field' (*LTI*, p. 124);[16] his treatment of that whole as a logical ground, without lapsing into any kind of foundationalism in which the given is regarded as the 'really Real' or as the source of indubitable knowledge; and, above all perhaps, his move from the ocular imagery and causal model of perception or representation, to 'function'. Moreover, he would admire the originality of Bradley's method in Chapter VI: examination of the individual problematic situation or specific 'enquiry' in which the total field or situation is, in Bradley's words, 'grouped round and centred in the object' or investigation (*ETR*, p. 180; cf. *LTI*, p. 124).

Beyond this point, however, our enlightened pragmatist would not go. He would indeed agree with Bradley that immediate experience itself is non-relational — but (cf. *LTI*, p. 124) he would hold it to be purely a matter of investigative practice whether we regard it as plural, i.e. as a matter of given 'existences' (*LTI*, p. 522), or as a total field. Again, he would agree that in the 'inquiry-situation' feeling functions as materials-source and critical corrective. But he would see it as no more than that, i.e. as no more than a phase of empirical method. For while he would grant that Bradley has escaped the Kantian fallacy of unification — locating the unity of the sensory manifold in a Transcendental Ego — he would see him as still enmeshed in the post-Kantian fallacy of unification: locating unity in an identical subject-object. And these are fallacies because, for the pragmatist, the problem of unification is solved by the nature of enquiry itself: the unification that our experience requires is constituted precisely by the consummatory outcome of enquiry. Thus with his theory of feeling Bradley is guilty of generalizing and hypostatizing the character that properly belongs to the resolution of individual problematic situations (*LTI*, pp. 533–4). To be sure, the pragmatist would readily admit that

in divesting himself of the cumbersome machinery of trans-
cendentals, intuition, and dialectic, and in resting his theory
of unification on the nature of 'enquiry', Bradley has placed
the traditions in which he works on a new basis. But he
would maintain that in doing so Bradley has also unwittingly
shown the bankruptcy of those traditions, for it is precisely
the nature of enquiry which renders a metaphysics of experience and Reality otiose. In other words, Bradley's transformation of the theory of the given, and his enquiry-based
regeneration of metaphysics, lead him — and with him both
British Empiricism and German Idealism — straight into
Deweyite pragmatism.

There is no denying the sweep and power of such a reading
of Bradley. Its legitimacy cannot of course be debated here,
but at least it indicates something of Bradley's significance
for contemporary philosophy: he keeps his old wine in
new bottles.

It does not, however, rest easily there. Indeed, Bradley
himself is always disarmingly ready to admit that his theory
of feeling, and the doctrines premised on that, are not without
severe difficulties. What, then, does he regard as the ultimate
rationale for such a confessedly intractable metaphysics?

V

Throughout all his writings, Bradley's tactic is to impale us
on the available alternatives, recapitulating the relative
advantages of his own position as he does so. He relies, in
other words, on what might be called historical-critical
considerations; the theory of feeling and its consequences
are established neither deductively nor inductively, but in
terms of their coherence and comprehensiveness in relation
to the extensive range of questions and difficulties in British
and German philosophy which constituted his problematic.
Bradley's reasoning is formed, to use Wisdom's words, 'not
like the links of a chain but like the legs of a chair'.[17]

Thus the theory of feeling provides a basis for a Reality
conceived in the post-Kantian manner as an identical subject-
object. Nevertheless, in Bradley's view the theory of feeling
allows him, not only to avoid what he regards as the abstract

Ego and dualism of Kant, but also to dispense with Hegel's dialectical logic (cf. *ETR*, p. 278). And while for Bradley as for Hegel the Reality is not as such a given, at least Schelling's insistence on the need for some kind of given remains, though without his guaranteeing mechanism of intuition (cf. *PL*, p. 654). This is replaced by Mill's feeling, which itself is transformed into a non-atomistic and functional doctrine of sensation. The theory of feeling further preserves the distinction between thought and existence, while knowledge and truth (not discussed here) can be regarded both with Hegel as expressions of the one Reality, and with the empiricists as a matter of practical efficacy. Similarly, the doctrine that Reality is experience is not the assertion of some strange world-stuff or hidden essence, but an indication of positions rejected and a complex register of the Lockean and post-Kantian traditions in which Bradley stands. And as he himself says, his metaphysics breaks down the barriers between nature and spirit, 'poetry and fact' (*ETR*, p. 444; cf. *AR*, pp. 434–9).

Now it is, I suggest, this historical-critical rationale that Bradley would have us weigh and which sustains him through all his turnings and windings. And it is on this basis that, alongside his ready acknowledgement of the difficulties involved, he can also maintain of his doctrine of Reality, 'to doubt it logically is impossible' (*AR*, p. 459). Bradley is not here claiming that his metaphysic has the status of a body of logically necessary truths, nor is he endowing it with a spurious finality — he does not remove philosophy out of history in the manner of post-Hegelians like Schopenhauer or Kierkegaard (cf. *AR*, p. 5). Rather, the logical indubitableness of a metaphysic is for Bradley a matter of its coherence and comprehensiveness in relation to the range of issues and alternative positions in philosophy (cf. *ETR*, pp. 17–18). And the point is, it can only be met in those terms. The formal logician's disjunction 'true or false?' is as inappropriate to the complex historical-critical structure that constitutes a metaphysic as is either the claim to atemporal necessity or a mere historicist reductionism.

I conclude, then, that Bradley is engaged upon the transformation of empiricist and post-Kantian philosophy into a metaphysics of feeling. So understood, he is not an aberration, nor a surrogate for less digestible thinkers; his elaboration of the theory of feeling and its implications gives him the status of an original. Indeed, unless the theory of feeling is recognized as the core and centre of his thought, he will continue to haunt Anglo-Saxon philosophizing like an unlaid ghost. And, where it is recognized, he will be seen to be a much more considerable figure in twentieth-century philosophy than is usually held to be the case. Certainly, the theory of feeling shows him to be something other than a perpetrator of instructive confusions who did all that could be expected of him in generating the realist and pluralist reactions. Even if his metaphysic is to be regarded largely as a transitional form, preparatory to Russellian logical atomism, Deweyite pragmatism, or Whiteheadian cosmology, it nevertheless relates to those developments not merely as their remote source or occasion, but also as a standing comparison and critique. In developing a theory of the given that is anti-foundational (cf. *ETR*, p. 210), a theory of knowledge that is anti-epistemological (cf. *AR*, p. 65), and all the while elaborating a monistic doctrine of Reality upon the basis of a functional analysis of enquiry, his metaphysics of feeling holds together 'traditional' and 'modern' concerns in a unique fashion.

NOTES

1. See James Ward, *Naturalism and Agnosticism*, 2 vols., London, 1899.
2. See M. Arnold, 'The Function of Criticism at the Present Time' (1885), in *Essays in Criticism*, First Series, London, 1886, pp. 7, 17, and 39; and E. Caird, 'The Problem of Philosophy at the Present Time' (London, 1889), in *Essays in Literature and Philosophy*, 2 vols., Glasgow, 1892, vol. i, pp. 179 ff.
3. For the effect of astrophysics, see David Masson, *Recent British Philosophy* (1865), 3rd edn., London, 1877, pp. 141-7; also of course Tennyson's 'Locksley Hall Sixty Years After', 1886, and H. G. Wells, *The Time Machine*, 1895.
4. T. H. Green, *Works*, London, 1885, vol. i, p. 142.
5. T. H. Green, *Prolegomena to Ethics*, Oxford, 1883, p. 51.
6. See G. R. G. Mure, 'Oxford and Philosophy', *Philosophy*, vol. xii, 1937, pp. 291-301.
7. See W. Wundt, *Human and Animal Psychology* (Leipzig, 1863), 3rd edn., London, 1908, tr. J. E. Creighton and E. B. Titchener, p. 218; compare *AR*, p. 80 n. *ETR*, pp. 161-71 owes a great deal to Wundt's analysis of oscillatory and discordant feelings in op. cit., p. 219. For a historically accurate but critically dubious account of the German psychological background to Bradley's feeling, see James Ward, *Psychological Principles*,

242   *James Bradley*

Cambridge, 1920, p. 42 n.
8. J. S. Mill, *An Examination of Sir William Hamilton's Philosophy*, London, 1865, 6th edn., London, 1889, p. 248.
9. The Scots professor Masson had already perceived how easily Mill could be taken to a post-Kantian conclusion; see David Masson, op. cit., pp. 219-60.
10. See G. W. F. Hegel, *Science of Logic*, London, 1929, tr. Johnston and Struthers, vol. ii, pp. 143 ff.; and *Encyclopaedia of the Philosophical Sciences: Logic*, Oxford, 1892, tr. Wallace, pp. 245 ff.
11. There is evidence (I admit) that in paragraph 3 Bradley is hankering after an argument which is like Hegel's, not in the sense that it depends purely on the fact of logical distinctness, but to the extent of being symmetrical in form (i.e. that works equally from the side of terms or relations). But it is not until some time after *Appearance and Reality*, when the theory of feeling has been completely freed from all taint of psychological atomism, that this becomes possible. Only then can Bradley move directly from the position that the given is (unreservedly) a non-relational whole, to the view that, merely as distinct, both terms and relations must be condemned as abstractions from that whole (*CE*, p. 634 ff.). So his argument becomes more Hegelian (symmetrical) in character only as his anti-Hegelian theory of feeling develops. *AR* III, in contrast, is still overshadowed by atomistic sensationalism, at least to the extent that it treats terms as elements in the sensory whole and does not quite regard them as ideal products on the on the same level as relations (compare *AR*, pp. 25-6, and *CE*, pp. 630-4).
12. See James Ward, 'Bradley's Doctrine of Experience', *Mind* vol. xxxiv, 1925, pp. 13-38; and William James, *A Pluralistic Universe*, London, 1909, Lecture VII, and *Essays in Radical Empiricism*, London, 1912, I and II.
13. G. F. Stout, 'Bradley's Theory of Judgment', 1902, in *Studies in Philosophy and Psychology*, London 1930, p. 208.
14. In this respect, as also with the doctrine of finite centres (not touched on here as belonging to his *ratio essendi*), Bradley's feeling operates in much the same way as Kant's Transcendental Ego — a register both of the extent of the 'shift' and of the problems involved in his sensationalist treatment of German Idealism. See E. E. Harris's superb article, 'The Problem of Self-Constitution for Idealism and Phenomenology', *Idealistic Studies*, vol. vii, 1977, pp. 1-27.
15. See F. C. S. Schiller, 'The New Developments of Mr. Bradley's Philosophy', *Mind*, vol. xxiv, 1915, pp. 345-66; R. Kagey, *The Growth of Bradley's Logic*, New York, 1931; R. D. Mack, *The Appeal to Immediate Experience*, New York, 1945; and J. H. Randall jun., *The Career of Philosophy in Modern Times*, vol. ii, *The Hundred Years Since Darwin*, New York, 1969, chap. 8.
16. See W. James, 'Bradley or Bergson?', London, 1910, in *Collected Essays and Reviews*, London, 1920.
17. Quoted by Renford Bambrough, *Reason, Truth and God*, London, 1969, p. 58.

CHAPTER 13

Scepticism, Ideal Experiment, and Priorities in Bradley's Metaphysics*

Stewart Candlish

I

In order fully to understand a metaphysician it is necessary to determine the order of priority amongst his various doctrines; and it is natural then to look for those which are fundamental to the rest. Bradley, though, appears to warn us off:

I will however begin by noticing some misunderstandings as to the method employed in ultimate inquiry by writers like myself. There is an idea that we start, consciously or unconsciously, with certain axioms, and from these reason downwards. This idea to my mind is baseless. The method actually followed may be called in the main the procedure used by Hegel, that of a direct ideal experiment made on reality. What is assumed is that I have to satisfy my theoretical want, or, in other words, that I resolve to think. And it is assumed that, if my thought is satisfied with itself, I have, with this, truth and reality. But as to what will satisfy I have of course no knowledge in advance. My object is to get before me what will content a certain felt need, but the way and the means are to be discovered only by trial and rejection. The method clearly is experimental (*ETR*, p. 311; cf. also *ETR*, p. 312, *AR*, pp. 127-8 and 509).

In view of this we need to tread very carefully in seeking the foundations of Bradley's thought. But the quotation itself contains clues. What are we to understand by 'certain felt need' and 'ideal experiment'?

*I am grateful for the hospitality of the Rockefeller Foundation for part of 1981 when this paper was written.

II

In a passage (*AR*, pp. 491-2) comparable to the one above Bradley speaks of 'satisfying the intellect' and the context makes clear that this is the 'certain felt need'. But what is it to satisfy the intellect?

What satisfies the intellect is truth (*ETR*, pp. 1 and 311), and such satisfaction is the practical criterion of truth; that is, the function of the notion is to enable us to determine when we have arrived at truth. The criterion is not intended to be a touchstone which applies to any statement or inference taken in isolation (*PL*, pp. 619-20), but, because of the nature of what does satisfy the intellect, is operative only when a statement or inference is considered in relation to others. Satisfaction is not just feeling pleased about things (*ETR*, p. 242, *CE*, p. 671):[1] it is satisfaction of the *intellect*, and that is arrived at only in a quite definite way, for the intellect demands unity (*AR*, p. 511). What kind of unity? It is the ideal self-development or self-completion of an object (*PL*, p. 598, *AR*, p. 507), the object being an ideal content taken as real (*PL*, p. 598). Now this terminology does not need to be fully understood yet to be recognized as that in which Bradley gives his final account of inference (*PL*, p. 598), and where there is genuine inference there is also implication (*PL*, p. 600).

The point is plain: Bradley is satisfied that he has arrived at truth only if his propositions express implications, that is, necessary connections (*AR*, pp. 349, 501, 509, and 511; *PL*, p. 600).[2] And our practice of intellectual enquiry does reflect this. A typical empirical explanation of some particular phenomenon works by conferring on it a kind of necessity, one relative to the truth of a general proposition under which the phenomenon is subsumed. If an explanation of the truth of the general proposition is then sought, a natural response is to render it in turn relatively non-contingent by subsuming it under a higher order proposition — and so on until we come to rest at the limits of our empirical knowledge on some law which is not similarly explicable. But, and this is Bradley's point, when we reach this position and 'conjoin aliens inexplicably' (*AR*, p. 502) we are still not satisfied, but rather struggle to find a way of rendering intelligible our presently fundamental laws by finding something more embracing yet. Our intellect is genuinely not content to rest in mere contingency.

All this is of course familiar, and it is no accident that the Covering Law Model of explanation flourished in a period when the prevailing tradition, of logical atomism and logical empiricism, gave a large place in its metaphysics to contingency; for the function of that model within that tradition is to pander to the Bradleian demand for intellectual satisfaction — which the tradition by its nature cannot meet — by giving, in the way just described, the appearance of necessity within an overall framework of utter contingency. But the provision of this appearance, while admittedly seeming quite plausibly to reflect the reality of scientific practice, fails to do more than pander to the demand; for the intellectual satisfaction it affords is partial and temporary, merely disguising the ultimate and perpetual frustration posed by the ineradicable contingency. (And here we see one of the grounds for Bradley's hostility to science as a basis of metaphysics). However, the goal postulated by the Covering Law Model, of a coherent system of logically related propositions as comprehensive as possible, clearly corresponds to Bradley's idea of perfect truth (*ETR*, pp. 203 and 223), even if it is in the end unsatisfactory because flawed with contingency at the highest level of explanation. And what Bradley says here can in principle be detached from his Coherence Theory of Truth and the notions of degrees of truth and reality, and be recognized as in essence fairly simple and plausible despite the difficulty of his language, for we can see it as offering something perhaps more satisfying to the intellect than truth (at least as we have learned to think of that notion under more recent influences), namely, explanation and understanding.

III

Now that we have some grasp of what satisfaction of the intellect consists in, let us have a look at the other fundamental feature of Bradley's philosophy, the notion of *ideal experiment*. Bradley says very little in a general way about what an ideal experiment is, and does not give a formal explanation of the notion at all.[3] But despite his recorded opinion that to give illustrations is dangerous (*ETR*, p. 339, n.) he does give some examples. The examples are nearly all in the chapter of *The Principles of Logic* entitled 'Fresh Specimens of Inference' (pp. 394–430); they include various species of reasoning and are summed up later:

Inference is an experiment, an ideal experiment which gains fresh truth (*PL*, p. 492).

However, the fresh truth cannot be a truth concerning a different subject-matter.

Inference is an experiment performed on a *datum*, which *datum* appropriates the result of the experiment (*PL*, p. 479; cf. also *PL*, p. 431).

This may tempt one to suppose that the notions of *inference* and *ideal experiment* are equivalent; but to say this without qualification would be misleading. For Bradley also calls supposal an ideal experiment (*PL*, p. 86) and in the above quotations he always says '*an* experiment', as though there are others.

Nevertheless this tempting supposition is at bottom correct. For supposal is, Bradley says, 'thinking for a particular end' (*PL*, p. 85), 'with a view to see what the consequence is' (*PL*, p. 86), and is thus not to be detached from inference. And when Bradley comes, under the influence of Bosanquet, to his later, more considered account of inference as 'the ideal self-developement [*sic*] of an object' (*PL*, p. 597, written for the 1922 edition), this object being 'an ideal content before us, taken to be real' (*PL*, p. 598), i.e. an affirmed judgment, he stresses the fact that inference cannot lead you to a completely different subject, neglecting the reference to experiment in his original account. And what I think this means is that by 'inference' Bradley is talking, as many logicians do, of *valid* inference only (even though he thinks that, *ultimately*, all inference is invalid (*PL*, pp. 588 and 621)), and that, if we take the general form of inference as 'If A, then B', ideal experiments are simply thoughts of this form, some of which are valid (that is, genuine inferences, corresponding to implications and preserving truth (*PL*, pp. 423, n. 3, and 598)) and some of which are not.

In other words, we find Bradley maintaining what, despite

the difficulty of the surface language, is something rather simple and uncontroversial. Why then is the language difficult? Why describe inference as 'ideal experiment'?

'Ideal' is fairly easily explained. Ideas belong to thought: 'the idea in judgment is the universal meaning', says Bradley (*PL*, p. 10; cf. also *AR*, p. 526), and an ideal experiment is an experiment which concerns connections between universals (*PL*, p. 441) which could, unlike a physical experiment, be accomplished solely in thought, though a physical version may be employed (*PL*, p. 423, n. 3). Roughly, it is a process in which we posit premises and then see what appears to follow.

But why also 'experiment'? I think the answer here is that for Bradley the outcomes even of deduction are in some sense or senses not guaranteed (*PL*, pp. 259, 266-71, and 530). If this sounds absurd, remember the difficulty which Wittgenstein had in making people understand just such a point[4] (and compare the similar problem concerning the non-relational character of experience, in the next section below). What Bradley means here is perhaps several things at once for which he gives some variety of reasons, but a reasonably clear summary comes in this passage:

The idea of a complete body of models of reasoning, to be followed as patterns and faithfully reproduced to make and guarantee the individual inference, I set down as a superstitition. No such code of rules and examples could, as we have seen, warrant its own infallible application; and, in the second place, no collection of models could conceivably be complete, and so anticipate and prescribe beforehand the special essence of every inference (*PL*, p. 618).

Bradley, like the later Wittgenstein, was interested in reasoning as a human activity, even, despite the strict anti-psychologism which he learned from Frege's teacher Lotze, to the point of thinking it proper to investigate the psychological accompaniments of the activity; and it is this which underlies the above remarks. (Unlike Wittgenstein, however, he draws a parallel here in moral philosophy.)[5]

Consistent with this is Bradley's refusal to put the so-called laws of logic on to an exalted plane.

A principle will neither demonstrate its applications nor can it be demonstrated *by* them. The principle is demonstrated when we see it *in*, and as the function of, an individual act (*PL*, p. 531).

The degree in which the various types [of inference and judgment] each succeed and fail in reaching their common end [of contributing to the width and coherence of the body of our knowledge], gives to each of them its respective place and its rank in the whole body (*PL*, p. 620).

And here we see Bradley taking up a position very similar to that associated with Quine.

Now, however, we come to a difficulty. As we have seen, for Bradley reasoning is ideal experiment. But in several places he appears to *contrast* ideal experiment with reasoning. For example, in maintaining against Russell that one cannot think without inconsistency of a relation on its own and devoid of terms, Bradley says (*ETR*, p. 303; cf. also p. 289), 'This is, however, not so much a matter for argument and discussion as for actual experiment.' In the famous proof of idealism (*AR*, pp. 127-8) he gives not a deduction but a series of instructions to the reader as to the conducting of an ideal experiment, an experiment whose results in his own case he reports with the apparent expectation that the reader will produce the same ones, and in a clear reference back to this proof he says (*ETR*, p. 316 n.):

We have here a matter for observation and experiment and not for long trains of reasoning ... if Prof. Perry wishes to get an idea as to the view which he is anxious to refute, why should he not suppose (for a moment) that on my side there is no argument at all, and that on his side there is an inference by way of vicious abstraction?

What can be made of this? I think the appearance of contradiction can be resolved, though Bradley himself does not seem to notice the tension in his thought here. In the places where he draws the contrast with experiment, he refers to argument, not to inference, and typically to argument from some axiom he is supposed to hold (for example *ETR*, pp. 289, 259, and 311), while in the quotation he speaks similarly, making the added reference to 'long trains of reasoning'.

What he seems to have in mind is a contrast between, on the one hand, those inferences which one can grasp with, as it were, one movement of the mind, and on the other, those inferences which proceed step by step to a distant conclusion and which cannot just be *seen* to be valid; but he also seems at the same time to be thinking of the contrast between conditionals, whose antecedents are of course not separately asserted, and arguments, which have a categorical first premiss, particularly arguments with premisses of a very general and all-embracing kind. We may be seeing as well the influence of one of the orthodoxies of his time, introspectionism in psychology.[6]

But now, we may ask, if this is all that the difference between argument and ideal experiment amounts to, if they both belong, roughly speaking, to the sphere of logic, why make such a fuss about the difference? An argument must begin from a premiss which within the context of the argument is taken for granted. But Bradley's experiments are meant to be free of presupposition, to be made directly on reality (*PL*, p. 563, *ETR*, p. 311), and moreover on reality as experienced and not as served up, already sliced, in sentences.

Despite this difference, however, I think that his ideal experiments are meant to reveal what these days we should be inclined to call logical or conceptual truths; and, furthermore, truths which are either what has been called self-evident or are self-evidently directly underpinned by something itself self-evident.[7] This would explain why he says (*ETR*, p. 289) that he cannot see how to argue about these matters, and does not argue downwards to the truths he wishes to maintain. We must not forget, too, that for him logic, while not reducible to psychology, works through ideas, which always possess a psychical aspect (*PL*, p. 38 n. 8) and are thus to be studied through introspection rather than through the linguistic expression which is subsequently (*PL*, p. 32) grafted on to them. Philosophy written in a psychological climate can be about the same things as that written in a linguistic climate; but the products of the former can often be understood from the perspective of the latter only by a translation into the more familiar idiom. So here are some examples to demonstrate my claim that Bradley's ideal experiments were meant to reveal self-evident conceptual truths.

First, Bradley says that by experimenting he cannot find that any relation survives the total removal of its terms (*ETR*, p. 295). Put in another idiom not alien to Bradley, this is the claim that relations are not substances, that is, not complete or individual (*PL*, pp. 71 and 187; *AR*, pp. 9 and 509; *ETR*, pp. 227 n. and 289–90), and the notion of substance gives us the clue to how the point appears in modern dress: producing a relational expression like '. . . is a compatriot of . . .' is not a complete linguistic act. It is not an assertion, nor is it a referring expression introducing some object of which we can go on to predicate something. The parallels with points made by other philosophers of language from Frege onwards are obvious.

Secondly, he says 'In actual experience we can never find a thing by itself; it is obvious that some context will always be present there' (*PL*, p. 563). This again is a logical point. If we interpret 'experience' as 'perception', then picking something out logically involves a background against which it is picked out. If we generalize 'experience', in the manner typical of nineteenth-century idealism, to include all psychical activity,[8] then we get instead the logical claim on which Bradley's idealism is partly founded and which is outlined in the next paragraph.

Thirdly, in his proof of idealism (*AR*, pp. 127-8), Bradley, after instructing the reader to try the experiment of thinking of something in the absence of all perception and feeling, says:

When the experiment is made strictly, I can myself conceive of nothing else than the experienced. Anything, in no sense felt or perceived, becomes to me quite unmeaning . . . I cannot try to think of it without realizing either that I am not thinking at all, or that I am thinking of it against my will as being experienced . . . The fact that falls elsewhere seems, in my mind, to be a mere word and a failure, or else an attempt at self-contradiction (*AR*, p. 128).

Here again the ideal experiment is designed to reveal a logical point. Bradley invites us to try to conceive of an unexperienced object. This seems straightforward enough, until we remember that for idealists, 'experience' and 'feeling' cover all forms of psychical activity, and the instruction thus comes to 'Conceive of something unconceived'. And this description of what we are to do is plausibly regarded as either 'a mere word' or an instruction to attempt something self-contradictory or self-defeating.[9]

Fourthly, he claims that the non-contingency of the fact that a term is not diverse from itself is revealed by ideal experiment, saying that the contrary supposition 'either is meaningless or self-destructive' (*ETR*, p. 290).

It seems clear from these four examples that ideal experiment is, as Bradley conceives it, a method of uncovering what

we might call relatively self-evident conceptual or necessary
truths, even though he might himself resist this description
of it. With these examples behind us we can now afford to
let in others which may seem less apparently self-evident
to us by reminding ourselves that they may have appeared
rather differently to Bradley: the impossibility of purely
external relations as revealed by ideal experiment (*ETR*,
p. 290), for one — which is clearly to Bradley an *obvious*
impossibility — and, for another, the impossibility of reflexive
relations through the revelation by experiment that relations
imply diversity (*ETR*, p. 289).

IV

Our result so far, then, is this. In his own view, at least,
Bradley's metaphysics rests on no assumption. Instead,
it is an as far as possible presuppositionless enquiry into
the nature of reality, pursued by ideal experiment and
with the goal of satisfying the intellect. The intellect, it
turns out, is satisfied only by a system of necessarily connected
propositions which is as comprehensive as possible. (For
'propositions' we may substitute 'truths' if we do not like
the Coherence Theory of Truth.) And ideal experiments
are conditional postulations revealing what are standardly
recognized as necessary truths, that is, on Bradley's view,
propositions which are high up in the system.

It may be suggested here that this is already to prejudge
the issue of the nature of reality in favour of some sort of
monism; but although this charge turns out to have something in it, it is, when stated baldly, unjust. For as we saw,
even metaphysics of contingency like logical empiricism pay
lip-service to this conception of intellectual satisfaction; and
Bradley is so far prepared to admit the bare possibility of an
ultimate contingency and atomism as to feel obliged to argue
against it (*AR*, pp. 500–11). What convinced him initially
that one would not have to admit it was the fact that experience did not present him with terms, qualities, and relations
in the manner in which thought (or language) is obliged to
represent that experience.

I have said that 'in his own view' Bradley's metaphysics is

assumptionless. We shall find that this requires qualification. However, I think it only fair to him to take him seriously and to find out how far we can get in deriving and understanding the main features of his metaphysics on this slender basis. Bradley starts, then, by taking experience as it comes, allowing himself to perform ideal experiments on it, and retaining those results which satisfy the intellect. And the first thing he notices about experience is that it is non-relational (*ETR*, pp. 230-1). He does not mean that it is simple, and lacking variety (*AR*, p. 508, *ETR*, p. 311). What he means is hard to explain, in just the way that his suggestion that deduction does not guarantee its outcome is hard to explain, for he is making that typical philosopher's move of denying a confusion which has no clear explanation; and this always leads to mis-understanding, for one is inclined to think that he is denying obvious facts instead. What Bradley is rejecting is the assump-tion that language mirrors reality. When we take an experience of an object — a green leaf, say, to use his example (*CE*, pp. 633 and 656) — experience has both a unity and a diversity which are not and cannot be adequately reflected in the language we use to describe the experience, language which necessarily deploys the tools of term, quality, and relation (cf. *AR*, p. 512, *CE*, p. 630). For with that language we must say things like 'Here is a leaf', which both splits the object from its background and fails to reflect its diversity, or 'The leaf is green', which again abstracts certain features of the actual experience leaving others unmentioned and furthermore splits up these features in a way in which they are not split in reality. While such sentences attempt to restore the original unity (they are not merely lists of their constituent words), they necessarily fail. Of course we cannot say clearly what it would be for them to succeed, for success in this matter is, as Bradley with his talk of perfect truth requiring thought's suicide recognizes, inconceivable; and therein lies the urge to misunderstand him, to take him as denying the obvious truth that in some sense the experience is relational since it con-tains diversity.

It may look as though Bradley is, right at this early stage, making assumptions, for to us, who see as it were almost through the eyes of our language, it can seem just perverse to deny that experience reveals to us objects in relation.

But this is precisely the point: the way we think of experience is affected by our language. (Although Bradley might want the point put the other way round, with the blame falling on thought rather than on language.) And Bradley's 'great problem' is the relation of thought to reality (*AR*, p. 492). So he cannot, as so many philosophers have done, take for granted that the categories of thought are automatically reflected in reality. And if it is said that he cannot take for granted that they are not, and his appeal to the evidence of experience is rejected, then it must be pointed out that his metaphysical views do not rest just on this observation of experience's non-relational character.

They do not rest on this alone, because his subsequent arguments about predication and relations are meant, *inter alia*, to show that any attempt to prove the apparent non-relationality of experience misleading and to analyse it relationally is doomed to failure. What the observation does is, when combined with his determination not to make assumptions, to license the weak form of what I have called his sceptical principle.[10] I say 'the weak form' because there are three distinct forms discernible in his work and although he appears not to distinguish them himself the weak form is the only one to which he is so far entitled. The principle is stated in various places but perhaps the closest approximations to the weak form are these:

For, if the qualities impart themselves never except under conditions, how in the end are we to say what they are when unconditioned? (*AR*, p. 11).

And you cannot ever get your product standing apart from its process. Will you say, the process is not essential? But that is a conclusion to be proved, and it is monstrous to assume it . . . And, if we have no further information, I can find no excuse for setting up the result as being fact without the process (*AR*, p. 23).

Each of these is a more particular version of the general principle which is at work in both cases and which I take to be formulable as follows:

One is not entitled to *assume* of something which always comes in combinations with something else, that it is capable of existing uncombined.

This version of Bradley's sceptical principle, although I have characterized it as weak, does quite a lot of work in his philosophy, for it licenses one form of his long-standing hostility towards *abstraction*. Bradley employs this form quite explicitly against Mill's Method of Difference (*PL*, pp. 560-2), and argues that while abstraction is legitimate in certain contexts and for certain limited and practical purposes, it takes the performance of an ideal experiment to prove this legitimacy in each case. Thus, ideal experiment shows that for the purposes of arithmetic one may treat an integer as a whole consisting of separable parts, since the sums involved do work in practice, despite the fact that numbers form an internally related system, a fact that cannot be forgotten when we come to give a philosophical account of number rather than merely do arithmetic. But the work that the principle in this form does, which is of immediate interest to us, is to open the door to both monism and idealism, because it places the burden of argument on those wishing to oppose these doctrines. However, before monism and idealism can be actually proved, the weak form must be replaced by stronger ones. In order to see what licenses this replacement, we must first proceed to an apparently independent matter: Bradley's attack on predication and on the correlative idea that we can understand reality as consisting of things which have qualities.

V

What underpins this attack is the demand for satisfaction of the intellect, that is, for a logical connection between different things if their coexistence is to be understood (*ETR*, pp. 314-15). This is not just a refusal to accept bare contingency as 'our ignorance set up as reality' (*AR*, p. 517). It is the result of a claim to find such contingency self-contradictory, both in general (*AR*, pp. 345-9) and in the case of predication (*AR*, pp. 500-11). Let us look at the case of predication. Suppose we have a billiard ball. It is both white and round. These properties are, in the object, in some way unified, and at the same time in some way held apart. Now according to Bradley, we are forced by the need for intellectual satisfaction to find a logical connection between the ball's whiteness and its roundness, and this leads into attempting to identify the two properties with each other, to attribute them as it were to the same feature of the ball. (Again, this is hard to understand because it is an identification whose possibility Bradley rejects. One could compare Wittgenstein on the subject of private designation.)

Why does the need for intellectual satisfaction force us to try to identify the two different properties? This happens because, in ordinary predication ('The ball is white and round') the link between them is presented as bare co-presence, and recognizing that this is inadequate since it does not do justice to their unity, and lacking knowledge of the true explanation of this unity (an explanation which will also show how they are not only linked but also kept apart), the intellect falls back on the only remaining logical connection which can guarantee the unity, namely identity.

It is idle from the outside to say to thought, 'Well, unite but do not identify'. How can thought unite except so far as in itself it has a mode of union? To unite without an internal ground of connexion and distinction is to strive to bring together barely in the same point, and that is self-contradiction (*AR*, p. 505).

It is this kind of reasoning which led Russell to accuse Bradley of confusing predication with identity. Whatever one thinks of the reasoning, the charge is quite unfair.[11] Bradley's point was that predication seems to link things quite arbitrarily and that such arbitrariness both seems not to do justice to the phenomena and is intolerable to the philosophical understanding. Identity removes the arbitrariness, but at the cost of self-contradiction. Hence ordinary predication is, while perfectly satisfactory for everyday business, ultimately unintelligible.[12]

The same point holds where we attempt, not to attribute two different, 'compatible' predicates to a single subject, but to attribute one to a designated subject. For Bradley argues (*PL*, I, I, II) that all designation proceeds through universals and that even the most apparently recalcitrantly singular, designatory proposition must be understood as combining predicates. (The idea is the same as that behind Quine's proposal for the elimination of singular terms, a proposal usually connected with Russell's Theory of Descriptions.)

Bradley sums up his view thus:

A thing cannot without an internal distinction be two different things, and differences cannot belong to the same thing in the same point unless in that point there is diversity. The appearance of such a union may be fact, but is for thought a contradiction (*AR*, p. 501).

He does not mean, as we would, that this, being a contradiction, is impossible, 'for the intellect can always accept the conjunction not as bare but as a connexion, the bond of which is at present unknown, . . . can accept the inconsistent if taken as subject to conditions' (*AR*, p. 503). He means that experienced facts cannot be understood; for the conditions can never all be filled in.

VI

We have now seen how the demand for satisfaction of the intellect, interpreted as the demand for connections of implication between diverse but related things, leads directly to the rejection of predication as unintelligible except subject to unknown conditions. Bradley's next move, the attack on external relations, has the same foundation.

That any external relations are impossible is revealed by ideal experiment (*ETR*, pp. 290–1 and 295); and the tendency to believe the opposite is the result of ignoring the sceptical principle (loc. cit.) in its weak form. How is it so revealed? First we must see what an external relation is.

We have here, I presume, to abstract so as to take terms and relations, all and each, as something which in and by itself is real independently.[13] And we must, if so, assume that their coming or being together in fact, and as somehow actually in one, is due in no way to the particular characters of either the relations or the terms . . . the fact is somehow there, but in itself it remains irrational as admitting no question as to its 'how' or 'why'. Or, if you insist on a reason, that would have to be sought neither in the terms nor the relation, but in a third element once more independently real and neither affecting, nor again affected by, either the relation or the terms (*CE*, p. 642).

With this understanding of the nature of externality we find by ideal experiment that a diversity of independent but limited 'reals' is self-contradictory:

Relational experience must hence in its very essence be called self-contradictory. Contradiction everywhere is the attempt to take what is plural and diverse as being one and the same, and to take it so (we must add) simply or apart from any 'how'. And we have seen that without both diversity and unity the relational experience is lost, while to combine these two aspects it has left to it no possible 'how' or way, except one which seems either certainly less or certainly more than what is relational (*CE*, p. 635; cf. *AR*, p. 126).

The point here is the same as that concerning predication, merely substituting the unity of a relational fact for that of an object as what requires explanation. And once it is seen that externality makes explanation impossible, requiring an intolerable contingency between the related elements (*AR*, pp. 514 and 517), the complaint is the same: that the attempt to remove the contingency and truly understand the unity results in self-contradiction. (I take the obscure last clause of the quotation to refer to identity.)

VII

At this stage, Bradley has sufficient to license the two stronger versions of his sceptical principle. As I said earlier, he distinguishes these neither from each other nor from the weak version to which he was only entitled at a prior stage of the development of his system; so we find the accounts of all the versions run together, and a tendency to move from the intermediate, what we might call an agnostic, version of the principle, to the strongest or atheist version in the same breath. Indeed, in one place (*AR*, p. 11) he moves straight from the weak to the strong version. But in another he starts with the intermediate version and moves directly to the strong.

If a thing is known to have a quality only under a certain condition, there is no process of reasoning from this which will justify the conclusion that the thing, if unconditioned, is yet the same. This seems quite certain; and, to go further, if we have no other source of information, if the quality in question is non-existent for us except in one relation, then for us to assert its reality away from that relation is more than unwarranted. It is, to speak plainly, an attempt in the end without meaning (*AR*, p. 13).

The intermediate version, then, is:

No argument can *prove* of something which always comes in combination with something else, that it is capable of existing uncombined.

And the strong:

> It is *meaningless* to suppose of something which always comes in combination with something else, that it is capable of existing uncombined.

These versions of the principle are justified by the attack on external relations. For to suppose something separable from something else with which it always comes combined is to suppose that that relationship of combination is external, one which can be broken with indifference to its terms. This is because separability without damage implies the independence of the terms, that their being in a given relation is nothing logically to do with their natures. Abstraction, then, can now be seen not merely according to the weak version as a blind, unjustified leap; it is a definite destruction of its subject-matter, which always leads to philosophical (though still not necessarily to practical) error. And furthermore, these stronger versions of the principle provide another basis, alternative to the one outlined in section III above, for the claim crucial to the demonstration of idealism, the claim that reality is internally related to experience.

But now we see Bradley reject internal relations as well.

VIII

That Bradley does this is so clear from his published writings (for example *ETR*, pp. 238-9; *CE*, pp. 641, 646, 665, and 667-8) that it is puzzling that he still has a reputation for adhering to the 'Doctrine of Internal Relations', i.e. the view that all relations are internal.[14] In any case, the rejection is sharp and quick. The notion of an internal relation is one which depends on the distinction between internal and external relations. But this distinction is untenable, not because the attack on external relations has shown that all actual examples fall on one side of it, but because it depends in turn on the distinction between a term's original or intrinsic nature and the nature as qualified by the fresh external relation into which it has entered. But this means that the term must have two respects, and the original argument against predication showed that the attribution of two different qualities to a single thing leads to contradiction.

Curiously, Bradley does not consider the objection that if there are no external relations then the problem of relating their consequent relational qualities to the intrinsic qualities of the object just does not arise. Perhaps this is because the reply would be so obvious: that the problem of relating to each other different intrinsic relational qualities will pose precisely the same difficulty, one which as we have seen Bradley regarded as insoluble.

Again, as is usual with the notions he rejects as inadequate for philosophical understanding, Bradley allows the external/internal distinction a limited value, for it corresponds to our useful distinction between accident and essence. But the place at which we draw this distinction is one determined by convenience and not by reason, and every relation is, he says, both internal and external; a philosophy which draws a hard distinction here is bound to go wrong.[15]

At this point we see how Bradley's metaphysics reaches inexpressibility. What he rejects is tolerably clear; and in general terms we can go on to see what he embraces. But the detail will necessarily elude us. For the consequence of the demand for necessary connections between diverse things has been to deprive us of the means for expressing those connections, since this task requires predication and expressions for internal relations. Thus the intellect alone is incapable of achieving what would meet its own requirements; and Bradley was forced to resort to metaphor whenever it came to setting out what reality is like. But he saw this coming himself, and well in advance: 'this ideal may itself be a thing beyond the compass of intellect, an attempt to think something to which thought is not equal, and which logic in part refuses to justify' (*PL*, pp. 489–90; cf. *AR*, p. 508).

Nevertheless, the outlines of some of Bradley's most famous and characteristic doctrines should now be becoming apparent; and indeed his monism is only one step away. For, given that relativity necessarily infects everything it touches with contradiction, and that we can admit as real only what is not contradictory, it follows straight away that what is real must be, in one sense of the several that the word possesses, a substance. This move is described succinctly by Bradley himself:

From this I conclude that what is real must be self-contained and self-subsistent and not qualified from the outside. For an external qualification is a mere conjunction, and that, we have seen, is for the intellect an attempt of diversities simply to identify themselves, and such an attempt is what we mean by self-contradiction (*AR*, p. 509).

This doctrine appeared in his thought as early as 1883 (*PL*, pp. 188-9); but there, drawing back as usual from metaphysics in the attempt to confine himself to logic, he refrained from continuing the argument to its inevitable conclusion.

IX

The move to monism is now immediate, for a plurality of such substances with no relation between them is ruled out by their very diversity being itself a relation (*AR*, p. 25); while a plurality of internally related substances is logically impossible since their internal relations would undermine the independence that makes them substances (*PL*, pp. 696-7; *AR*, pp. 124-5); and a plurality of genuinely independent substances would imply their being externally related[16] and that is already proved self-contradictory (*AR*, pp. 125-6):

And, since diversities exist, they must therefore somehow be true and real; and since, to be understood and to be true and real, they must be united, hence they must be true and real in such a way that from *A* or *B* the intellect can pass to its further qualification without an external determination of either. But this means that *A* and *B* are united, each from its own nature, in a whole which is the nature of both alike. And hence it follows that in the end there is nothing real but a whole of this kind (*AR*, p. 510).

And the very next sentence makes it clear that 'a whole' does not mean 'one amongst others'.

We have, then, reached the monism for which Bradley is famous: 'The universe is one in this sense that its differences exist harmoniously within one whole, beyond which there is nothing' (*AR*, p. 127). But this whole has the nature of its constituents (*AR*, p. 510), for their properties are not completely lost when we abandon predication and relations (*AR*, p. 114); and as a constituent of every (partial) whole is experience, it follows that reality as a whole is experiential:

But to be utterly indivisible from feeling or perception, to be an integral element in a whole which is experienced, this surely is itself to *be* experience (*AR*, p. 129).

So, finally, if rather obscurely, and via Bradley's version of monism, we have reached idealism;[17] not of course subjective idealism, for as Bradley sees (*AR*, p. 128) this would involve a relation between experience and its possessor, but absolute idealism, in which finite possessors of experience are regarded as mere appearance along with everything else familiar to us. And accordingly we have seen how the principal tenets of his metaphysics are derived from the narrow basis of the performance of ideal experiments on reality as experienced with the goal of achieving satisfaction of the intellect. Perhaps this basis, and what is derived from it, is not always as crisply delineated by Bradley as one would wish. Nevertheless, we should take seriously his claim to have started virtually from nothing in deriving his notorious conclusions. 'Precisification' can be falsification: rather than sort out in detail the theoretically separable strands of his thought, I have tried here to understand *Bradley*, and thereby provide a perspective from which the details of the derivation can be evaluated without distortion.

X

There is an obvious objection to Bradley's claim, which should be considered before closing: that he is assuming what he needs to prove, that ultimate contingency is not a given fact about the world. If he is, his views rest, after all, on an assumption not merely grand but with insufficient independent plausibility, the Principle of Sufficient Reason. This was Russell's allegation,[18] and followers of Bradley have been content to acknowledge the Principle as 'the real and sole basis'[19] of their claims, even if Russell's own version of it was too idiosyncratic for them.

Bradley faced such an objection quite explicitly:

To me such a doctrine is quite erroneous. For these ultimates (*a*) cannot make the world intelligible, and again (*b*) they are not given, and (*c*) in themselves they are self-contradictory, and not truth but appearance (*AR*, p. 502).

What he seems both to need and to want to show is that the Principle of Sufficient Reason is not an assumption, nor even a methodological postulate, but something unavoidable.

Would his three points above, if established, prove this? Point (*a*) is not going to worry an advocate of ultimate contingency, for he would probably himself be happy to deny that the world is intelligible in Bradley's sense of the word. So Bradley's defence must rest on the remaining two points.[20] I shall take (*c*) first.

The proof that things conjoined by bare contingency are self-contradictory, as we saw in sections V and VI, rests on the claim that in seeking to provide an account of the conjunction satisfactory to itself, the intellect, failing an account of the link between the things that is one of implication, seeks to identify the things with each other, which is self-contradictory. But this contradiction is derived purely from a claimed intellectual dissatisfaction with a bare, contingent, external conjunction; and this dissatisfaction itself can be rationalized only in terms of the conviction that the world cannot exhibit such conjunctions. Thus this defence of the Principle of Sufficient Reason rests upon that principle itself, and hence is useless.

One could try to respond to this charge of uselessness by arguing that conjunctions, as I said in section IV, belong, for Bradley, essentially to the way language or thought presents things as being and not to the way they actually come in experience, and that, linked as things are in a manner which language cannot adequately represent, conjunctions cannot be treated merely as having links of the kind which language *can* represent. While this response may yet leave it open to an opponent of Bradley to insist that the links are nevertheless possibly contingent, it does seem to point to the fact that the real corner-stone of Bradley's objection is (*b*), the claim that ultimate contingencies are simply not given in experience; and so, presumably, there is no need to suppose, without proof, that they exist.

Let us assume, then, with Bradley, that in some sense this is true: in the sense that experience is a manifold, presenting diversity in unity of a kind to which linguistic representation cannot do justice. Now, employing the weak version of Bradley's sceptical principle, the only version he is entitled to, *prior to* accepting the very arguments (concerning predication and relations) which the advocate of contingency is challenging, we do not have sufficient to justify his claim that ultimate contingencies will not be unearthed, in science or philosophy, in attempting to account for the content of experience. For the justification of this claim, the stronger versions are needed — and indeed in considering (*b*) Bradley refers disparagingly to the abstraction that 'discovering' such ultimate contingency would require and which those versions prohibit — but what in turn justifies those versions is, as was just said, the very set of arguments which the believer in contingency is attacking.

So with the only justified — i.e. virtually assumptionless — form of the sceptical principle, then, Bradley cannot rule out the possibility of the ultimate contingency of the way things are. And I think he half sees this, as his hesitancy (*AR*, p. 503) on the subject suggests. In this way, then, Bradley eventually pays the price for, as we saw, failing to distinguish clearly the three versions of the sceptical principle which plays such a determining role in the production of his metaphysics.

There is, however, another passage (*ETR*, pp. 15-17) which could be interpreted as an attempt on Bradley's part to argue that we must, to think at all, reject the idea that ultimate contingency is possible. Philosophy demands, and in the end rests on, faith, he says: philosophical activity lacks sense unless it is assumed that its goal is attainable. He is talking of truth, but we have seen that this Truth is closer to our Explanation.

Hence the only scepticism in philosophy which is rational must confine itself to the denial that truth so far and actually has been reached. What is ordinarily called philosophical scepticism is on the other hand an uncritical and suicidal dogmatism (*ETR*, p. 17).

Perhaps, then, the Principle of Sufficient Reason is for him not so much a grand assumption on which his other views are based,[21] as a rationalization of that restless spirit of enquiry which is the hallmark of all intellectual endeavour and which reaches its quintessence in metaphysics. It was, after all, Bradley who wrote the second as well as the first part of this famous sentence (*AR*, Preface, p. x): 'Metaphysics is the finding of bad reasons for what we believe upon instinct, but to find these reasons is no less an instinct.'

APPENDIX

The Publishing History of *Appearance and Reality*

The first edition of *Appearance and Reality* appeared in Muirhead's Library of Philosophy which at that time was published by Swan Sonnenschein. It has always been rumoured that the book had originally been offered to, and rejected by, the Clarendon Press. On receipt of information from the Press, Richard Wollheim has attempted to scotch this rumour (*F. H. Bradley*, rev. edn. 1969, Supplementary Note to Chapter Five). He says, *inter alia*, 'In consequence, the story retailed, for instance by J. H. Muirhead that the book had been turned down is without foundation. Indeed, the most likely explanation of Bradley's new course of action is that he wanted to accommodate Muirhead, who was editor of the new Library of Philosophy.' This suggests that Muirhead was not only mendacious but irrational, in that he was prepared falsely to advertise the contents of his own Library as rejected material. Two things are clear from the Bradley Papers in Merton: one is that Muirhead claimed to have the story of the rejection from Bradley himself. The other is that it was important to Bradley's literary executors, in the legal battle with Stanley Unwin (of George Allen & Unwin, who had taken over Swan Sonnenschein) over the transfer of the book from Allen & Unwin to the Clarendon Press as part of the project of publishing a collected edition, to establish that the Press had not rejected the original manuscript. And indeed the Press's records showed no such rejection. But this is not surprising, since according to a typewritten copy (held in the Bodleian Library, where it is recorded that the original had been up for auction) of a letter from Bradley to a publisher (presumably Swan Sonnenschein), he says quite unequivocally that he had withdrawn the book prior to its official consideration by the Clarendon Press since he had been requested to do so by friends amongst the Delegates who told him that the book would be rejected, albeit with regret. They apparently found it 'controversial'. Quoting from this material is problematic, since no one now appears to know whose permission must be sought; but what I have said here is readily verifiable in the Bradley correspondence. What I have not been able to determine the truth of, or even the source for, is the further story that the Delegates viewed *Appearance and Reality* with disfavour because its Supreme Being is not the God of religion. Of course, given the clericalism of the Oxford of the period, the story is highly plausible.

NOTES

1. Nor is it, *pace* Wollheim (*F. H. Bradley*, Harmondsworth, 1959, rev. edn. 1969, pp. 282 and 277 respectively), feeling *especially* pleased about things.

2. Even this will not do *ultimately*, but 'ultimately' is the point at which his metaphysics reaches complete inexpressibility. Cf. *PL*, p. 487, and sec. VIII below.

3. One may think here that in view of Bradley's attribution of the method of ideal experiment to Hegel, one should look to Hegel himself for explanation. But to find such an explanation in Hegel turns out to be even more difficult than finding one in Bradley. The interpretation offered below is corroborated in an entry in the Bradley papers in Merton College Library (Bradley Papers, III B 2, p. 115).

4. This is not the sole anticipation of Wittgenstein one can find in Bradley. Compare, for example, *PL*, III, II, I, with the doctrine of saying and showing.

5. *PL*, pp. 266–71. This is only one of several ways in which Bradley's work, despite a few notable changes of mind, is all of a piece in a way that Russell's, for example, is not. For other parallels, see S. Candlish (a), 'Bradley on My Station and Its Duties', *Australasian Journal of Philosophy*, vol. 56, 1978, sec. 8. It is this unity of Bradley's work which makes it possible to proceed as I have done by citing temporally widely scattered writings in illustration of a single thesis. Bradley did not change his mind a great deal (cf. *AR*, p. 356, n. 1), and when he did, usually said so (cf. *PL*, p. 38, n. 7).

6. Herbart influenced both Bradley and Wundt.

7. Russell interpreted Bradley the same way (letter to Bradley, dated 2 March 1911, held in the Bradley papers at Merton). Bradley's reply (dated 15 March 1911, held in the Russell Archives at McMaster University) considers and does not reject Russell's interpretation.

8. Cf. S. Candlish (b), 'The Status of Idealism in Bradley's Metaphysics', *Idealistic Studies*, vol. 11, 1981, sec. 2 and n. 3.

9. Commentators on this experiment (for example Wollheim, op. cit., pp. 201–3, rev. edn. pp. 197–200; Cresswell, 'Reality as Experience in F. H. Bradley', *Australasian Journal of Philosophy*, vol. 55, 1977, p. 183; and Montague, 'Wollheim on Bradley on Idealism and Relations', *Philosophical Quarterly*, vol. 14, 1964, pp. 158–62) have attempted to recast Bradley's loose and discursive presentation into a more or less complex argument. This seems to me a mistake. It also seems wrong to suggest (Wollheim, op. cit., pp. 202–3, rev. edn. pp. 199–200; and Montague, op. cit., pp. 160–1) that Bradley's experiment confuses conceiving with picturing. What the experiment may confuse, however, is the impossibility of conceiving with the conceiving of impossibility.

10. Candlish (b), sec. 7.

11. There is a curious tension, so far unnoticed, between Russell's usual charges that Hegelians first, confuse the 'is' of predication with the 'is' of identity, in favour of the latter, and second, assume that every proposition is of the subject-predicate form.

12. This is a summary of part of Bradley's own summary of the crucial parts of his reasoning (*AR*, pp. 504-6, *ETR*, pp. 226-9). Wollheim's view that Bradley thought that all subject-predicate statements are really identity statements can thus be seen to be a distortion of the truth. A rather different attack on predication is mounted in the very early chapters of *Appearance and Reality*. This is glossed in Candlish (b), sec. 9.

13. Wollheim (op. cit., p. 111, rev. edn. p. 109) says of this theory that 'it seems very unlikely that [it] engaged his interest'. But he gives no reason for believing this; and Bradley defines externality in this way in more than one place (including a letter of 5 February 1909 to Samuel Alexander, held in the John Rylands University Library, Manchester). Moreover, the second sentence in this quotation (*CE*, p. 642) together with other remarks (*ETR*, p. 291; and see too *AR*, pp. 507 and 559) implies that Bradley conceived the relationship between the two conjectures, of the independent reality of terms and relations on the one hand, and of the absolute contingency of their combinations on the other, to be one of mutual implication. Indeed, Wollheim's whole treatment of Bradley's discussion of relations is suspect, given that he believes, against the evidence – and indeed against his own admission of the contrary – Bradley to have adhered to something known as the 'Doctrine of Internal Relations' (Wollheim, op. cit., pp. 104-9, rev. edn. pp. 102-7), and that he deploys some of Bradley's arguments out of context. On the so-called Doctrine of Internal Relations, see below sec. VIII. I was unduly cautious about this interpretation of the externality of relations in Candlish (b), sec. 7. Russell too noticed the essential connection between externality and contingency in Bradley's thought (letter dated 9 April 1910, Merton College Library). Cf. also Bradley Papers, III B 14, p. 97.

14. A recent example comes in the few references to Bradley in R. M. Sainsbury's *Russell*, London, 1979. Even Wollheim, who notices that Bradley rejects the Doctrine of Internal Relations, cannot resist the temptation to say of all Bradley's arguments on the subject that they are 'arguments adduced in its favour' (op. cit., p. 109, rev. edn. p. 107). So strong, presumably, was the influence of Moore and Russell. However, for them and for Bradley's other contemporaries, there was a lot more excuse, for all the clear and explicit statements (which I know of) on this matter come from the posthumously published papers in *Collected Essays*, except for one passage on pp. 238-40 of *Essays on Truth and Reality*. (This is in a paper originally published in 1909. Russell admitted in a letter to Bradley dated 16 November 1900 that he had not read *Appearance and Reality* with the same care which he had devoted to *The Principles of Logic*, and had misinterpreted it in his *Leibniz*. There is no reason to suppose that he was more assiduous in 1909.) Perhaps the main original cause of the confusion is the Index to *Appearance and Reality*, which states 'Relations are all intrinsical'. However, none of the references there given actually states this or even implies it, and the index entry reflects only one-half of Bradley's real view that all relations are both internal and external (*CE*, p. 641). One might suppose simply that there had been a change of mind between 1892 and 1924, were there not in the same index an exactly parallel phenomenon with the entry 'Idea is what it means'; for here we have again only one-half of Bradley's real view (*PL*, pp. 6-7), and again the references do not support the entry. Bradley was right to reject his own index as 'useless, . . . faulty and incomplete' (*AR*, p. 565).

15. Cf. Candlish (b), n. 2.

16. Cf. Candlish (c), 'Idealism and Bradley's Logic', *Idealistic Studies*, vol. 12, 1982, sec. 7. On the importance of the notion of substance in Bradley's

thought, cf. Candlish (b), secs. 8 and 9.

17. David Stove has suggested that on my account of the priorities in Bradley's reasoning, Bradley could just as well have turned out a materialist as an idealist. I think the point has to be admitted (it is not clear that it is an objection), provided that the materialism were not of an atomistic kind. But the qualifications involved are heavy. Idealism, it is true, appears logically quite late in the canonical ordering of Bradley's views. But psychologically, I am sure, it appears early, as anyone familiar with any of the details of Bradley's education, reading, and manner of writing will recognize. Idealism is present, even before it is proved, as a goal, something awaiting justification. In a very real sense, a materialist monism could not be *Bradley*'s. And Stove's point requires a certain indifference to the question of whether Bradley's argument for idealism is sound.

18. Russell, *Philosophical Essays*, London, 1910, p. 164. He made the allegation also in a letter to Bradley of 29 October 1907 (Merton College Library). But the letters (of the period near this date) from Bradley to Russell which are held in the Russell Archives contain no reply on the subject.

19. C. A. Campbell, *Scepticism and Construction*, London, 1931, p. 25.

20. The Bradley papers in Merton contain other attempts to come to grips with the problem (I B 19, p. 149, and III A 24, p. 11-19). But they can hardly be said to be successful; and he must have recognized this himself, for they form a large part of the material suppressed from Chapter I of *Essays on Truth and Reality*.

21. Peter Forrest has pointed out to me that Bradley's views on deduction and the laws of logic (see section III above) could be used to defend him from the charge of presupposing the Principle of Sufficient Reason. Just as 'A [logical] principle will neither demonstrate its applications nor can it be demonstrated *by* them. The principle is demonstrated when we see it *in* and as the function of, an individual act' (*PL*, pp. 530-1), so the Principle of Sufficient Reason could, in Bradley, be not a general and *a priori* demand of a metaphysic that it make the world intelligible in a special sense, but a summing-up of a series of individual judgments about particular intelligibilities and unintelligibilities. I have consigned this interesting insight to a note, not because I think it unimportant, but because it is something not in Bradley's own doctrines even though it is consistent with them.

　　How much support does Forrest's suggestion give to Bradley at this crucial point? It certainly appears to offer a way of justifying Bradley's claim to have a metaphysics devoid of presupposition. But a price has to be paid for this, and the price is that he and a metaphysician of contingency now have nothing to say to each other in deciding upon the status of a putative example of ultimate contingency. As so often in metaphysics, the achievement of security against one's opponents leaves them equally invulnerable.

CHAPTER 14

Bradley's Contribution to Absolute-theory

J. N. Findlay

I

The aim of this paper is to assess Bradley's contribution to
a discipline which I shall call Absolute-theory. This is the
attempt to determine the nature of something whose being
and essence are wholly self-explanatory, and neither permit
nor need any external explanation, and whose being and
essence are likewise totally explanatory of the existence and
properties of anything other than the entity in question. An
Absolute is something in regard to which it is nonsensical
to ask 'Why does it exist?' or 'Is there a possibility that it
should not have existed?', and equally 'Why is it of such and
such a nature?' or 'Could it have had another quite different
nature?' An Absolute is something whose existence covers all
possibilities: there can be no possible state of things in which
it would not be present, whatever else was present or not
present. In the case of the Absolute the Ontological Argument
is valid, for, if there were any possibility that it did not
cover, it would not be a true Absolute at all. Either it exists
whatever exists, or it does not, and cannot exist in any
circumstances. Absolute Space as conceived by some people
is a true Absolute, for whatever may exist·or not exist *in* it,
it cannot, as Kant held, be conceived as non-existent or
thought away. Logical Space as conceived by Wittgenstein
in the *Tractatus* would likewise be a true Absolute, since it
covers all the possibilities of the combination of ultimate
simples, and cannot be thought away.

There is nothing absurd, *in the abstract*, about the notion
of an Absolute; it is only when we begin to determine its
character that doubt arises. For, though it is impossible that

an Absolute should not exist, or be other than it is, it does
not at all follow that *we* can readily see or prove that we have
a true Absolute in our hands, or even that having such an
Absolute *clearly* in our hands is at all possible *for us*. We have
therefore always to exert ourselves and to ask very earnestly:
'Is it thinkable that such and such a thing should not exist?',
could there be a state of things in which there was no space,
or no time, or no matter, or no consciousness, or no society,
or no language, etc., etc.? And plainly what would be deemed
an Absolute by one philosopher would not be so deemed by
another. It is even possible to have a kind of thought, whether
valid or not, for which *all* existence is contingent, and nothing
is therefore an Absolute: many modern thinkers would seem
to be of this opinion. It is not wholly clear, however, whether
the absence of a first-order Absolute would not itself amount
to a higher order Absolute: whatever is possible, the finite or
transfinite *sum total* of contingencies will be possible, and
therefore necessary, and not thinkable away. All this really
shows how far we are from having a well-worked-out doctrine
of modality, perhaps the most pervasively urgent of all
philosophical requisites.

Absolutes may, further, it is arguable, be of different
degrees of perfection according to whether they do or do
not permit contingencies to exist *alongside* of them, whether
these take the form of additional properties that they themselves can have or not have, or of additional existences that
might be superadded to them. Thus Absolute Space could,
on certain views, be variously occupied or unoccupied, and
Absolute Godhead could be variously creative or non-creative,
without prejudice to its own absolute existence. On the other
hand, we have a strong inclination to hold that a truly
Absolute could not have further properties or existences
superadded to it, but would have to include *all* properties
and existences in its own omnipossibility. I am not, however,
sure that this sort of all-necessary Absolute is not as self-
contradictory as the sort of Absolute all of whose separate
determinations are contingent. I am inclined to think that
a coherent Absolute will have to have a set of necessary
properties and existential accompaniments that it *could* not
lack, but also certain contingent properties and existential
accompaniments that might *very well* be absent, and that a

contrast between the necessary and the contingent is, even in this case, necessary to the sense of either.

The Absolute will then be necessarily related to contingencies of some sort — there is only an apparent contradiction in this — and contingencies will be necessarily related to some sort of Absolute. A Creator-God, for example, will necessarily be able to create a World or not to create it, but this necessity will leave unaffected the contingency of what he creates or leaves uncreated. I am further not sure that a truly viable Absolute will not have to be credited with something like an Aristotelian *power of opposites*, so that it can freely decide or determine *which* contingent possibilities will or will not be realized. Such a disjunctive power of opposites completely explains, without entailing, whichever alternative is decided upon, and this power would seem to enhance, rather than diminish, the dignity of an Absolute.

It is further clear, I think, that a viable Absolute, even if it includes a multiplicity of component aspects, must also be overarchingly unitary in relation to all of them. An Absolute can have any number of component aspects: it can be trinitarian or decadic or hendecadic or whatever, but, since all these aspects necessarily coexist, they must all in effect constitute a single Absolute which is merely being considered *qua* this or *qua* that. Whatever is or is not the case, it is, however, clear that no Absolute can permit *alternatives* to itself: like Jahweh on Mount Sinai, it tolerates no other rival Absolutes. We cannot say that there is *this* Absolute but that there *could have* been another one: an Absolute is only aspectually plural. To distinguish its aspects, however deeply different, is only to consider it, without division *qua* this and *qua* that. I cannot hope to improve on the wonderful logic of St Athanasius. But this does not mean that *we*, as human thinkers, may not entertain a plurality of alternative Absolutes, and even, as we mentioned before, the questionable alternative of there being no Absolute at all; Absolute-theory would not be so difficult a discipline if it were otherwise. I would further stress that Absolute-theory cannot be consummated in terms of merely epistemic modalities, and certainly not in terms of the analytic modalities of formal logic. It is in quest of modalities that are in some sense metaphysical or ontological and themselves absolute, and it presupposes the presence of a certain sort of insight in ourselves that we find it certainly hard to exercise, and that may enrich and sometimes transform the insights of formal logic. Because *we* cannot determine whether a given candidate for Absolute status is or is not truly viable, does not determine whether it is or is not truly viable. Could there, for example, be an Absolute without some relation to consciousness or to value? There is an answer to this question, but only an iffish answer for us. *A priori* synthetic truths are the most important of all truths, but it is impossible for us to reach agreement on the *a priori* synthetic, or even to become quite clear what it is.

I cannot, however enter into all these matters on the present occasion except to express my conviction that Absolute-theory is a valid and viable discipline, and that it is obligatory, and not just optional, to include it in philosophy. It is in fact our duty as philosophers to operate with some concepts that are not, and never can be made, quite clear. And I can support my view dialectically by indicating how practically every philosopher has an Absolute of some sort, whether existential or subsistential or axiological or spatio-temporal or material or spiritual or what not. Everyone has something, cast in some category, that he cannot think away, and this leads me to think that there is and must be something that *no one* can validly think away. And I think further that there have been many great exponents of Absolute-theory who must have dug down to some of its basic axioms and theorems, though I feel quite hesitant in commending them. There are Plato, Plotinus, and Proclus whose Absolute, i.e. Unity or Goodness, is at once mathematical and axiological; there is Aquinas whose Absolute *is* His essence and His existence and His goodness, and has many other fascinating properties; there is Spinoza with his fascinating contrast of a naturing and a natured nature, both unknowably infinite; there is Christian Wolff who perfected Leibniz as Aquinas perfected Aristotle; there is Hegel with his dialectical Absolute plunging marvellously from category to category; there is a modern Absolutist such as Whitehead; there are of course the oriental Absolutists of the Vedanta or Mahayana, whether ancient or recent; and there is last, but not least, our own home-grown F. H. Bradley, who is a much more original Absolute-theorist than is usually thought. Though his contemporaries called him a Hegelian, he rightly rejected this description. He is in fact much closer to Proclus and to Spinoza than to Hegel, and he has a stress on Feeling which is all his own. I am not however concerned on this occasion to determine the ancestry of his Absolute-theory, but to study its content and structure, and comment on its validity. Whatever he has produced, it is a domesticated, British Absolute, and must be cherished and admired as such.

Though Bradley was not a Hegelian, he was deeply influenced by his reading of Hegel, and great light may be thrown on his Absolute-theory by comparing and contrasting it with Hegel's. Like Hegel, Bradley believes that there is no firm and final truth about anything which is not the truth about the All, the Everything, the Total System to which all things belong. Only when a thing, concept, or state of mind has been given its place in the Total System of things can we arrive at the truth about it. Bradley's great difference from Hegel is, however, the absence of any gradualist ascent from finite things, concepts, and states of mind to the Absolute, any use of the 'dialectic method', which Bradley in fact explicitly rejected.

Hegel may have his Absolute up his sleeve throughout his dialectical progress, but he only produces it as a trump card at the very end. He endeavours to show that Being is impossible without distinctive Quality, that Quality is impossible without an indefinite progression into other qualities, that qualities require a quantitative basis to unify them, that qualities and quantities alike require underlying essences or laws to connect them, that essences or laws presuppose self-specifying, self-instantiating, notional universals, that these notional universals presuppose mind that can know and manipulate objects, and that behind everything is a basic teleology that externalizes itself in the form of nature, and which then can interiorize itself in the form of conscious spirit, and which then in the end can achieve complete consciousness of itself as being the Absolute, the Idea or Truth of things in which they all have their final end.

In Bradley there is no such dialectical unwrapping of the Absolute: it comes straight into the picture from the outset in his view that finite, independent things externally related to one another cannot exist, that their existence would involve an inner contradiction or discrepancy, that anything less than the total system of things is dependent on that total system for its existence and for all its properties, that it is really only a moment or aspect of that system, and that the relations which appear to connect it with other moments or aspects are not to be conceived of as external, contingent bonds, but as simple expresssions of the pervasive unity in which moments live, move, and have their being. This unity does indeed express itself in distinct, particular individuals, and in distinct universals which these instantiate, but such instances and universals have no true independence or self-sufficiency, but are merely the one Absolute undividedly lending its inalienable self-sufficiency to whatever it informs.

None the less, just as Hegel conceded the existence, both in Nature and Mind, of a principle called the Understanding, which could accord a *seeming* self-sufficiency and independence to the various aspects of the Absolute, and which was in fact necessary to their final unification by Reason, so Bradley concedes that the Absolute includes and sums up varied *appearances*, in each of which particulars and universals achieve a seeming independence, which will however have to be liquidated when they are fitted into their final place in the whole. All our higher mental acts of intellect and volition involve giving a show of independence to what, seen in the Absolute, is incapable of any independence, and such acts themselves also enjoy a seeming independence from their objects; and it is, moreover, a basic feature of the Absolute that it should be able to show itself in these abstractive activities, which are themselves only abstractly separable from the total system on which they practise their abstractions. There is thus a real existence *as* a moment, of what *seems* to erect moments into separate existents.

Bradley, however, differs absolutely from Hegel in that he does not believe in any overcoming of the false abstractions of the Understanding in a higher, rational form of intelligibility. He allows, as Hegel does, that the abstract lucidities of the intellect and the will have emerged out of an obscure matrix of feeling, a blended unity resembling the *petites perceptions* of Leibniz, but he also thinks as Hegel does *not*, that the higher forms of intellect, will and rationalized emotion, must *terminate* in a state which will have all the obscurity of primitive sentience, and of which we can form no clear conception since clear conceptions must commit suicide in reaching it. Vaguely and analogically we see what sort of consummation it must be, but we cannot, without liquidating ourselves and our intellects, actually conceive or intuit it. Plainly we are here moving in the region of Aquinas's accounts of the beatific vision, when the Divine Essence supersedes the concepts of the human intellect, or in the upper ether of Plotinian theosophy, where our acquaintance with the One is described as a *touch*, rather than as a conception or a vision.

To this sort of consummation Hegel is of course averse. While he does not shun the use of the term 'mystical' in regard to processes which reveal higher unities, they are also held to be activities of the *Vernunft* or Reason: these may transcend the Understanding, but they also have more affinities with that Understanding, and with its abstract diremptions, than with the immediacies of Feeling or Sentience in which diremptions are wholly lost. It is hard to say whether Bradleian or Hegelian Absolutism is more in accord with the formal logicism of contemporary thought. Bradley is perhaps more acceptable to the modern formalist since he is prepared to *break* with intelligibility in the modern formal sense — formal logicians are strangely ready to respect anything that proclaims itself as blind faith — whereas Hegel perpetrates the greater enormity of trying to be reasonable and intelligible in a field beyond the strict either–or and not–both of formal logic.

My own view is that there is no legitimate quarrel between rationalism and mysticism. Reason will show us where ultimate truth must lie, whereas mysticism will enable us to enjoy it. It is, however, doubtful whether Bradley was either consistently rational or consistently mystical. His arguments for the Absolute will not convince the rationalist, while his pallid descriptions will not inflame the mystic. I should like to point out, further, as a great weakness of Bradley's Absolutism in opposition to Hegel's, that, in making *all* relations internal, he does not allow us to distinguish between profound contrasts, entailments of essence, and conjunctions that only have a basis in fact. To suppose that John Smith might have smoked an extra cigarette is as self-contradictory as supposing that he might have been a puma. The activities of a Kripkean, possible-world theorist would be impeded in a Bradleian world, and so also would those of the Husserlian phenomenologist. Hegel here has the advantage. For he admits radical contingency and mere correctness in some superficial assertions, thereby lending greater significance to the categorial connections that he emphasizes.

It is worth while at this point to commend Bradley for his wide use of the term 'Feeling' to cover any sort of consciousness of a deeply blended, 'nutshell' character, a *Bewusstheit* or *Bewusstseinslage* in the sense of the Würzburg school, in which much intellectual content may be concentrated, without being teased out into lucid symbolism or imagery. We could have, on Bradley's use of the term (which agrees with ordinary usage) an obscure feeling that n is a prime number, that all will come all right in the end, that this should not be permitted in the circumstances, that this involves a contradiction somewhere, etc., etc. We are not limited to the feelings and sensations of laboratory psychology, which have unduly influenced even so genuine an introspector as Wittgenstein. It is also worth while to commend Bradley for the sort of idealism which rests on this conception of Feeling. For the form of epistemological idealism which believes that the knowing mind constructs the world, through its acts of perception and judgment, is as far from him as it is from common sense. The feelings we have of ourselves, and of the things and persons around us, are for him states which precede the distinction between the This and the What, or between subject and object. The world is there for Feeling before it is there for Intellect or for conscious Volition. And there may even be feelings claiming a place in the Absolute which are unconnected with any organized body, and which are, in fact, nobody's feelings. The primitive cataclysms of geology may for Bradley simply have been part of the Absolute's total sentience, without being part of any experience in which the distinction between subject and object was explicit. Hegel too, in his *Naturphilosophie*, believed in a vague geological sentience which antedated the emergence of animals and men, and Whitehead has likewise made great play with prehensions and feelings that anticipate the long-range intentionality of consciousness.

The Bradleian doctrine of sentience enables us to avoid a materialistic absolutism in which the emergence of life and consciousness is inexplicable, and also the late Victorian neo-Kantianism in which the world is a construct of the thinking mind. Sentience is a category which avoids the subject-object bifurcation of intentionality, and is, as it were, neutral between mind and matter, yet will permit either to emerge from its unity, in which both are implicit. There is an appeal in the equation between natural forces and kinaesthetic and organic sensations: pressure, density, resistance, attraction, velocity, even heat and cold, are things that we can feel; as sights and sounds, the objects of the distance-senses, are not. It is attractive to conceive of physical space as thickly peopled with tensions, pressures, shivers, resistances, etc., not unlike those which we feel, and which, while qualitative, always have a close relation to what is quantitative.

If it is a merit of Bradley to have built Feeling, as a primitive form of consciousness, into the deep structure of his Absolute, it is also a merit to have incorporated primitive feeling — forms of desire, will, and emotion — into the same deep structure. Teleology or teleonomy is a built-in feature of all the organic structures in our world, and a viable Absolute-theory is not possible if teleology is attached contingently or miraculously to what is not in any way purposive. Purpose, however interrupted, frustrated, and dispersed in the universe is so distinctive a feature in its structure as to demand a presence at its very centre, and, once there, can explain the non-purposive features of reality better than the latter are capable of explaining *its* presence. Value-free Absolutes have certainly been constructed, but they lack the inner coherence and unity which is surely characteristic of an all-explanatory Absolute, and Bradley has not erred in incorporating a nisus, not only towards pleasure, but towards all the higher intellectual, aesthetic, and moral ends which arise when we consider our striving and our action in their bearing upon everything and everyone. Bradley's Absolute is not a moral agent nor a self-concious artist, not a scientist nor a philosopher, but it can give birth to these remarkable products, so removed from anything limited, local, and transient that they must plainly spring from some feature central to the Absolute. Being themselves in aspiration absolute, and detached from anything contingent, they would seem to be authentically an expression of the Absolute, which is at all points beyond all contingency. If the Absolute therefore becomes somewhat in the nature of a religious object, this is surely appropriate, since religion is nothing other than the unified pursuit of those goals all of which carry detached universality to its limit, whether in thought, emotion, or practice. These propositions cannot be argued for on the present occasion.

II

In Book II of *Appearance and Reality* Bradley then sets forth various basic features of his Absolute, the first being that it has a positive nature, exclusive of all discord. Its nature is, in other words, a true universal which is also a true unity, something that explains its own existence and that of every-thing else; it is not, and cannot be, a trumped-up, adventitious complex of mutually irrelevant features such as might seem 'coherent' to a formal logician. (Professor Nelson Goodman, with his notorious 'bleen' and 'grue', provides the handiest example of such a complex.) In this true unity of the Absolute there will be many distinct appearances to which the intellect can give quasi-independence, and between which it may fail to spot necessary connections. In the Absolute, however, all these appearances will be ineluctably blended like the various savours in a well-made cocktail. (Example not Bradley's.) Since Bradley's fundamental category is that of sentience or feeling, out of which all physical and psychic categories must be separated, it follows that sentient experience is the basic stuff of reality. Its differentiated, abstractive forms are them-selves elements that can be lived through, and that contribute to total sentient experience.

We are, however, assured that, since in the Absolute all things are embraced in a felt unity, which does something better than explain or understand them, this felt side must also be *pleasurable*. Indefinite accesses of pain and disvalue may be present in sundered aspects of the Absolute, but, duly felt in context, they can only contribute to its pleasure. The thought of Nero fiddling while Rome was burning, here obtrudes itself, but is obviously irrelevant, for Nero himself did not even appear to burn. Bradley's Absolute, like Vedantic Brahman, has therefore Bliss as well as Being and a sort of Wisdom among its basic properties.

Further, the Absolute, like the God of Aquinas, has an essence inseparable from its existence: the distinction between exemplifying instance and exemplified universal here collapses into coincidence, to comprehend which would, however, involve intellectual suicide. This does not mean that Bradley, any more than Aquinas, countenances the Ontological Proof: *for us* the coincidence of essence with existence remains unintelligible, and God or the Absolute does something much better than understand it. Our thought merely strives towards the unity of an all-embracing concept with an instantial totality which it wholly illuminates, and it is in the light of this nisus that we after a fashion understand the Absolute's self-enjoyment, something as much above understanding as our feeling-life lies beneath it. In the Absolute, errors and false appearances will likewise have their place, and in fact all we call real and true is erroneous and false, since it fails to achieve the completeness of context essential to the real and the true. Many criticisms of Bradley by pluralists and realists are here wide of the mark. He would not deny that 'John Smith lives in Wimbledon' is a wholly correct statement, which may not, in any ordinary sense, require to be revised. It is only erroneous in failing to achieve a fullness of context to which all statement merely strives. Criticisms of Bradley too often fail to see how far from the ordinary is the sense of many of his basic concepts.

What is true of falsehood and error is also true of evil. There are countless untoward things which are perpetrated by, or which happen to, finite individuals, whose finitude consists in *their* not being seen in their context. In that complete context they will cease to be untoward, since they are aspects of an Absolute which provides teleological as well as causal reasons for everything, even if *we* find its providence inscrutable. Time and Space are next, because involving contradiction, they are dismissed from the inner core of reality, though appearances of the temporal and the spatial are essential parts of it. That appearances, in the sense of appearings of certain matters, are absolutely real, does not mean that appearances, in the sense of the matters apparent, are real at all. Bradley is aware of intentional logic, and believes that the self-discrepant, while entering into what is intentionally objective, need not therefore be accorded reality.

The immediacies of the This and the Mine, on the one hand, and of the universals they contingently illustrate, are next considered: in appearance these may be polarized in a senseless manner, but in the Absolute they must come into full coincidence. Universals and instances seen in full context are the same facets of the Absolute differently regarded. Solipsism, as the attempt to confine everything to the merely personal, or the merely momentary experient, is next dismissed: the particular self, and, *a fortiori*, the self of the moment, necessarily point to other persistent or momentary selves which will provide them with a context. Bradley by anticipation refutes the solipsism of the early Wittgenstein and others by holding that the notion of a self is essentially that of *one among others*: it can only be *this* and *mine*, because there are other 'thises' and 'mines'. A chapter on Nature suggests many interesting possibilities, for example of spaces and times completely independent of one another, but somehow coexisting in the Absolute, or detached bodies of feeling which belong to no finite centre, etc., etc.

Nature for Bradley, as for Hegel, is a side of the Absolute characterized by maximum opposition to self-dependence and unity: it is the region of externality and chance conjunction. The *nature* of the Absolute is, however, only such as to demand the appearance of such externality: in its show of the external and fortuitous, Nature provides a necessary contrast to its more systematically organized, conscious citizenry. The chapter on body and soul is likewise full of interesting suggestions, but Bradley does not accord any important place to the phenomena of hypnosis, telepathy, clairvoyance, etc., to which Hegel in the *Philosophy of Spirit* assigns such significance, seeing them as in some sort a half-way house between the disjoined externality of nature and the interpenetrating unity of Spirit. The notion of psychic survival is likewise countenanced as no more than an empty possibility: Bradley is particularly hard on those who, like Kant, see it as a necessary postulate of morality. But in Bradley's mystical theosophy a place might well have been found for a spectrum of states of imperfectly externalized, half-interpenetrating phenomena which would have led up, step by step, to the complete interpenetration of the Absolute fully itself. But perhaps anything like a belief in spooks would have sat ill on a Fellow of Merton College.

The three chapters XXIV–XXVI of *Appearance and Reality* make a number of weighty points, the first being that, in the Absolute, the copula and the sign of identity will come into full coincidence, thus liquidating what Russell was to call a 'disgrace to the human race', which has always been Bradleian on this point. In the appearances of the Absolute there will, further, be vastly many *degrees* of departure from such full coincidence, and we shall have, in consequence, vastly many degrees of truth and reality, i.e. approximations to truth and reality. Provided 'truth' and 'reality' are given Bradleian senses, there is nothing unacceptable in this opinion: most of Bradley's critics simply refuse to think in this manner. There are likewise, we are told, infinitely many degrees of goodness in phenomenal things and states: only in the Absolute will they all achieve maximum goodness. 'Nowhere', we are told,

is there even a single fact so fragmentary and so poor that to the universe it does not matter. There is truth in every idea however false, there is reality in every existence however slight; and, where we can point to reality or truth, there is the one undivided life of the Absolute. Appearance without reality would be impossible, for what then could appear? And reality without appearance would be nothing, for there is certainly nothing outside appearances. But on the other hand Reality (we must repeat this) is not the sum of things. It is the unity in which all things coming together are transmuted, in which they are changed all alike, though not changed equally. And, as we have perceived, in this unity relations of isolation and hostility are affirmed and absorbed. These also are harmonious in the Whole, though not of course harmonious as such, and while severally confined to their natures as separate . . . The apparent discordance and distraction is overruled into harmony, and it is but the condition of fuller and more individual development (*AR*, pp. 431–2).

I cannot improve on this passage, which gives poignant expression to a uniquely original form of Absolute-theory.

III

I shall round off this paper by briefly considering the merits and demerits of Bradley as an Absolute-theorist. That Absolute-theory is a meaningful, necessary enterprise I shall assume, even though it is impossible to pursue Absolute-theory by means of formal logic alone. But since natural science is likewise in quest of forms of explanatory unity that are not significant in terms of formal logic alone, this transcendence of the formal is not a reproach to Absolute-theory. An assessment of Absolute-theory must however raise the question as to the validity and coherence of the whole notion of an Absolute. For an Absolute stands in the unique position of being either a necessary existent, since there can be no possible state of things that its being does not cover, or, if we discern incoherence and ontological absurdity in its concept, of being wholly incoherent and impossible. For us this is an open question, and will probably always remain so.

For the Absolute, of course, if there is one — a possibility for us — this is not the case. It cannot but have something which is better than even a certainty of its own omnipossibility. For us also it will always be an open question with what sort of being the Absolute coincides, and there will be many alternative Absolutes that we have to consider, though for the Absolute, if it is coherent, and therefore real, there can be no such alternatives. Absolute-theory as a human enterprise therefore involves a multitude of alternatives, including the alternative that belief in an Absolute is incoherent and nugatory.

It is a defect of Bradley that he does not explore alternative Absolutes with sufficient zeal, and certainly not in the exhaustive way in which they were explored by Aquinas and Christian Wolff and Shankaracharya, to name only a few great Absolute-theorists. For the all-inclusive individual Absolute believed in by Bradley has many competitors: the One, the Form of the Good, Space-Time, Logical Space, the Transcendental Subject, the Ultimate Emptiness, the primitive proposition which generates all others, etc., etc. Bradley as an Absolute-theorist is rather an amateur and a dilettante. Like a man hurling darts in a pub-room, he aims at the

Absolute with random intuitions, and does not doubt that he has hit it.

Appearance and Reality plainly does not deserve a place beside Proclus' *Elements of Theology*, or Aquinas's *Summa Theologica*, or Spinoza's *Ethics*, or Hegel's *Encyclopaedia*, or Shankara's Commentary on the *Vedanta-sutras*. On the other hand, as the achievement of a late-Victorian, Oxford don, it has very great brilliance, and fits in well with the other brilliant products of that *fin de siècle*. I myself must confess myself charmed by a rereading of Bradley after some decades of neglect. He philosophizes in a very gay manner, and one develops a certain warmth towards his highly irresponsible Absolute. I find, further, that his Absolute largely coincides with a mystic mandala that I have worked out for myself, which may have been influenced in part by early readings of Bradley. For I believe myself that the dirempted world of our common experience, and the language which describes it, are the source of an infinity of philosophic puzzles, which will not yield to Wittgensteinian or similar types of therapy.

Other minds, causation, time, duty, etc., etc., are all the seats of antilogisms and antinomies, in whose case it is largely capricious which intuitive certainty one prefers to reject, and which to hold to. I have come to believe that these puzzles arise because we live, as it were, on the periphery where everything seems to stand apart from everything else. Such peripheral disjuncts can only be forced to make sense if we see them all as radiating from a centre where all disjuncts interpenetrate in unity. Many of our higher experiences emulate such a unity, and particularly our more widely ranging thoughts, emotional attachments, and momentous decisions. There, at the centre, as Bradley teaches, essence will coincide with existence, and goodness and beauty with reality, and the anguish of our separated selfhood will terminate in something better even than love. I believe in such an absolute centre, and conceive of it, with Bradley, as being as much parasitic on its disjoined periphery as the latter is parasitic upon it. I think, further, that, without such a centre, it is impossible to make sense of any phenomenal arrangement, and I also believe myself, in common with the most worthless things, to be on an ever open lifeline which unites me to that centre, from which I am constantly deriving comfort and refreshment. Our whole inner life moves along that lifeline, and we may perhaps go further along it when we leave this periphery for good. All these persuasions are mystical, and I also believe them to be the necessary pre-suppositions of rationality in every field. For rationality involves a deeper unity among all items than formal logic ever deems necessary. I also think that Bradley has set forth the requirements of a mystical rationality in a manner that is maybe far from cogent or intellectually mandatory, but which is none the less vastly delightful and refreshing.

CHAPTER 15

The Self and its World in Bradley and Husserl

T. L. S. Sprigge

According to Bradley the self is merely appearance, and unreal, though, like other appearances, it exists.[1] Quite what we are to make of unrealities which exist has always been a problem for Bradley's readers. However, part of what Bradley means is that there is an incoherence in the concept of things so characterized, but that the concept of such things, and judgments which ascribe existence to them, are an indispensable part of a way of thinking about reality which is appropriate and inevitable for universal human projects. The incoherences that Bradley finds in the concepts of things that he regards as unreal but existing are not all of the same kind, but the typical case is one in which there are clashing elements, between which we have to oscillate in our thinking, while abandoning any one element would destroy the utility of thinking which employs the idea of there being such things.

This suggests that it must be peculiarly difficult to give a coherent account of the concept of one of these things which is unreal but exists. To present it as a coherent concept is not to describe it correctly. With things of this sort (and Bradley thinks that all ordinary things *are* of this sort) a certain impression of confusion in saying what they are may be a mark that a philosopher has got their nature right rather than wrong. Thus it may be a sign that the commentator has failed to do justice to Bradley's position if he makes it seem too clear-cut.

It may be objected that the description of the incoherent need not itself be incoherent and that the fact that the concept of something, either in truth or as Bradley takes it, is incoherent does not mean that incoherence is an ideal in specifying it. Yet it is certainly difficult to be coherent about the incoherent (muddled views are harder to describe clearly than clear ones). More important, from a Bradleian point of view, the concepts we employ in analysing a concept are themselves bound to be elements in the incoherent way of thinking about the world which is normally our best way of dealing with it.

Thus the following account of Bradley's view of the self is probably rather lacking in the right kind of incoherence to do justice to Bradley. However, in the interests of simplicity I am going to concentrate on just one of the strands he finds in our concept of the self, ignoring its conflict with the others. This strand corresponds to what Bradley gives as the sixth meaning of 'self' in Chapter IX of *Appearance and Reality* and plays a role in various of his other discussions. It is the sense of 'self' in which self and not-self are equivalent to subject and object.

In dealing with Bradley's account of the self I shall also be concerned with the character of the not-self. I shall, however, confine my concern to that major component of the not-self, which is the self's surrounding physical environment, ignoring such other realms as that of mathematics, the imaginary, and so forth.

In discussing the relation between the self and its surrounding physical world, and in thinking about the contrast between the real environment and what one contrasts with it as imaginary, Bradley develops an account of what he calls 'my real world' which has interesting affinities and contrasts with Husserl's notion of one's surrounding world and of the life world. I shall make some comparisons later.[2]

A common philosophic view which Bradley attacks is that the contrast between the self and its environing real world is one between what belongs within experience and what falls wholly outside experience, known to the self only as something which somehow produces certain psychic effects. For Bradley the contrast between the self and its world falls within experience, even if there is more of the world outside too. The hither side of the world, so to speak, is actually an ingredient of my centre of experience as it is at any moment.

Though Bradley uses the expression 'my real world' to suggest that reality in this sense (to be distinguished from that sense in which reality is lacking in ordinary things) stands in contrast with other realms thereby treated as unreal only from a particular personal perspective, Bradley is not implying that it is necessarily private to me. Your real world and mine may be shared so as to be our real world, though we should not forget that for Bradley 'it takes two to make the same' and that identity always implies a difference.

The distinction between self and not-self occurs within *a centre of experience*. We must now consider what Bradley means by such centres which became increasingly important element in his system (*ETR*, chap. XIV). Readers of Bradley diverge in how they take this conception. I shall offer my own account, and of the role these centres play in Bradley's system, without fully justifying my interpretation. We must remember that here, as with more everyday concepts, we have what for Bradley is an inevitable way of thinking about reality (for those who plumb it metaphysically), but there are incoherences. I shall continue to use simplifications which somewhat disguise this.

As a first attempt we might say a finite centre of experience is either the total experiential reality which constitutes one total phase in a stream of experience, or that it is an enduring reality whose history is a stream of experience. The Jamesian and Husserlian expression 'stream of experience' is not used by Bradley, and is a little misleading, but it is helpful in a first reconstruction of Bradley's position.

Of the two ways of understanding a finite centre the first seems more basic for Bradley. The enduring centre is an 'ideal construction' which comes about by identifying certain centres, posited in addition to the one in which the positing is carried out, as that centre's past, and perhaps other ones thought of as somehow possible as that centre's future. Thus different centres in the first sense are the same centre in the second sense, because relations hold between them on the basis of which identifications of one with another occur within them. Centres of the first kind are therefore more basic, in the sense that we can better explain the status of the second kind by reference to the first kind than vice versa. I think that Bradley holds that there can be a less full case of a centre of the second sort, enduring across time, but where the identification is made from outside it.

I shall call centres in the first sense momentary, and in the second sense enduring, though this is not Bradley's terminology. He allots a double status to centres of experience of either kind. Firstly they may be taken as existing in the 'real' world of space and time, in the object world. It is evident that when we take them thus, centres of the first sort will be momentary, those of the second sort enduring. Thus these expressions are convenient ones for distinguishing them more explicitly than Bradley does. Secondly, and more fundamentally, centres of experience may be taken as the focus within which the object world is experienced, envisaged, constructed, the object world being nothing other than what in some manner or other is presented within these focuses.

Each centre, we might say, tells itself a bit of a world story, one fragment of the story told in some detail, the rest merely adumbrated. The object world is the whole story on which all these fragments of story converge. In that whole story the centres themselves figure as things or events, but their more fundamental status is as fragments of story-telling. As tellings of the story, and thus as out of the story, they are not in the story's time ('real' time). Hence Bradley says that, speaking strictly, they are not in time. It remains the case that the centres which, taken as elements in the story, come out as momentary are metaphysically more basic for Bradley than those which, taken as elements in the story, come out as enduring. They may, indeed, be less basic in the story, inasmuch as we can better explain what the momentary ones are within the story by saying they are phases of the enduring ones — none the less the actually experienced tellings of the story, in which the story has its fragmented home, is in the centres which the story calls momentary. (The whole story is, however, experienced by the Absolute via its fragmented tellings within the 'momentary' centres.)

The kind of contrast which I have been trying to explain here is found in other philosophers too. It is explicit in Husserl's thought, where the pure ego finally inserts itself into the object world it constitutes, though as something whose nature, even as an object, is illuminated by the kind of understanding it can gain of itself by practising the epoché and seeing itself as the ultimate constitutor of the world. But there is an interesting difference. For Husserl there is a genuine internal or subjective time within which each phase of experience has a definite position not derivative from the part allotted it in the object world, while Bradley inclines to think that momentary centres only stand in temporal relations to one another, perhaps even only belong together as the same enduring centre in different states, in a manner derivative from their role in the object world.

This is one of several related reasons why it is misleading to use the expression 'stream of experience' in presenting his theory, for it is associated with philosophers, such as James and Husserl, who believe that the flowing on of one experience from another is a basic experienced datum, not something constructed or 'ideal'. By contrast, the relation which for Bradley makes a centre of experience own another one as belonging to its past, is a suitable identity of character, together with just the right difference of character for the one to lend itself to interpretation as a transformed version of the other, whether directly or via intermediaries. It would seem, indeed, that the relations between their characters (including the content which makes them both perspectives on different phases in the history of the object world) are supposed to do more than merely settle which past experiences belong to a present centre as its past, but determine even that they are in the past rather than in the future.

What are these relations between the characters of 'momentary' centres which must achieve so much? In developing a Bradleian view for myself I should lay great stress on memory, including that primary memory which is the sense on the part of one phase of experience of itself as having just emerged from a previous one of the distinctive character of which it retains a taste. This can be understood as a relation between their characters, even though the only brief way of expressing it is in language which presupposes what it is supposed to explain. Some of what Bradley says lends itself to this interpretation, but he also expresses scorn for theories which take memory as basic in explaining anything.

This is related to his insistence that memory is an inference (for example *ETR*, chaps. XII and XIII). We should bear in mind, however, that for Bradley the process of reproduction or redintegration (his substitute for the association of ideas) is a form of inference, one in which a certain experienced or judged universal content is supplemented by further universal contents with which it has been united in the past. We may well object that this lacks the universally accessible type of validity expected of inference; it is really a case of memory in a broad sense. Bradley up to a point recognizes this, but thinks that broad sense improper (*ETR*, pp. 353 ff., 384 ff.). Still, his insistence that memory is inference could have been presented as the claim that memory of specific events is derivative from memory, in the sense of empirically acquired knowledge, of universal connections.

This may suggest that it is the fact of redintegration which constitutes identity of a centre across time (*AR*, p. 97). That would imply that redintegration is an ideal echoing of connections of content between distinct momentary centres, which puts them in a temporal series as phases of one enduring centre, rather than something to be explained by their being such phases. I doubt that Bradley clearly held this, and can only say that his rather vague view of a centre's transtemporal identity is best thus made precise. With regard to the identity of a self, which may or may not persist throughout the duration of the centre to which it belongs, Bradley seems to think that memory of a particular past is an essential factor (*ETR*, pp. 451-9).[3] (If such memory derives from redintegration, a self, in its core being, is thus tied to one centre.)

Although for Bradley the persistence of an enduring thing, whether a centre, a self, or anything else, requires a series of particulars which somehow follow on from one another, one must not think of him as simply eliminating the enduring thing and substituting a succession of differents in Humean or Whiteheadian fashion (for example *PL*, pp. 61 and 289-94; cf. also *ETR*, p. 195). Rather is the enduring thing a concrete universal actualized all along the series. (Since Bradley thinks that such an identity of character, in the case of a centre, is part of the real basis of redintegration, there is, after all, an aspect of the identity of a centre which founds rather than is founded on redintegration.)[4] The enduring centre is not a fiction, nor is it other than the momentary centres; rather each momentary centre is the enduring centre actualized in a fresh determination. Or at least this would be so if identity lived up to its name, as Bradley thinks it fails to do with selves, and perhaps with centres.

Does a momentary centre have any duration? Bradley tells us that there may be 'a lapse and a before and after' within a centre (clearly a 'momentary' one). (*ETR*, p. 410; cf. *PL*, pp. 53-5). Such remarks suggest that they last for 'a specious present' and are intensive unities stretched out in a time dimension with a unity not belonging to the constructed sequence of such centres, just like the pulses of experience of James, Whitehead, Santayana, and others. Bradley's actual position may be more tortuous than this, but we come nearer to it by thinking of them thus rather than as 'instantaneous' (see esp. *AR*, chap. V).

We must now consider the role these centres play in Bradley's system. It is tempting to say that they are the basic building blocks of the universe, that taken together they form the Absolute, or total self-experiencing reality, and that everything else which in any sense exists does so only in virtue of in some manner falling within, or exhibiting itself within, them.

This is, indeed, the sole status allowed by Bradley to anything not either a centre or the Absolute itself (though Bradley allows the bare possibility, which I shall ignore for now, that there may be a margin of feeling in the Absolute not filtered through a finite centre). (*AR*, pp. 241-4 and 467; also *ETR*, p. 350, n. 1.) As I tried to suggest by my talk of a world story, the surrounding world of physical objects exists only because it is exhibited piecemeal in different finite centres. Bradley speaks of what is thus exhibited as being 'in' these centres — a use of the preposition we shall be considering. (Whether some things exist as merely thus exhibitable will be discussed later.)

Finite centres, then, do play a basic role in Bradley's system. It is perhaps misleading to speak of them as the building blocks of the universe; this suggests that what only exists as falling or exhibited within them is necessarily a less fundamental reality, which is not Bradley's view. Indeed, the word 'only' gives a wrong impression. Certain eternal values, for example, are more real than the finite centres within which they must occur in order to be (for example *ETR*, pp. 468-9).

Selves, like these other realities, can only exist within finite centres. It seems that a self exists by occurring in some one finite centre as that to which whatever is exhibited there as an object is exhibited. In order to grasp this conception we must distinguish between the fact that something is experienced and that it is an object of consciousness. A whole momentary centre, I suggest, is something of the kind one is trying to get a grasp of if one tries to imagine what it is like being a certain organism. The ones we know about figure in the object world as some organism's personal perspective upon it. If there are any which do not pertain to an organism, they are experiential unities of the same essential kind. Each centre, at least in familiar cases, is experienced as a unified multiplicity of elements with certain specific sorts of togetherness with each other, which we conceptualize, if we do, as relations, and which, following Bradley himself, I shall simply call relations (for example *ETR*, p. 417). Among these is the relation of being conscious of. The self is a totality experienced as standing in this relation to other elements, without there being anything experienced as thus related to it. (We may confine ourselves to the simple case where there is just one such self.)

So the self is not an object of consciousness, but it, and its relation to that of which it is conscious, is experienced. One may ask 'experienced by what or whom?' Bradley's answer would seem to be that, from one of view, it is the whole centre which experiences itself and the way in which its elements are related, and from another point of view, it is the Absolute which experiences itself through this centre. Setting the Absolute regretfully aside for now, this notion of a total experience which experiences itself takes us, I believe, further into the depths of things than we can get by more standard locutions.

So far I think Bradley's view illuminating. However, his official view of this relation of consciousness which sets off the self against the not-self does not seem quite satisfactory, though it is near to a view I would endorse.

I should like him to have held that the contents of a centre of experience fall into two groups. First, there are contents directed upon other contents. These are either modes of attention or feeling towards them, or some kind of attention which singles out some characteristic present in them and somehow projects it on to reality not presently experienced but continuous with what is so, either as a characteristic supposedly occurring there in another relational context, or as somehow symbolizing some characteristic found there. Secondly, there are contents which are not themselves directed at any other content, but which may have contents of the first kind directed at them. It would fit in with the usage of some philosophers (for example Husserl) to call the first contents active, and the second passive, but these are labels not offering further explanation of their status.

On this view, the self consists in the active contents within the centre, and the immediately experienced not-self of the passive contents, together with, as an introspected aspect of the self, any active elements which are also objects on which other contents are directed. The more organized into a unity the active elements are, the more there is a single coherent self.

This is certainly a fairly Bradleian conception, but it is not quite Bradley's.

This is not just because Bradley was suspicious of any use of the words 'active' and 'passive' to express supposedly fundamental concepts, since this suspicion is misconstrued if he is taken to hold that experience consists merely of a union of equally charged sensations (cf. his discussion of the experience of the expansion and contraction of the self; see, for example, *CE*, chap. XIV). The clash is rather with the suggestion that whatever has not been made an explicit object of attention belongs to the self, once granted that there is something which has been made an object, with which it thereby contrasts; in short, that infantile immediacy has been surpassed.[5]

This suggestion was hardly satisfactory. First, it is surely incorrect to identify merely not being an object with being a subject to which whatever does occur as an object appears. This would lump together contents of such different status as a feeling of sexual excitation in response to some visible object, a mere ache not in response to anything, and the noise of the traffic outside, provided that they all belonged in the background of experience and were not attended to as objects. Second, even if we took it as an account of the contrast between self and not-self, while dismissing an equation of this with the contrast between subject and object, it remains unsatisfactory to think of such elements in the unnoticed background of experience as a mild ache and the noise of the traffic as equally elements of the self.

It may be suggested that, for Bradley, the noise of the traffic, when not attended to as an object, is mere sensation, thus not part of the not-self object world. Yet for him sensation, when made an object, belongs to the not-self, so that it does not, as such, belong to the self. It seems that both Bradley's own view, and the one I have adumbrated, require supplementation by reference to the *me* which, belonging to the object side of experience, is still experienced by the self as belonging to it in a way which the mere not-self does not. The ache and the noise of the traffic contrast then as potential objects of consciousness as me and as mere not-self.

Although Bradley's account of the contrast between the object side of experience and the subject side for which it is an object may be unsatisfactory, his key claim that the contrast between them is a distinction within experience, and that the relation between them is experienced but not something of which any subject is conscious, is surely an insight of enduring value. The same goes for the contrast between self and not-self, obviously so if this coincides with that between subject and object but also if it is taken in any other at all promising way. Elsewhere Bradley puts more stress on the role of other features in the constitution of an intra-experiential contrast between self and not-self which do not seem to coincide with it, for example he treats association with pleasure and pain, or some kind of special identification which the experiential whole accomplishes with a particular part of itself, as distinctive of the 'group of contents' constituting the self (see especially AR, chap. IV).[6]

One valuable application of the view that the contrast between self and not-self holds within total experience is found in the thesis that contents may pass between the two sides of experience. Here is a basis for a phenomenological investigation into different ways in which one's body may be experienced, and also for a comparison with the Husserlian view that higher noetic acts may initiate fresh layers of noema.

I turn now to the not-self as Bradley conceives it, and more particularly to the environing natural world. This, Bradley seems to hold, consists for each of us of a sensibly given core of spatially and temporally patterned sensory quality, together with an indefinitely conceived more of the same sort of thing of which this core is a fragment and which is linked to it by spatial and temporal relations of the kind that hold between elements within that core. Thus the physical world exists for us as that which is specified in analytic and synthetic judgments of sense as these are explained in *The Principles of Logic*, Chapter II.

We are able to make these judgments about a reality which runs on beyond what is present in immediate experience, beyond what is part of the actual filling of the present centre, because the centre within which the judging self falls is merely a fragment of a larger whole and feels its own incompleteness and even self-contradictory character, as something detached as an entity in its own right, a feeling which supplies the self with its directedness upon the beyond as a subject of judgments in which the predicates are abstracted elements of its own contents.

Bradley, indeed, thinks that these judgments are ultimately incoherent, for all sorts of reasons, including the paradoxes of space and time on which he so much insists; they disguise the character of the real whole of which we are fragments and which is that cosmic unity of organized feeling known as the Absolute. However, they certainly have a degree of truth suited to normal purposes, providing us with a practically and emotionally suitable rendering of the context in which each of us must work out his destiny. This concept of the world as an extension of the perceptually present replete with the so-called secondary qualities, and drenched in emotional and workaday values, is truer as the dominant way of conceiving it than what we arrive at if we try to form a strictly scientific conception.

Bradley here adumbrates a conception which has much in common with part of what Husserl speaks of under the heading of 'the life world'. Both insisted that our conception of nature is impoverished if we regard it as totally describable by physical science, and see the nature of daily experience as a mere subjective appearance of the world which we actually inhabit. For Husserl the surrounding world is composed of the very things which we encounter in perception, possessing the very properties we encounter them as having. Scientific descriptions either provide an extension of our concept of this world, or an idealized set of concepts in which to construe it for specific purposes. Far from annulling the validity of the life world their point lies in their enhancement of our ability to deal with it.

Bradley's development of a kindred theme is less thorough and set in the different context of his concept of the Absolute, but I believe it constitutes a contribution to a kindred phenomenological enterprise with its own special merits. Consider the beautiful passage in *Appearance and Reality* in which he contrasts the nature of the poets and the nature of the scientists and claims that the former is in many respects more real (*AR*, pp. 435-9).

He insists here that even if for scientific purposes an abstract mathematical description of nature is required, in which the traditional secondary qualities, aesthetic qualities, and the qualities things wear for emotional feeling, are regarded as not really there, or as merely subjective, still all these qualities and the felt inwardness of organisms must remain part of our non-specialist idea of that true nature in the understanding of which science plays but one role. Bradley adds that, once one supplements the abstract characterizations of science with more concrete specifications of the nature of actual experience, there is no definite stopping point before one's conceptions dissolve into the metaphysical insight that nature is but one aspect in a total spiritual reality which goes beyond it. Yet he holds, I take it, that that insight, which in any case is always in danger of being grasped so abstractly that it distorts our sense of reality as much as materialism, cannot be made the basis of our normal practice and emotion. For this what is required is a conception of nature, half way between the idealist and the materialist one, for which 'its beauty and its terror and its majesty are no illusion, but qualify it essentially' (*AR*, p. 437), and in which justice is done to the full-blooded concreteness of the context in which we have our being.

Bradley's contrast between the nature which 'as studied by the observer, and the poet and the painter, is in all its sensible and emotional fullness a very real Nature' and the nature which is 'the strict object of physical science' and which 'is a mere abstraction made and required for a certain purpose' (*AR*, p. 438), is akin to Husserl's contrast between the life world in which we carry on the ordinary affairs of life and the 'objectively true world' of science which is there solely as the object of a particular kind of intellectual activity carried on in the life world, and intriguingly comparable to Heidegger's contrast between the ready to hand and the present at hand. However, while Bradley is more concerned to stress that what nourishes our emotions and aesthetic sense must not be treated as unreal compared to the world of science, Husserl and, still more, Heidegger are more concerned to emphasize the foundational character of the nature we encounter in 'praxis'.

A Marxist or a Heideggerian might have a field-day in exhibiting how Bradley's musing sense for nature's wonders as a deeper reality than that met with in scientific research suggests the passive aestheticism of one who, removed from physical labour, forgets that nature is for most men primarily experienced as what must be manipulated if we are to survive. However, elsewhere Bradley does insist that the basic character of 'my real world' lies in the fact that, as continuous with my body, it is the field of action in which value must be realized (cf. *ETR*, chap. XVI).[7] All in all, Bradley's conception of the way we are in our real world is not so different from the later Heidegger's.

Another possible criticism is that Bradley belittles the beauty of the world that scientists have present to their minds even when they exclude all that is not required by the scientific enterprise as such, remarking that it can possess at best 'a kind of symmetry' (*AR*, p. 435). Perhaps Bradley had insufficient appreciation of the appeal of the scientific picture even then, but he has a point when he says that the scientist himself will insist that feelings which nature, as he describes it, arouses in him are not the awarenesses of any values which pertain to it, while it is nature as actually possessing the values we feel in it whose superior reality Bradley is above all stressing. And surely he is right that it is only when the world of science is 'made real by flesh and blood of secondary qualities' (*AR*, p. 438) that it can be a home for aesthetic or other value qualities.

Granted that 'my real world', or, as shared, 'our real world', as conceived by Bradley, contrasts with the world of science as does Husserl's life world, how far are their views of how this, our primordial world, relates to consciousness the same?

Husserl's position is phenomenalistic. What is not perceived is there in the sense that it would be perceived or would have been perceived by subjects who gave themselves the right kinds of kinaesthesia. Certainly there are differences between Husserl and phenomenalists in the empiricist tradition, but in the appeal to 'if ... then ...' propositions here they are close.

It is far from clear how far Bradley also thinks of that presumably large unperceived part of the physical which we postulate as continuing on from that perceived part of it which has our felt body at the centre, as either really, or in our common opinion, having an existence which consists in the fact that it would be perceived if we, or others, took appropriate steps. His hearty dislike of seeming to approximate to a position held by J. S. Mill, and his general belief that appeals to possibility or potentiality are usually the resort of bankrupt philosophies, may explain his obscurity here. His position sometimes seems to be that although we normally think of the unperceived parts of nature as really there, in a sense not reducible to the availability of various perceptions for us, on reflection we realize that it can only be true that some circumstance holds which is the real possibility of such a part of nature, that is, is something which combined with appropriate activity on our part would produce this part of nature as an object of perception for us (cf. *AR*, p. 245). It is not too clear what such a circumstance would be. The view that it must be some experience occurring within the Absolute points to a kind of panpsychism which Bradley dallied with rather than endorsed. A Bradleian might well say that our ordinary conception of the physical as unperceived contains as one of its many incoherences a shilly-shallying between thinking of it as there because available for perception and thinking of it as available for perception because there, and that within the limitations of ordinary thought this cannot be replaced by a more stable conception.

I turn now to a contrast between Bradley and Husserl in which Bradley is allied with such radical empiricists as Hume and William James, and with respect to which I would rather suspect that contemporary opinion would wrongly, as I think, tend to favour Husserl.

Husserl insists that the physical world, whether we think of it as made up of the objects of the life world or of scientifically posited entities (or even of some primordial 'ownmost' world private to myself) is transcendent, in the sense that no part or element of it can intelligibly be identified with any element which is a literal (*reell*) ingredient in one's stream of consciousness.[8]

In the case of all non-introspective awareness, nothing then present in the stream of consciousness pertinent to such awareness is identical with its object. Even in imagination of a non-existent object, as Husserl often urges, that object is to be distinguished from the image of it literally *in* consciousness. The one case, for Husserl, where the mental act is directed upon something within current consciousness, as a real ingredient thereof, is in 'immanent perception', where the object is a mental act or sensory datum, such, for instance, as may support awareness of external things. But in the case of perception in the ordinary sense, that is perception of the physical, though it is indeed essential to it that in some sense its object is present in *propria persona* (and not as something merely symbolized) it is impossible for it to be present as an actual element of consciousness.

Though this view of the transcendent status of the objects of perception, as of all non-introspective mental acts, is sometimes used to justify the denial that Husserl was an idealist, it goes hand in hand with his view that the real existence of a physical thing is a matter of its being true that appropriate sequences of perception of it from different points of view are possible for the community of egos to which I belong.

So far as non-perceptual awareness goes, Bradley's view is not so different from Husserl's. The physical which we do not perceive but know of, is there for us as something specified in synthetic judgments of sense; this means that some characteristic present in our experience is projected on to a region more or less vaguely indicated as continuous with what is perceptually present. Thus the psychical stuff in which the characteristic inheres is not the physical reality of which it mediates awareness, and is related to it in a manner somewhat similar to that in which the hyletic data, for Husserl, underpin consciousness of external objects. Perception is another matter, however, for here on Bradley's view the actually perceived is sensory stuff which belongs to the not-self aspect of the centre of experience as part of what is literally there, though what is there spills over into what is not there in a manner which allows of no neat dividing line. This is essential to the possibility of taking it as part of that larger whole characterized in synthetic judgments of sense (in a manner which the metaphysician sees as finally only a useful fiction, since the real whole to which our experience belongs is not *physically* structured).

As a description of how we ordinarily conceive the physical world this seems more satisfactory than Husserl's. It makes it much plainer how we can think of the perceived thing as there *in propria persona* in perception; it complies with the trump card of empiricism that there should be instances of our most basic concepts which we confront as directly as we do anything within experience; and it does better justice to our 'being in the world'. Husserl's strong Cartesian contrast between consciousness and all its works on the one hand and its transcendent objects on the other hides this, as Heidegger has taught us.

The view that the most directly perceived parts of the physical world are the very stuffing of our sense experience and that its unperceived parts are a postulated more of the same sort is close to Hume's view that the unperceived physical is an incoherently posited system of unperceived perceptions. It can be associated, however, with a stronger sense than Hume's, and even than Bradley's, of the extent to which the qualities and forms immediately present in sense experience owe much of their character to past acts of interpretation.

The obvious difficulty in this view is that it makes us call identical, what is, in fact, different, for example the same surface of an object as seen by you and by me. It is not clear, however, that philosophers such as Hume and Bradley who are explaining a conception they regard as finally incoherent need resolve such difficulties. Yet Bradley does have an answer, namely that all identity is identity in quality, and that identity in quality is compatible with, indeed requires, an element of difference, and that the physical is one sort of concrete universal actualizable with differences in different centres of experience — actualizable rather than exemplified by, since the latter expression implies a non-Bradleian contrast between universal and instances (cf. *AR*, pp. 248-50).

Though he has an answer to this difficulty, in general Bradley is only too pleased to agree that the physical world thus conceived is riddled with contradictions. But he is also concerned to establish that, as the experienced environment we as it were inhabit, and in which we must work out our destiny, it is more real than any world we may try to conceive, under the leadings of the scientific attitude, as purged of anything 'subjective'.

This is only one strand in the complicated windings of Bradley's thought. One could also cite passages in which he denigrates judgments which lie below the level of intellectual development represented by science. There is a similar, if more deliberate, ambivalence in Husserl as to whether we should think of the life world as a basis on which we advance to the more serious business of science, or whether science is but one attitude within the life world which must prove itself by the service it provides to existence within the latter. Upon the whole, however, Bradley and Husserl unite as opponents of the supposition that one gets nearer to things as they really are by trying to think of a world characterizable only in ways in which all qualities and forms which reflect human modes of sense experience and human valuings and practices are set aside.

NOTES

1. The main sources for this account of positions of Bradley are: *Appearance and Reality*, chaps. IX, X, XV, XXI, XXII, and XXVI, and *Essays on Truth and Reality*, chaps. XIV and XVI. Also relevant are *Collected Essays*, chaps. XII and XXVI-XXIX, and *The Principles of Logic*, chaps. I-II. Helpful comments by the editors of this volume on an earlier draft have made me clearer in my mind, and I hope my exposition, on a number of important points.

2. For Bradley's conception of 'my real world' see particularly the passages indexed under 'Real world, my' in *Esssays on Truth and Reality*. Chief works of Edmund Husserl drawn on in my discussion are: *Ideas*, London, 1931, tr. Boyce Gibson; *Ideen Zu Einer Reinen Phanomenologie*, Zweites Buch. The Hague, 1952; *The Crisis of European Sciences*, Evanston, USA, 1970, tr. David Carr; and *Cartesian Meditations*, The Hague, 1969, tr. Dorion Cairns.

3. See *PL*, pp. 61 and 289–94, for example. Cf. such remarks on personal sameness as *ETR*, p. 195.

4. It can only be an aspect of the identity, since presumably redintegration does not occur simply as a result of identity of character, as, for instance, when there is an identity of this sort occurring in your experience then and mine now.

5. This is only one of seven meanings of 'self' which Bradley develops in Chapter IX of *Appearance and Reality*, namely the sixth, that in which self and not-self correspond to subject and object. This, or meanings of self closely related to it (or perhaps the same meaning differently explicated), is the one relevant in a discussion of the self and its world. For this present suggestion regarding that meaning see *AR*, pp. 75–87, esp. 78–9.

6. In his 1887 essay 'Association and Thought' (*CE*, chap. XIII) he describes the emergence of a contrast between self and not-self within experience in a manner which suggests that it is distinctive of the former that its contents are especially intertwined, or 'one with', pleasure and pain (*CE*, p. 223). There seems a difference here from the account in *Appearance and Reality*, in spite of a reference in the latter suggesting that they are meant to be the same. In this essay he notes, incidentally, that unconscious, but of course experienced, sensations 'for all that, make part of the object group' (*CE*, p. 224 n.).

7. The role Bradley ascribes to the body as the centrally experienced core of 'my real world' invites comparison with Husserl's conception of the lived body and its role in awareness of the world. They diverge over the possibility of alternative worlds surrounding lived bodies in no spatial relations to each other, something ruled out by Husserl.

8. See, for example, *Ideas*, sect. 41.

CHAPTER 16

Bradley and Frege

Anthony Manser

It has been generally assumed that Frege and Bradley differ so greatly that a comparison between them would be of little philosophical interest. Bradley is described as an 'idealist' and Frege as a 'realist'. These two labels are seldom precisely defined, so the differences they are meant to mark can hardly be considered clear. Certainly the bland application of such labels is evidence of a failure to read either writer closely. However, at least one philosopher, Gilbert Ryle, detected an important similarity between them; in his introduction to the lectures published under the title *The Revolution in Philosophy* he described both as putting the notion of 'meaning' in the forefront of the philosophic scene,[1] a development which he regarded as central to the modern movement in philosophy. Most subsequent English philosophers have been aware of Frege's contribution to this area, but they have not looked at what Bradley said on the topic. Although many who have written on his later metaphysics have referred to the role played by logic in his arguments, few have investigated what he said about meaning in his *Principles of Logic*.

Besides that mentioned by Ryle, there is another important similarity between the two; both were strongly opposed to the logical views of Mill. His *System of Logic* constituted the major statement of empiricism in the nineteenth century. For a work of philosophy it was extremely popular; it went through eight editions in Mill's lifetime. He made it plain in his *Autobiography* that the object of the book was to oppose the 'German School', by which he meant the Kantianism that had been imported into England by Coleridge and Carlyle. In the place of this view which based knowledge on *a priori* or innate ideas, he wanted to found 'metaphysical and moral science' on a 'basis of analysed experience'. (The German word *Geisteswissenschaften* was in fact a translation of Mill's 'moral science'.) In Mill's own words:

The German or *a priori* view of human knowledge and of the knowing faculties is likely for some time longer . . . to predominate . . . But the 'System of Logic' supplies what was much wanted, a textbook of the opposite school — that which derives all knowledge from experience.[2]

One reason for the plausibility of the German importation was its ability to explain the necessity and universality of mathematics and physics, which had always constituted a weak point of empiricism. Mill set out to explain their necessity in terms of experience, without invoking innate ideas or other 'metaphysical' entities. His contemporaries obviously judged his efforts successful. In a period when the sciences were becoming the dominant intellectual influences, Mill seemed to provide a foundation for their work. One writer expressed this:

So the advancing sciences of modern times looked upon the Inductive Logic of Mill in the light of a new revelation . . . The enormous influence of the physical sciences saw itself reflected in a distinct logical outline: and the new logic became the dominant philosophy.[3]

Mill's attempt to explain logic 'naturalistically' was to account for it by 'mental mechanisms', in particular by the 'association of ideas', a doctrine which he had inherited from Hume. Only in this way could he explain logical necessity without invoking some form of an *a priori*. The situation in Germany was not perhaps too different; there the dominant idealism had collapsed not long after Hegel's death. What replaced it was a rather vague scientifically oriented naturalism, equally reliant on a psychological explanation of necessity. Both Frege and Bradley were opponents of this kind of philosophy, and it is hard to understand the writings of either without bearing it in mind. Far from it being true that Frege's target was idealism, it might be said that he was engaged in reviving a form of it in order to establish a firm foundation for mathematics. In a review of Michael Dummett's *Frege*, Hans Sluga says:

Frege's work was not a response against a 'dominant idealism,' but rather it was a response against a set of philosophies that had arisen out of the collapse of German idealism in the nineteenth century.[4]

In his book on Frege, Sluga connects him with Kant, and describes the former's views as a variety of idealism.

If Frege's theory of objectivity can be interpreted in this Kantian sense, we can credit him with an understanding of the shortcomings of metaphysical realism or Platonism while holding on to the belief in the objectivity of logic and mathematics. There is a sense in which that position can be called realism but its realism is not incompatible with idealism: it is a form of idealism.[5]

Sluga is making a polemical point against Dummett here. I must admit to a degree of unclarity about the differences between 'realism' and 'idealism' as labels, and I doubt whether any substantive philosophical issue hangs on their application. What is clear, however, is that the empiricists' weak point had always been logic, whereas those who have been labelled 'idealist' made it central to their philosophies. Indeed, it might be said that this was the core of their opposition to empiricism. If we divide philosophers into those who rely on psychological accounts of logic, and those who oppose this tendency, then Frege and Bradley come out on the same side, as do Kant and Hegel. The extent to which Kant relied on the traditional formal logic in writing his *Critique of Pure Reason* is well known. Hegel too gave logic a high place and also wanted to substitute it for the old metaphysics. If 'realism' means that a judgment's truth or falsity is dependent on facts or a reality which do not depend in any sense on the maker of the judgment, then it is clear that Bradley was a 'realist'; it is equally clear that he was an anti-empiricist. What I have been concerned to point out so far is that both Frege and Bradley began their considerations of logic from a similar point, a rejection of 'psychologism'.

Apart from this similarity in their background, there is another point of contact between Frege and Bradley; both read the work of Lotze. Bosanquet thought that Bradley had departed from the pure line of Hegelian thought under Lotze's influence, and characterized the latter as a 'writer of the German reaction', presumably meaning 'reaction against Hegelianism'. Indeed, he wrote a book of some three hundred pages, entitled *Knowledge and Reality* immediately after the publication of *The Principles of Logic* in order to recall Bradley to the correct line. Lotze's writings were widely read, and Bosanquet himself translated the *Logic* not long after its publication. Sluga finds many similarities between Frege and Lotze:

It is known that Frege attended one of Lotze's courses when he was a student at Gottingen (though one on the philosophy of religion). The precision and logical rigour on which Lotze insists in his writings may have appealed to the young Frege. There are several important theses in Lotze's *Logic* of 1874 that are familar from Frege's writings. Not only does Lotze insist on the sharp separation of logic and psychology, he also maintains that mathematics must be regarded as an extension of elementary logic. Like Frege Lotze gives a formal characterization of the notion of an object. Lotze also insists that one must distinguish between the objectivity and the reality of objects. Identity-statements are distinguished by him into informative and trivial ones, and he accounts for this difference by distinguishing between the content and the reference of the terms in such a statement.[6]

Interestingly, Lotze makes use of the mathematical notion of a function when dealing with concepts and syllogisms. He says that the 'appropriate symbol' for the structure of a concept is 'not the equation $S = a + b + c + d$, etc., but such an expression as $S = F(a, b, c, \text{etc.}) \ldots$'.[7] Later he says of the syllogism: 'The only symbol of a more exhaustive kind would be that of the mathematical function in general, which we used before . . .'[8] However, he makes no formal use of this suggestion, and I quote it merely as a matter of interest.

To establish that the background, and even some of the reading, of two thinkers is similar does not prove a similarity between them; it is only to point out that they started from the same, or similar, points. There are obvious and radical differences; Frege was above all interested in the foundations of mathematics. Bradley admitted that he did not understand the subject at all. Frege introduced a new formalism into logic; Bradley was cavalier in the symbolism he used and clearly regarded it as of little importance. So it might be thought that there was nothing further to be done after their similar backgrounds have been indicated, no profit to be gained by pursuing the comparison. However, noticing a likeness between the two is going to change our view of both. Also it may serve to correct that lack of historical understanding of Frege and his situation which is manifested by Michael Dummett in his monumental *Frege*. It is not just a matter of getting the historical facts straight; some of the arguments that Dummett uses are vitiated by his failure to grasp the context in which they were put forward by Frege.

Both thinkers, however, differ from Lotze on the subject-matter of logic. Traditionally books on logic had been divided into three parts, Words or Concepts, Propositions or Judgments, and Inferences. Kant had followed this pattern in his *Logic* of 1800. Lotze's first chapter was entitled 'The Theory of the Concept'. Both Bradley and Frege considered that logic should deal only with judgment and inference. Bradley was even willing to go further and suggest that there was no need to make a radical separation even between these two, but that each faded into the other. *The Principles of Logic* is divided into two main sections. The first book is about judgment, the second and third on inference. Bradley starts by saying that it is arbitrary to select either to begin a study of logic, and later adds that the two parts form a concrete whole which analysis artificially divides.

For both Bradley and Frege the reason for not including a separate section on words or concepts was an acceptance of the 'contextual principle', that a word only has meaning in the context of a proposition. Frege's use of this is well known, though there is some disagreement about the extent to which he followed it in his work after the writing of 'On Sense and Reference'. It is not easy to find in Bradley any statement of the principle which is as explicit as that of Frege, but it is clear from his failure to include a section on words that he held it, as well as from what he has to say about the difference between grammatical and logical form, a topic I will deal with below.

The nearest he comes to an explicit statement is in his denial that judgments consists of the copulation of two or more elements: 'It is not true that every judgment has two ideas. We may say on the contrary that all have but one' (*PL*, p. 11). This passage also implies that logical and grammatical form do not coincide. However, there are clear statements in other Anglo-Hegelian writers. Green said in his 'Lectures on Logic':

Apart from propositions, then, the distinction between 'general' and 'singular' names is a distinction between names that have a meaning and those that have none. And the meaning of those that have meaning is always resoluble into propositions. Only in propositions has a singular name significance.[9]

In an elementary logic text, Bosanquet expressed the principle thus:

We ought not to think of propositions as built up by putting words or names together, but of words or names as distinguished though not separable elements in propositions.[10]

It is not surprising that many philosophers should agree on the contextual principle; the connection between logic and language had long been known; even Hegel had said:

The forms of thought are, in the first instance, displayed and stored in human *language*.[11]

More important, the principle was a commonplace among grammarians. One English philosopher, Mansel, reviewing in 1850 a book on Universal Grammar, writes:

That there ever was a period in the history of man, as Reid conjectures, when every single word represented a sentence, when the noun and the verb themselves held the same place which their several syllables hold now, as fractional and imperfect in speech as they still are in thought; this is a hypothesis which we may reasonably hesitate to admit. But logically the proposition is true. The sentence, we may go farther, the enunciative sentence, is the unit of speech, as the judgment is of thought; and it behoves us to remember, that the verbal analysis of the thoughts we utter, like the chemical decomposition of the air we breathe, exhibits only the forced and unnatural dissolution of parts whose vital force and efficacy exists only in combination.[12]

Frege, after a statement of the contextual principle in an unpublished paper: 'And so, instead of putting a judgment together out of an individual as subject and an already previously formed concept as predicate, we do the opposite and arrive at a concept by splitting up the content of possible judgment', remarks in a footnote:

In this connection I find it remarkable [the English translation says 'extraordinary', but this seems to distort Frege's meaning] that some linguists have recently viewed a '*Satzwort*' (sentence-word), a word expressing a whole judgment, as the primitive form of speech and ascribe no independent existence to the roots, as mere abstractions. I note this from the *gottinschen gelehrten Anzeigen* 6 April 1881: A. H. Sayce, *Introduction to the Science of Language* 1880 by A. Fick.[13]

There are several passages in Sayce's book which make the contextual point; perhaps the clearest is the following:

The Greek Logos was not the individual word, which, apart from its relation to other parts of the sentence, has no meaning in itself, but the complete act of reasoning, which on the inward side is called a judgment, and on the outward side sentence or a proposition. The single word is to the sentence what syllables and letters are to the single word. We may break up a word into the several sounds of which it is composed, but this is the work of the phonologist, not of the speaker. So, too, we may break up a sentence like 'Don't do that' into the four words *Do-not-do-that* but this, again, is the conscious procedure of the grammarian. Sentences may be of any length; they may consist of a single syllable, like *go!* or yes, or they may have to be expressed by a large number of separate 'words'; what is essential is that they should be significant to another, should adequately convey to his mind the whole thought that is intended to be expressed. Unless the sounds we utter are combined into a sentence, they have no more meaning than the cries of a jackal or the yelping of the cur; and until they have a meaning, and so represent our thought, they do not constitute language. The sentence, in short, is the only unit which language can know, and the ultimate starting point of all our linguistic enquiries.[14]

I have quoted this at length because contemporary philosophers, although well aware of recent work in linguistics, do not seem to realize what had been done on the subject in the nineteenth century and that many philosophers were familiar with this work.

Perhaps the important point about the grammarians' stress on the judgment as the unit of meaning is that it presented a powerful argument against empiricism. Kant had already argued that concepts were to be regarded as predicates of possible judgments as part of his attack on it. One of the few German philosophers to present a different view was Lotze.

Thus it is that every developed language possesses ... numerous ideas which could not have been framed ... without employing judgments and syllogisms ... This obvious reflexion has given rise to the assertion, that in logic the theory of judgment at least must precede the treatment of concepts, with which it is only an old tradition to begin the subject. I consider this to be an over-hasty assertion, due partly to the confusion of the end of pure with that of applied logic, partly to a general misconception of the difference between thought and the mere current of ideas.[15]

Frege's comment in a letter of 1882 seems almost a reply to this remark:

I do not think that the formation of concepts can precede judgment, for that would presuppose the independent existence of concepts; but I imagine the concept originating in the analysis of a judgeable content.[16]

Lotze's argument was basically the empiricist one that what is complex in our mental life must be constructed out of simple atoms. Bradley saw the point that higher concepts seemed to depend on lower ones, and these in turn rested on the flux of impressions that came via the senses. His interest in psychology led him to devote much attention to this. However, he was also clear that there was a distinction between the genetic and the logical, and that in the latter it was a set of considerations other than the historical that should prevail. His adherence to the 'contextual principle' consisted in the denial of Lotze's point. I should stress that the 'contextual principle' must be regarded as anti-empiricist. All philosophers who used it were opposed to the tenets of Mill; Green saw clearly, in the passage from which I quoted above, that to defeat the 'psychologizing' of logic it was necessary to attack the idea that simple names or words were prior to propositions or judgments.

It is noteworthy that the 'contextual principle' makes judgments the subject-matter of logic, because the judgment is the minimum meaningful unit. Hence the sentence becomes an abstraction, something which belongs to grammar only. Neither Frege nor Bradley would have committed the solecism of talking of 'the use of a sentence', with its implication that there might be a stock of ready-made sentences which were learned and then brought out when the occasion demanded. Of course it is possible to treat a foreign language in that way; a person who knows no French may be provided with a stock of French sentences to use under appropriate circumstances, but speaking one's native language could not be like that. More important for my concerns here is the fact that the principle makes it possible to separate grammatical from logical form. Although previous logicians had been aware of the fact that grammatical form was not always a good guide to 'logical form', they had only used this principle in a relatively trivial way. What they had meant by the phrase was the shape a sentence had to be in order to function as a premiss in a syllogism, to indicate correctly which of the four traditional forms it represented. Thus 'All is not gold that glitters' required to be reformulated as 'Some things that glitter are not gold'. It was an 'O' proposition, not an 'A'. Bradley and Frege have a more radical approach; they are both prepared to deny that grammar is any guide at all. Nor should this be surprising; if the 'grammatical form' is extracted from what is a unity for the purposes of the grammarian, there is no reason to suppose that it will serve the very different aims of the logician. In Frege's words:

> Again in the two sentences 'Frederick the Great won the battle of Rossbach' and 'It is true that Frederick the Great won the battle of Rossbach', we have, as we said earlier, the same thought in a different verbal form. In affirming the thought in the first sentence we thereby affirm the thought in the second, and conversely. There are not two different acts of judgment, but only one.
>
> (From all this we can see that the grammatical categories of subject and predicate can have no significance for logic.)[17]

Judgment constitutes a unity for Frege; it is an expression of what he calls 'thought', which he sharply distinguishes from 'idea'.

For Bradley the judgment is also a unity, though he does not characterize it in quite the same way as Frege:

> Judgment proper is the act which refers an ideal content (recognized as such) to a reality beyond the act. This sounds perhaps harder than it is.
>
> The ideal content is the logical idea, the meaning as just defined. It is recognized as such, when we know that, by itself, it is not a fact but a wandering adjective. In the act of assertion we transfer this adjective to, and unite it with, a real substantive. And we perceive at the same time, that the relation thus set up is neither made by the act, nor merely holds within it or by right of it, but is real both independent of it and beyond it (*PL*, p. 10).

Bradley's 'ideal content' seems to correspond to Frege's 'thought', though there is one point of difference. Frege distinguishes between judgment and assertion.

> Therefore two things must be distinguished in an indicative sentence: the content, which it has in common with the corresponding sentence-question, and the assertion. The former is the thought, or at least contains the thought. So it is possible to express the thought without laying it down as true. Both are so closely joined in an indicative sentence that it is easy to overlook their separability. Consequently we may distinguish:
> (1) the apprehension of a thought – thinking,
> (2) the recognition of the truth of a thought – judgment,
> (3) the manifestation of this judgment – assertion.[18]

The Fregean 'thought' is in some sense a single entity, and Bradley emphasizes that a judgment contains but one idea (or 'ideal content'). In both cases there is a problem about what kind of an entity they are talking about. Frege stresses that the thought is an objective entity; for him ideas or sensations are subjective: 'every idea has only one bearer; no two men have the same idea.'[19] Thoughts belong to a 'third realm':

> Thus the thought, for example, which we expressed in the Pythagorean theory is timelessly true, true independently of whether anyone takes it to be true. It needs no bearer. It is not true for the first time when it is discovered, but it is like a planet which, already before anyone has seen it, has been in interaction with other planets.[20]

It is difficult to know quite what such an entity is, for it seems in some sense to exist independently, for 'it needs no bearer' unlike ideas which need men to have them. In a sense this view is forced upon Frege by his adoption of the contextual principle; it is the unitary 'meaning' of a sentence. There are ideas in men's minds, but these are subjective and hence cannot be considered true or false, are of interest only to psychology, part of each person's inner world.

Bradley was similarly forced to separate 'ideas' as mental entities from 'meaning'.

> For logical purposes ideas are symbols, and they are nothing but symbols. And, at the risk of common-place, before I go on, I must try to say what a symbol is.
>
> In all that is we can distinguish two sides, (i) existence and (ii) content. In other words we perceive both *that* it is and *what* it is. But in anything that is a symbol we have also a third side, its signification, or what it *means* (*PL*, pp. 2–3).

Ideas are mental events and can be described. The word 'horse' may call up in my mind a particular image of a horse, a black stallion with a white blaze on its head, for instance. But this is not the meaning of the word 'horse' as is shown by the fact that I can identify a white mare *as* a horse. The same applies to other kinds of thing that can have meaning. Bradley instances the Victorian 'language of flowers', in which a message could be spelt out by sending one's beloved a certain collection of blooms. These could be enjoyed as flowers, for their colour or scent. But then the message would be lost. For the thought behind the bunch to be grasped, the individual blooms had to be considered not as blooms but as symbols. Similarly we can consider the actual shape of the written characters on the page, but in so doing we are not attending to what they say:

> The word dies as it is spoken, but the particular sound of the mere

pulsation was nothing to our minds. Its existence was lost in the speech and significance. The paper and the ink are facts unique and with definite qualities. They are the same in all points with none other in the world. But, in reading, we apprehend not paper or ink, but what they represent; and, so long as only they stand for this, their private existence is a matter of indifference. A fact taken as a symbol ceases so far to be fact. It no longer can be said to exist for its own sake, its individuality is lost in its universal meaning. It is no more a substantive, but becomes the adjective that holds of another. But, on the other hand, the change is not all loss. By merging its own quality in a wider meaning, it can pass beyong itself and stand for others. It gains admission and influence in a world which it otherwise could not enter. The paper and ink cut the throats of men, and the sound of a breath may shake the world (*PL*, pp. 3–4).

Thus both believe in mental contents, which are not the same as 'meanings'; it would seem that what Frege meant by 'the thought' was virtually identical to what Bradley meant by 'meaning'. We can see how the attempt to eschew psychology forces both into similar positions. Logic is concerned with meanings, not with what is private and peculiar to individuals. But it is hard to say much about what such meanings are, for they are part of the presuppositions of language and consequently difficult to express in it. The attempt to do so is bound to produce what borders on nonsense.

There remains a problem of how the thought or meaning relates to the world. Here again it is clear that both thinkers are reacting against the kind of view that Locke put forward, in which 'ideas' in the mind go proxy for objects in the world. Such a view reduces logic to a branch of psychology. Part of the problem is how these ideas 'hang together' to make up coherent propositions. In spite of the fact that he devoted a considerable amount of space to concepts, Lotze was forced to admit that, in the last resort, the combination of concepts could only take place in judgments.

Kant himself in his search for the *a priori* forms which were to give the unity of an inner coherence to the empirical content of our perceptions, made the mistake at starting of developing them in the form of single concepts, the Categories, and that in spite of the fact that he derived them from the forms of the judgment itself. And now having got them, as he thought, in his Categories, it became the more evident that there was nothing to be made of them, and thereupon followed the attempt to derive judgments out of them again, and so he arrived at the 'Principles of the Understanding' which it was now possible to apply as major premises to the minor premises furnished by experience. It seems therefore that this disposition to bring into the inadequate form of a single concept truths which can only be adequately expressed through the proposition, is natural to the imagination at all times, and is not peculiar to the plastic mind of ancient Greece. It may however be remarked in passing how dangerous a tendency it is, leading the mind as it does away from the full concrete reality which is the true aim of its enquiries to a barren playing with empty ideas which have become separated from their natural foundations.[21]

There is a reason for talking in terms of concepts. If it is accepted that we recognize the meaning of a new judgment or proposition by understanding the words out of which it is composed, then it seems to follow that the judgment consists of a combination of elements which in some sense pre-exist the judgment which makes use of them. It is this which lead Dummett to remark:

in the order of *explanation* the sense of a sentence is primary, but in the order of *recognition* the sense of a word is primary.[22]

The 'contextual principle' seems to make it impossible to give a sense to individual words, and yet we do come across words whose 'meaning we do not know', and deal with the problem by looking them up in a dictionary. This enables us to understand the utterance which contained the unknown element. Frege's talk of the sense and reference of words also seems to point in this direction, and to pull against his use of the 'contextual principle'. Bradley too makes remarks like 'A word, we may say, never quite means what it stands for or stands for what it means' (*PL*, p. 168), apparently putting meaning on to the individual words which make up a judgment. But if words are only the artificial products of grammatical analysis and the unit of meaning is the whole judgment or proposition, then it should be impossible to make such remarks.

One thing that can be said straight away is that the question of what a word is, is not altogether easy to answer, as can be seen from the work of philologists or grammarians. It can be said that a word is the smallest unit of language considered from the grammarians' or philologists' point of view, but it by no means follows that this should be a unit which is of interest to philosophy. The general tendency of empiricism has been to equate words with the 'atoms' which form the basis of all subsequent discourse, regarding them as playing in language the role that sensations or ideas do in the mind. But language-learning is not a matter of first acquiring a vocabulary and then learning to say things by means of it. The child learns by hearing things said, propositions or judgments, and these are normally expressed by fully-formed sentences. It is only later that the child comes to realize that these 'units' can be separated into sub-units. There is no primary process of 'ostensive definition', where a word is correlated with an object. This is not to deny that ostensive definition can take place once a language has been learned. I could put the point here by saying that although a theory may lead us to say that certain things are logically simpler than others, it does not follow that these are, as a matter of fact, the building blocks out of which the whole is constructed.

Here it may well make a difference if a philosopher talks in terms of sentences rather than propositions or judgments. The former are grammatical units, the latter logical. Some of Frege's difficulties seem to come from his failing to observe this distinction. I am thinking here of the problems of sense and reference and of 'unsaturated' elements. There were particular reasons why Frege should have been forced into talking of sense and reference, but these arose from his mathematical, rather than his philosophical, concerns, notably the problem of identity statements. There is no space to discuss this issue here. The question of 'unsaturated elements' is more relevant, for these were introduced to solve the problem of the unity of a judgment. Previously logicians had believed that the copula provided a kind of 'logical cement' to hold the subject and predicate together. Frege saw rightly that this was not needed, but nevertheless still thought that some device was needed to account for the way in which the two parts of a judgment cohered. On his own views this seems a mistaken idea. In a passage written in 1919, Frege said:

What is distinctive about my conception of logic is that I begin by giving pride of place to the content of the word 'true', and then immediately go on to introduce a thought as that to which the question 'Is it true?' is in principle applicable. So I do not begin with concepts and put them together to form a thought or judgment; I come by the

parts of a thought by analysing the thought. This marks off my concept-
script from the similar inventions of Leibniz and his successors, despite
what the name suggests; perhaps it was not a very happy choice on
my part.[23]

This seems to imply that, as in earlier statements of the
'contextual principle', concepts are in no different position
than any other parts analysed out from the unity of the
thought. The problem becomes more complicated as Frege
tries to explain this remark, as the nature of the 'parts' of a
thought remains unclear. But this is a difficulty in Fregean
exegesis, not for this paper.

Bradley did not have the same problems, because he was
clear about the unity of the judgment, nor was he led to talk
of the sense and reference of words. This is not to deny that
he fell into other difficulties which might be said to be
analogous to those of Frege, for instance his talk of the
'concrete universal' which was introduced to solve certain
logical problems. But discussion of these belongs to a study
of Bradley, just as full consideration of the doctrines of
sense and reference and 'unsaturatedness' belong to a detailed
examination of Frege.

There is one final comparison to be made. Bradley believed
that the correct form of a judgment should be rendered
'Reality is such that S − P' rather than simply 'S − P';
reality is the real subject of all judgments. This was a particular application of the doctrine that the logical form of a
proposition need not be represented by its grammatical
form. There seems to be a similarity between this view and
Frege's belief that the reference of a sentence was 'The true'
or 'The false'. Bradley said that the subject and predicate
should be regarded as mere adjectives applied to the subject
of all judgments, reality itself. It seems possible to represent
Frege as saying that a true judgment was a description of
'the true'. In other words we could see Bradley's 'reality'
and Frege's 'The true' as fulfilling the same function. Again,
this mode of talk was forced on both of them by the use
of the 'contextual principle'.

In conclusion, I do not claim that I have shown that one
or other thinker was superior or more insightful. I have
rather tried to point out some unnoticed analogies between
certain of their views, and to suggest that these analogies

had a similar origin, the attempt to rid logic of psychological elements. There is no need to stress the differences between them; they are many and obvious. One point, however, might be picked out as significant; Bradley used no formalism, so it may be that Frege's views depended less on his reliance on formalism than has been generally believed.

NOTES

1. *The Revolution in Philosophy*, London, 1956, p. 7.
2. J. S. Mill, *Autobiography*, New York, pp. 169–70.
3. *The Logic of Hegel*, Oxford, 1874, pp. lxxvi–lxxvii.
4. 'Frege as a Rationalist', *Studien zu Frege*, vol. I, Stuttgart – Bad Cannstatt, 1976, p. 45.
5. H. Sluga, *Gottlob Frege*, London, 1980, p. 107.
6. 'Frege as a Rationalist', p. 37.
7. *Logic*, Oxford, 1888, tr. B. Bosanquet, vol. I, p. 48.
8. *Logic*, p. 146.
9. *Works*, ed. Nettleship, London, 1890, vol. II, p. 203.
10. *The Essentials of Logic*, London, 1914, p. 87.
11. *Wissenschaft der Logik*, Frankfurt am Main, 1969, vol. 5, p. 20.
12. *Letters, Lectures and Reviews*, ed. H. W. Chandler, London, 1873, p. 12.
13. *Posthumous Writings*, Oxford, 1979, tr. P. Long and R. White, p. 17.
14. *Introduction to the Science of Language*, 3rd edn., London, 1890, p. 112.
15. *Logic*, vol. I, p. 23.
16. *Posthumous Writings*, p. 141.
17. 'The Thought', *Mind*, vol. 65, July 1956, p. 294.
18. 'The Thought', p. 300.
19. 'The Thought', p. 302.
20. *Logic*, vol. II, pp. 210–21.
21. Lotze, *Logic*, vol. II, pp. 220–1.
22. *Frege*, London, 1973, p. 4.
23. *Posthumous Writings*, p. 253.

Index of Names